# BE A SUCCESSFUL
# RESIDENTIAL LAND DEVELOPER

# BE A SUCCESSFUL RESIDENTIAL LAND DEVELOPER

## R. DODGE WOODSON

**McGraw-Hill**

New York  San Francisco  Washington, D.C.  Auckland  Bogotá
Caracas  Lisbon  London  Madrid  Mexico City  Milan
Montreal  New Delhi  San Juan  Singapore
Sydney  Tokyo  Toronto

Cataloging-in-Publication Data is on file with the Library of Congress

## McGraw-Hill

*A Division of The McGraw·Hill Companies*

ISBN 0-07-134160-9

The sponsoring editor for this book was Zoe G. Foundotos, the editing supervisor was Steven Melvin, and the production supervisor was Sherri Souffrance. It was set in Melior by Constance M. Tucker of Lone Wolf Enterprises, Ltd.

Printed and bound by Quebecor/Martinsburg.

 This book is printed on recycled, acid-free paper containing a minimum of 50% recycled de-inked fiber.

McGraw-Hill books are available at special quantity discounts to use as premiums and sales promotions, or for use in corporate training programs. For more information, please write to the Director of Special Sales, McGraw-Hill, Two Penn Plaza, New York, NY 10121-2298. Or contact your local bookstore.

For Afton and Adam, my balance points in life.

# CONTENTS

# INTRODUCTION

Land developers have a reputation for making a lot of money. Many of them do. Developers who expand into being builders or general contractors can create tremendous wealth. They can run their business interests on a full-time or part-time basis. Even as a part-time developer, you could make some very serious money in a short period of time. There is a risk involved with developing land, but many of the risks can be kept to a minimum with the proper procedures.

Home builders often buy their lots from developers. In doing so, they may be paying twice as much for the building lots as they would have to pay if they did their own development. It's not common for land developers to double their money on land sales. For example, a building lot that cost a developer $15,000 to create might be sold for $30,000. Builders who develop their own building lots can see much higher profits.

How complicated is it to become a land developer? Well, almost anyone with reasonable intelligence can do it. You don't have to be an engineer or an architect to become a developer. There are many experts who may be needed during the development process, but these people can be hired or contracted for their services. A depth of knowledge in the construction trades is not needed to be a successful developer. General intelligence is enough to get you started in the potentially lucrative business of land development.

Are you worried that you don't have enough money to cash in on the big money possible with land developing? You may not need nearly as much money as you think. It can take substantial money for a development project, but there are many ways to get a project moving with limited funds. Even if your credit isn't perfect, you can still make things happen with the right approach.

There are many steps to be taken in the venture of developing land. Some of the work is extremely technical, but this work can be done by experts. So what is required of you, the developer? Some developers take very active roles in their work. Other developers are more passive and depend on others to do most of the work. The choice is yours. Doing more of your own work may result in higher profits, but there is plenty of money to be made either way.

I've been involved with real estate for more than 24 years. There have been years when I built more that 60 single-family homes. I'm also the owner of a real estate brokerage. Starting with raw land and creating viable projects ranging from building lots to completed construction packages has been my professional life. And, I'm just an average guy with a basic education. If you want to become land developer, the opportunity exists.

This book is not a technical manual for land planners, architects, or engineers. The purpose of this book is to show you, and the experts, some real-world angles to the business that most books on the subject don't cover. I'm not going to tell you how to sift soil and rate it, but I will tell you how various soil types can impact your project. You will learn how to understand and work with the professionals that you will need during the course of a development project. Consider this your guide to down-to-earth developing.

You could read a number of technical books on the subject of developing and still find yourself confused and possibly intimidated. Much of what I know about developing has come from hands-on experience, which is hard to beat. But first-hand experience is often expensive. A lot of mistakes are made during the learning curve. By reading this book, you can benefit from my life experience without the costly mistakes that you might otherwise make. Are all the answers to successful developing contained in these pages? No, of course not, but a great deal of them are.

Look at the table of contents. Notice how it is laid out to cover topics as you are most likely to encounter them. Thumb through the chapters. Notice the sample forms that will help you to protect yourself when dealing with subcontractors and experts. Read a few paragraphs to see just how reader-friendly the text is. It won't take long for you to see that this is not your typical book on land developing. It's different, and the difference might make you an extremely successful developer, even if you work only part time at it. Go ahead, take a few minutes to decide for yourself, but I don't think that you will find another book quite like this one. If you are serious about becoming a developer, this is your chance. Go for it!

# ACKNOWLEDGMENTS

Special thanks are extended to the United States government and the Southern Building Code Congress, International, Inc. for permission to reprint illustrations placed in this book.

# Why Should I Get into Land Development?

**W**hy would anyone get into land developing? Money, of course. The profit potential of land development is incredible. There is substantial risk attached to some development deals, but there usually is risk when there is the potential of rich rewards. Home builders need land to build on. Most builders buy their building lots from developers. This is fine, but builders can increase their profits considerably by developing their own building lots. How much extra money can builders make when they develop their own lots? It depends on many factors, but some builders have cut their land cost in half when they developed their own lots. I know it is true, because I am one of those builders.

Developers work in many ways. Some of them concentrate on large commercial deals, such as shopping centers. Creating a large subdivision of building lots for homes can prove very lucrative. Small developers can do well by subdividing small parcels of land into just a couple of building lots. Whether you are cutting a single parcel into two building lots or developing hundreds of acres into a sprawling subdivision, there is plenty of money to be made with land development.

Almost anyone can learn to be a land developer. However, developing the skills to create profitable land deals may take a lot of time and effort. The money from developing does not usually come easily. Many developers fail before they see their first projects completed. Getting financing for a land development can be extremely difficult for anyone who has not previously established a successful track record. There are many obstacles between a developer who buys raw land and that same developer seeing a prosperous completion to a project.

You don't have to be an expert in any particular field to make money as a land developer. Anyone with reasonable intelligence can carve a place in the world as a developer. Having money and good credit is an advantage to an aspiring developer, but with creative partnering, a person can rely on others for cash and credit. A feel for real estate is important, and the willingness to work hard, learn daily, and make adjustments as you go along all help a person to become a successful developer.

## How Much Money?

How much money does it take to become a land developer? The amount of money needed varies from deal to deal and developer to developer. It's possible for developers to begin their work with very small amounts of money. If a person has good credit, the need for cash on hand is greatly reduced. Some developers are able to create projects with nearly none of their own cash. Some money is usually needed, but the amount can vary considerably.

As a builder and developer, I have done deals of all sorts. I've taken 200 acres of land and turned it into ten 20-acre lots. Working with a partner, I participated in the development of a shopping center, a large housing tract, and similar deals. On a smaller scale, I have purchased small pieces of acreage to cut in half to create two building lots. My past experience includes working with other developers to control dozens of lots in a particular subdivision. Most of my experience has been with residential developments.

In addition to being a builder, I also own a real estate brokerage. During my work as a broker I've helped investors and developers structure numerous land deals. Some projects that look great on the surface turn out to have severe development problems. It's common for a piece of property that seems to be only what it is to have a higher and better use. This is what land developing is all about—finding a higher and better use.

During all of my various types of experience, I've seen deals done with as little as $100 coming out of a developer's personal bank account. Developers should plan on needing much more than a hundred bucks, but the out-of-pocket expense can be kept minimal. Developers who don't have cash or credit can turn to partners to see a project come together. Almost anyone with determination can find a way to develop real estate.

Large development plans can require thousands upon thousands of dollars before any hope of creating income can be seen. It's not unusual for tens of thousands of dollars to be spent before the first shovel is filled with dirt to break ground. Developers working on a plan for a shopping center might spend $100,000 just to get approval for a project. On the other hand, a builder who is splitting one building lot into two lots might not need any cash before financing can be arranged.

Builders with good track records can often include the cost of land acquisition in their construction loans. This is the way I've normally done my business over the years. If you create a good relationship with a lender, you may be able to start developing land with the only money out of your pocket being for an earnest-money contract deposit to buy the land.

## How Do I Get Partners?

How do I get partners if I don't have enough money to work on my own? Potential partners for land developers are everywhere. Some of the partners are basically money investors. If you have a good plan, an investor may put up the money and credit to get the job done. Of course, there will be a need for the investors to see profits. The investors may want a percentage of all profits made, or they may want to earn interest on the money that they are putting up. But money investors are not the only way to get what you need.

There are many types of professionals needed in some land development deals. Surveyors, engineers, architects, and others may be needed in the planning stages of a development. These professionals are sometimes willing to perform their services without immediate payment. The pros might be willing to gamble their time and skills to get a piece of the action. Even banks may be willing to participate as partners with land developers.

Not all home builders are developers, but any builder who builds in volume may make a great partner for a land developer. Builders need land to build on. If the builders can turn extra profits by working with a developer, they may be willing to lend their reputation, cash, and credit to create a new development.

Finding partners for land deals is not difficult. However, developers must be careful when choosing partners. And it makes the most sense to limit the partnership to one particular development. Partnerships often end on a bad note. It's usually best when the partnership is limited to single deals so that ongoing deals can be done together but are not required to be.

## More Control

Money is not the only reason for home builders to expand into land development. Builders can gain much more control over their businesses when they develop their own building lots. A builder who is not a developer has to buy building lots where they can be found and for whatever price it takes to get them. But builders who create their own developments have unlimited access to the lots that they are developing.

It's not uncommon for a developer to option or sell large blocks of building lots to selected builders. A subdivision of a hundred lots might be limited to just four builders. This kind of deal is common. Selling to just a handful of builders is convenient for developers. It is also cost-effective in terms of marketing. The downside of this for builders who are not invited to buy into a development is being essentially locked out of the subdivision.

Some developers limit the number of builders allowed to build in a subdivision to maintain quality construction. It could be that each builder will offer four to six model homes that can be built in the subdivision. If there are 100 lots and four builders who will build four to six types of houses, this works out to 16 to 24 house styles. This practice is very controlling, but it goes on all the time. And it can shut down small builders who can't afford to build in high volume.

Successful developers generally have a following of builders. For a new builder to break into the loop can be very difficult. But if the new builder can develop building lots personally, the heat is off. Builders who do their own developing have much more control over where and what they will build, and they normally make a handsome profit on the land.

## How Much Risk?

How much risk is involved in developing land? There can be substantial risk, but the risk can be managed. Some types of developments create more risk than others. Assuming that all zoning and local code requirements are in order, doing a subdivision of a single lot shouldn't be very risky. Planning to develop a shopping mall is a very different matter. Large commercial ventures can be extremely risky, as can large residential developments.

Many investors feel that risk is directly in proportion to potential reward. Sometimes this is true, but it's not always a fact. A lot of money can be made without exposing yourself to excessive risk. Risk management is crucial to enduring success as a developer. A lot of people assume that small projects equate to small risk. This is not always the case. Risk is risk; it is not always tied to the size of a project or the potential profit of a deal.

There is risk involved with developing land. Of course, there is risk in all types of business. Builders who build on speculation take risks all the time. There can be a lot more risk involved with opening a restaurant than there is in developing land. Basically, the skill, experience, and knowledge of the developers curve the risk factors. Inexperienced people who jump in headfirst and don't take the time to learn what to do beforehand are at much higher risk than seasoned developers are. Fortunately, learning to reduce the risk of land developing is not all that difficult. With the right research, you can turn the odds in your favor quickly.

## How Can I Compete?

How can I compete with the big guns of the business? Don't established developers have their pick of all the prime property? Developers who have been in the business have certain advantages, but they don't hold all of the cards, especially when home builders are turning into developers. Many business owners become lazy once they have enough business to satisfy themselves. This can leave a door wide open for aggressive new developers. As for prime property, new developers who dig deeply can find ideal properties before they are offered for public sale. Yes, the big guns will be looking for the same treasure, but it is a race against time, and anyone can win it.

You don't have to possess a long line of credentials to get into land development. If you choose to break into big-time development, you may well be biting off more than you can chew. But there are plenty of opportunities for small investors to take advantage of. Little land deals can turn big bucks, so they should not be overlooked. In fact, this is one reason why new developers have a fair shake. Once developers grow to large proportions, they probably will not pay much attention to a piece of property that can be cut into four building lots. It's not that there isn't money to be made or that the money couldn't be very good. Usually, it's a matter of the big developers being too busy on major projects to ferret out small deals.

Developers who are not builders have to make all of their money from the sale of building lots. There can be plenty of money to be made in this way, but builders hold an advantage. Builders can profit from both the markup on building lots developed and on the sale of any homes sold. This, in essence, gives builders an added edge of security. If the profits from the land are not as strong as projected, the profit from the houses can still make a project fly. Having the dual earning ability definitely gives builders an advantage over standard land developers.

## Red Tape

Isn't there a lot of red tape involved with land development? There can be. Many state, federal, and local agencies may have a say in whether or not a piece of land can be developed for a specific purpose. Cutting through the red tape can take years for some projects, but other projects can zoom through the approval process without much fuss. The work required to gain approval for development is worthwhile for projects with strong potential, but it can be a bank breaker on marginal deals. Learning to estimate the amount of red tape to be cut is just part of becoming a successful developer.

What type of trouble can a developer run into from various agencies? Depending on where land is located and what the intention for its development is, the obstacles in front of a developer vary. You might have trouble getting approval from a zoning board, but this is something that should be set aside as a contingency in the purchase contract for the property. If there is a possibility that zoning regulations will not allow the intended use, you should have a clause in your contract that allows you to void the purchase agreement. Be warned, this is not standard language in most boilerplate contracts. You, your broker, or your attorney must make provisions for it.

Environmental agencies can wreak havoc on development plans. Usually, intervention from these agencies is well warranted. However, stopping the development of a large tract of land because there is a frog pond in the back corner of it may be excessive. Normally, developers can find a way to work with environmental issues so that everyone wins, but it can take a chunk of real estate that was originally slated for profitable development.

The extent of red tape reaches into deed restrictions and covenants, too. A previous developer may have created rules that are not easily broken. Politics can be a factor in developments, as can noise. A developer who is required to install a noise barrier that was not planned for can see profits shrink quickly. The cost of connection to municipal utilities can cut heavily into development profits. Plenty of research is needed to avoid costly problems, but this should not be a deterrent. If a project shows viable potential, the time spent will be well rewarded.

## The Transition

The transition from home builder to land developer is a natural one. Builders who build in volume can benefit greatly from doing their own development work. You don't have to be building 60 homes a year, like I used to, in order to justify land development. Being a developer is enough in itself, but when you factor in the builder profit, the deal gets sweeter. Most experienced builders have enough industry knowledge to step into the role of a developer without much trouble.

If you are a builder, getting into land development shouldn't be too difficult, and it could prove to be extremely profitable. Are you working a full-time job and wishing you had a business of your own? Would you like to work part-time and make a full-time income? People who hold down day jobs can be developers in their spare time. That's right, you don't have to be available full time to make major money as a developer. Nights and weekends can provide plenty of time for you to get active as a land developer. Let's move into the next chapter and see more about how you can cash in on the big money being made with land development.

# I'm No Engineer: Can I Really Do It?

A lot of people wonder if they have what it takes to break into land development. Many of these people write themselves off as unsuited to the business. In some cases they may be, but you might be surprised at how little it takes to get a piece of the action in land developing. You don't have to be an engineer or a licensed real estate broker. Developers are not always builders, so you don't have to know how to hammer nails. In fact, there are no real minimum qualifications to meet on an official level. This is not to say that developing land is easy. But, you can train yourself to be a developer and start making money as quickly as you are ready to.

What qualities must you possess to be a successful land developer? Well, we're going to talk about advantageous traits throughout this chapter. Basically, you don't need any form of professional licensing and you don't need a college degree. To survive, you need special skills, but they can be learned as you are earning money as a developer.

Many business owners have to complete years of study to be able to own their own business. It can take years to obtain a license as a master plumber. Getting a license to operate a real estate brokerage can also take years. Earning a college degree takes years. Seems like everywhere you turn, you need to invest time and money to gain the credentials needed to run your own business. There are plenty of exceptions, of course, but there do seem to be time factors associated with many business opportunities in the construction and real estate industry.

Real estate investors don't need special licenses. If they have money or credit, they can buy and sell real estate. The brokers with whom they may work are required to be licensed, but the investors are not. Neither are developers. In fact, developers are real estate investors. But, instead of just buying and selling, developers change the condition of a property. They don't necessarily build anything. Sometimes they acquire property, get it zoned for development, and then sell it for a hefty profit. There are many variations on which to work as a developer.

People are often intimidated by real estate. Many people remember trying to buy their first home. It's common for people to be paying more in rent than what a home loan would cost, but these people may not be able to qualify for a home loan. If they can make the payments, why not? There are rules to abide by. Borrowers usually are required to have a down payment and to meet qualifying ratios. Having enough income to make the payments isn't enough if the other criteria aren't met. This situation can be compared to others. Someone may be a great electrician, but without the proper license, doing electrical work for others is a no-no. Fortunately, real estate investors are not weighted down by licenses. If they have the ability, they can play the game.

Okay, if it's so simple, how is that more people are not developers? Becoming a successful land developer is not always easy. In fact, it rarely is. But, it can be much easier than earning a college degree, and it can prove to be much more profitable. Even with a degree, graduates usually have to work for years to repay their college loans and to climb the financial ladder to their prime income potential. A developer can jump into a six-figure income in a matter of months. But, just like the college student, wise investors and developers spend hours reading and doing research to ensure their success.

So, who can become a land developer? Almost any adult can delve into development. The background of some people is better suited to the business than others. If you have experience in real estate, building, the trades, engineering, surveying, or other skills related to development work you have an advantage. However, the advantage may be slight. Unless you have worked closely with developers, your learning curve will be about the same as it would be for anyone else. Bottom line: Almost anyone who is willing to put in the time for personal study can become a land developer.

## Ideas

Ideas are one of the most important tools in a developer's arsenal. Taking a piece of land and cutting it into four equal pieces qualifies as land developing. This type of project can produce good profits and does not require much creative thought. Planning a full subdivision is a very different job. Few developers create their own development designs. Usually, landscape architects come up with developmental designs. But, developers who are involved in their own designs are often happier with their projects and, sometimes, more profitable.

It is often assumed that developers don't need design skills. This stems from the fact that experts in design features are usually retained for such work. While it is true that experts often do the actual design, good developers have to have an eye for design to see the potential of a prospective property. If you have no creative ability to see something that does not yet exist, you may have trouble as a developer. Successful developers can look at a tract of raw land and see glowing images of what could be in the future for the land. Call these people dreamers if you like, but they can see visions and then move forward to make the dreams come true. This is a natural talent for some developers and a learned skill for others. I'm fortunate to have the natural ability, but if you don't, you can learn to see into the future with the right training.

Vision has so much to do with developing that it's difficult to explain. Almost any piece of land has some potential for development. Some years ago, a CPA and I were looking for land to develop. I found a great tract on a good road and was excited. Then, I found that the land didn't have city sewer or water available to it. Things got worse. Much of the land was not prime building terrain. We had been looking at the piece with an intention to build houses on it. However, after enough research, I wrote the piece off as being too much of a risk, because of the extensive development costs.

After sitting in my office for a few hours, after voiding the offer for the land to build on, I came up with another vision. Remember that this was years ago. Paint-ball games were just becoming popular in the area where I lived, in Virginia. The land that was too wet, too inaccessible, and too rocky to build on profitably could have been turned into a great paint-ball battleground. Since the land had so little suitability for building, it probably could have been purchased at a very low price. My vision of taking a somewhat worthless piece of land and turning it into a battlefield for rent could have paid big dividends. At the time, I was concentrating on building houses in volume and had no interest in running such a business. But, the point is that I was able to see a potentially profitable use for the land that others were not seeing. This is the kind of vision that is very helpful to land developers.

## Money and Credit

As I said in the last chapter, you don't need a lot of money or credit to get involved with land developing. It certainly helps to have both, but determined developers can find ways to overcome a lack of cash or good credit. Doing a partnership deal is often the easy way to circumvent problems of limited resources. But, working with the seller of the land for purchase terms is also an option, and it can be a much better way of going.

Some sellers are quite willing to offer very agreeable terms to developers. In fact, there are sellers who are happy to participate as something of a partner with developers. Raw land can be difficult to sell. This can make sellers more receptive to creative financing options. This is especially true if you are able to spot a piece of land that is not easily identified as a desirable property. Most sellers are willing to accept small deposits and they don't often run credit checks on buyers. Let me give you a few examples of how you might involve the seller of land in your development plans when you don't have much money or good credit.

### Seller Financing

Seller financing is one way to involve a seller in your development plans. A lot of land is sold with seller financing. All financing agreements should be reviewed very carefully. In the case of seller financing, an attorney should review all terms of the loan agreement before any final commitment is made. But, when you can arrange good seller financing, it can make it possible to get a good jump ahead in the development game.

If a seller is willing to work with you and is in a position to offer seller financing, you can do just about any type of land deal that you can agree to with the seller. A tiny deposit could give you contractual control over a nice parcel of land. Once you have the land secured, you can move on with your preliminary development work. It can take months, sometimes years, to get all approvals needed for a development plan. A seller may be willing to hold a piece of land for you during this period time, and you might not have to make monthly payments. The seller might agree to let payment amount accrue until you gain development approval.

It's fairly easy to get interest-only loans from sellers. This type of loan is advantageous because of lower monthly payments. You might have to offer the seller a higher sales price to get more attractive terms. The added cost of the land may be a small price to pay in order to get attractive financing. Buyers and sellers can create almost any type of deal between themselves.

## Options

Options are another consideration in dealing with a seller. It's possible to control vast amounts of real estate with nearly no money when you use options effectively. A $50 bill can give you control of hundreds of acres of land. The problem with options is that the money that is given as option money is usually forfeited if the optioned property is not purchased. But the option money can sometimes be kept low. An advantage to options is that the option money is all that is at risk, so the pendulum swings both ways.

## Seller Participation

Seller participation in development deals is certainly not unheard of. When you can work directly with a seller you may have any number of opportunities. Some sellers may be very happy to work with a developer as a partner. When this is the case, the developer doesn't have to buy the land. Avoiding the cash outlay to purchase property may be enough of an advantage to bring a seller into a partner position. If you have a solid development plan you may even find a seller who will help you pay the predevelopment costs in return for a percentage of the overall profits. It never hurts to ask a seller for some form of participation in a deal. The worst that can happen is that your request will be denied.

## Organizational Skills

How are your organizational skills? Being well organized is a major plus for a land developer. If you have trouble remembering appointments, getting to work on time, or finding personal papers when they are needed, you could be in for a rough ride as a developer. Good developers are well organized and meticulous in their record-keeping matters. Of the many skills needed to be successful as a developer, strong organizational abilities are certainly high on the list of top priorities.

Getting organized is difficult for some people. But it's not terribly hard to gain satisfactory organizational skills. If you are not already comfortable with your ability to file and find material, put some effort into learning how to manage your business matters. Once you start developing land, there will be plenty of material to keep up with. You can improve organizational skills by reading books, attending seminars, and practicing your skills until you find ways that work for you.

## Research

Research plays a vital role in land developing. It is often deep research that turns up outstanding deals. Rarely is a prime deal advertised for sale in a newspaper. Real estate brokerages are a source of land for sale, but like ads in a newspaper, the deals offered by brokerages are probably not the best deals available. Savvy investors ferret out their own deals. They do this by going over tax records, riding around to find suitable properties, and then looking up the owners, and by networking with local people who may know of something that is coming to market soon. Lawyers are a good source of hidden deals. When estates have to be settled, there can be land for sale. It's common for lawyers to handle the settling of estates, so getting to know local lawyers is helpful. Just as attorneys dispose of land, so do banks. Beating the bushes at banks can turn up some good foreclosure deals.

Developers who work with real estate brokers may not do a lot of research. Personally, I think that this can be foolish. Unless a developer's time is extremely valuable and in short supply, personal research should not be omitted. It's fine to let brokers bring deals to you, but don't forget who is affected most by finding good deals—you are. If you want superior opportunities, you may have to create them yourself. Relying on others to do research for you can result in lost time and frustration.

## People Skills

Having good people skills is very helpful for a land developer. There are many people who must be dealt with during most development projects. If you are uncomfortable talking to people, you are going to find yourself at a disadvantage. Lacking general communication skills is a detriment in most careers, and it can be a severe hindrance to developers. Someone has to talk to sellers, brokers, builders, buyers, surveyors, engineers, code officers, and a lot of other people when it comes to developing land. If you can't manage this, you may have to consider hiring someone to do your talking for you. This can be done. But it's better to work on your own abilities and rise to a level of comfortable communication on your own.

## Time

How much time must be devoted to doing a development? The amount of time needed for a development depends on everything from what the project is to the skill of the developer. Simple development plans may be ready to work with in just a couple of months. Complex developments can require years of preliminary work before the land can be developed. How much time must you have to devote to developing on a regular basis? Again, the answer is elusive for many reasons. However, small development deals can generally be managed by people who have full-time jobs. It's very possible to get into land developing on a part-time basis.

If you can't make yourself available during normal business hours of a week you will be at a disadvantage. At the very least, you should try to be available for phone calls. Some parts of the preliminary developing work can be done after regular business hours. Brokers, sellers, subcontractors, and others are often willing to work evenings and weekends. You are not likely to find engineers and code officers so accommodating. It is difficult to do all aspects of land developing if you don't have some flexibility in your schedule for appointments during normal business hours.

The amount of time needed for a development is very difficult to predict. You may find one project that will almost run itself and then hit a deal that requires your attention almost constantly. If you will be working with a real estate broker, you may be able to use the broker for some of the daytime requirements of meetings and deliveries. It's pretty easy to enter developing on a part-time basis, but flexibility during the day can be a big factor in how quickly your projects come to life.

Much of the work done during predevelopment tasks is done by people other than the developer. Once the development team is in place and working, the requirements on a developer diminish. You can limit the amount of time required of you if you build a good team of professionals to work with. Turn to the next chapter and I'll show you what I mean.

# Developing Your Development Team

Developing your development team is a task that you should take on as soon as possible. Even if you don't have any idea of the exact property that you will be developing, you should start to assemble your team right away. This is a process that takes time, and it's such an important element to developing that you should never rush it. Depending on what your basic plans for development are, you may need a large group of professionals to get your project off the ground.

It's easy enough to open a phone directory and hire a surveying firm, but finding a firm that you are comfortable with could take weeks, or more. Then, finding a firm that will work with your personal needs may take even longer. Large projects require a diversified list of talent. Some of the players may be land planners, architects, landscaping architects, engineers, designers, drafters, tax attorneys, accountants, marketing experts, project managers, and a host of other specialists. Soil scientists, environmental experts, geologists, hydrologists, real estate brokers, builders, and various consultants may be needed. Small projects don't usually require such extensive talent. But there will be a need for experts, and you should find them long before you need them.

If you are new to developing, you may not realize how important it is to have a good relationship with the members of your development team. Working with people whom you like and whom you can communicate well with makes every project more enjoyable. Compare the situation to going to a dentist or a doctor. Most people have had bad experiences at one time or another with dentists or doctors. Often it's not that the medical professional was inept; more likely, it is that the patient and doctor just didn't have a good rapport. Personalities are a factor in life and in business. It can take time to find the right people to work with, but the advantages of having a comfortable team offsets the time that must be invested to build it.

## The Experts

The experts needed for your team will depend on what you are developing. A simple subdivision of a building lot will not normally require a lot of technical attention. If you have plans to develop a large subdivision, you can expect to need a lot of experts on your team. Another factor in the experts needed is the location in which you will be doing your development. Some regions require different types of talent. Code requirements and zoning requirements can also affect the type of experts required for a project. Depending on your skills, you may fill some of the slots that would otherwise be held by experts. For example, you may have all the skill needed to act as your own project manager or as your own marketing consultant. Let's look at some of the experts that might be needed on your project.

### Attorneys

Attorneys are almost always needed in some capacity for a development deal. You may consult with tax attorneys prior to making a decision to do a development. A good real estate attorney should be involved in contract issues and the settlement procedures of purchasing property. If you are unfortunate enough to run into litigation, you may need an attorney to represent you in court. Don't expect a single attorney to fulfill all of your needs. It's better to deal with specialists in each field that representation is needed in.

## Accountants

Accountants are often consulted prior to major developments. Certified public accountants (CPAs) are the standard choice for expert tax advice. Most developers depend on their CPAs to stamp their approval on a project before much effort is put forth in development. When partnerships are created, accountants may be used to render accountings to each partner on a regular basis.

## Marketing Consultants

Marketing consultants may be used to determine the viability of a project. The consultants can range from real estate agents to general marketing consultants. Many developers learn to be their own marketing experts. They do this to have an increased comfort level in the proposed success of their projects. Small projects don't generally have enough profit in them to justify a large budget for intricate market studies and sales plans. This is normally when builders, brokers, and developers put their heads together and come up with figures. Large projects may not be approved for financing without a formal market study. These studies can be very expensive. Don't forget to budget for this expense if you have any reason to believe it will be needed.

## Builders

If you will not be doing your own building, you may have to talk to a number of successful home builders during your planning stage. The builders should be able to give you an idea of the types of homes and the price ranges of the homes that they might build in your development. As a rule of thumb, land value is usually thought of as being worth about 20 percent of the total appraised value of a home. So, a house that sells for $200,000 could be built on a lot that sold for $40,000. If you are hoping to get $50,000 for each of your building lots and find that the builders would be building houses that didn't exceed $175,000, you would be hard pressed to get your price for the building lots. This could kill your deal. Of course, your marketing consultants should be able to help you with this aspect of your planning, too.

## Project Planner

You may be your own project planner or you may hire one. If you do contract with or hire a planner, you should have your arrangements in writing (Figs. 3.1 and 3.2). The planner bears a lot of responsibility. If you hope to be your own planner, make darn sure that you are competent to get the job done properly. If you hire an outside planner, choose one that has a long, successful track record. Project planners pull in data from other team members and then put it all together as a master plan. If you are thinking in terms of home building, you could compare a project planner's role to that of a general contractor.

Your Company Name
Your Company Address
Your Company Phone and Fax Numbers

**LETTER OF ENGAGEMENT**

Client: _____

Street: _____

City/State/Zip: _____

Work phone: _____ Home phone: _____

Services requested: _____
_____
_____

Fee for services described above: $_____

Payment to be made as follows: _____

By signing this letter of engagement, you indicate your understanding that this engagement letter constitutes a contractual agreement between us for the services set forth. This engagement does not include any services not specifically stated in this letter. Additional services, which you may request, will be subject to separate arrangements, to be set forth in writing.

A representative of _____ has advised us that we should seek legal counsel prior to using information or materials received from _____
_____

We, the undersigned, hereby release _____,
its employees, officers, shareholders, and representatives from any liability. We understand that we shall have no rights, claims, or recourse and waive any claims or rights we may have against _____, its employees, officers, shareholders, and representatives. We further understand that we will pay all costs of collection of any amount due hereunder including reasonable attorneys' fees.

_____     _____     _____     _____
Client                                          Date     Client                                          Date


_____     _____
Company Representative          Date

**FIGURE 3.1**

Letter of Engagement.

## Architects

Architects are often instrumental in the design stage of a development. Landscape architects play an important role on projects that will require extensive landscaping. However, cutting up rural land into

---

Your Company Name
Your Company Address
Your Company Phone and Fax Numbers

### EARLY TERMINATION AND
### MUTUAL RELEASE OF CONTRACT

For good and valuable consideration had and received and the mutual promises and releases herein contained, the parties known as _____ (Contractor) and _____ (Customer) do hereby release each other, now and forever, in and from all further promises, liabilities, warranties, requirements, obligations, payments, and performance of the contract dated _____, 19 _____, entitled _____ and made for the purpose of _____ _____ as reflected in said contract between them.

    The parties each acknowledge all matters between them regarding the said contract have been satisfactorily adjusted between them, and the contract has been terminated prior to its entire fulfillment and performance, as the parties have agreed such early termination is mutually desirable.

    Accordingly, said contract is hereby SUPERSEDED AND ABSOLUTELY TERMINATED.

    Each party warrants each's own full power and authority to enter into this Early Termination and Mutual Release of Contract, which shall become effective only upon the signature of both parties.

Date: _____    Date: _____

Customer: _____    Contractor: _____

by: _____ (Seal)    Title: _____

                           by: _____ (Seal)

State of _____ of _____

The foregoing Early Termination and Mutual Release of Contract was sworn to and acknowledged before me by _____ and _____ on _____, 19 _____.

_____
Notary Public

My commission expires:_____          (Notary Seal)

**FIGURE 3.2**

---

Early termination and mutual release of contract.

building lots for a few houses will not likely justify the services of a landscape architect. If your development plans include building a structure, architectural plans will probably be needed to obtain full development approvals. As with all of your experts, written agreements should be in place for the services rendered and the payment offered (Fig. 3.3).

| | |
|---|---|
| **ARCHITECT-ENGINEER CONTRACT** | 1. CONTRACT NO. |
| | 2. DATE OF CONTRACT |
| 3a. NAME OF ARCHITECT-ENGINEER | 3b. TELEPHONE NO. *(Include Area Code)* |
| 3c. ADDRESS OF ARCHITECT-ENGINEER *(Include ZIP Code)* | |
| 4. DEPARTMENT OR AGENCY AND ADDRESS *(Include ZIP Code)* | |
| 5. PROJECT TITLE AND LOCATION | |
| 6. CONTRACT FOR *(General description of services to be provided)* | |
| 7. CONTRACT AMOUNT *(Express in words and figures)* | |
| 8. NEGOTIATION AUTHORITY | |
| 9. ADMINISTRATIVE, APPROPRIATION, AND ACCOUNTING DATA | |

NSN 7540-00-181-8326
PREVIOUS EDITION NOT USABLE

**STANDARD FORM 252** (REV. 10-83)
Prescribed by GSA - FAR (48 CFR) 53.236-2(a)

**FIGURE 3.3**

Architect-engineer contract.

## Civil Engineers

Civil engineers are frequently involved in development projects. The engineers may work with geotechnical conditions and infrastructure requirements. It is fairly common to find civil engineers working in firms with other types of talent that will be needed for developing

10. The United States of America (called the Government) represented by the Contracting Officer executing this contract, and the Architect-Engineer agree to perform this contract in strict accordance with the clauses and the documents identified as follows, all of which are made a part of this contract:

If the parties to this contract are comprised of more than one legal entity, each entity shall be jointly and severally liable under this conract. The parties hereto have executed this contract as of the date recorded in Item 2.

| SIGNATURES | NAMES AND TITLES *(Typed)* |
|---|---|
| 11. ARCHITECT-ENGINEER OR OTHER PROFESSIONAL SERVICES CONTRACTOR | |
| A | |
| B | |
| C | |
| D | |
| 12. THE UNITED STATES OF AMERICA | |
| Contracting Officer | |

STANDARD FORM 252 (REV. 10-83) **BACK**

**FIGURE 3.3**

**Architect-engineer contract. (*Continued*)**

land. For example, a firm that I used to use could handle all of my engineering, drafting, and surveying needs. It helps to keep as much of the work as you can under one roof. Have your attorney draft a working agreement for all of your dealings with engineers (Fig. 3.4).

Form RD 1942-19
(Rev. 10-96)

UNITED STATES DEPARTMENT OF AGRICULTURE
RURAL DEVELOPMENT

FORM APPROVED
OMB NO. 0575-0015

**AGREEMENT FOR ENGINEERING SERVICES**

This Agreement, made this _____ day of _____ , 19 _____ ,

by and between _____ , hereafter referred to as the OWNER,

and _____ , hereinafter referred to as the ENGINEER:

THE OWNER intends to construct a _____

_____ in _____ County, State of _____
which may be paid for in part with financial assistance from the United States of America acting through Rural Development of the United States Department of Agriculture, pursuant to the consolidated Farm and Rural Development Act, (7 U.S.C. 1921 et seq.) and for which the ENGINEER agrees to perform the various professional engineering services for the design and construction of said system.

WITNESSETH:

That for and in consideration of the mutual covenants and promises between the parties hereto, it is hereby agreed:

SECTION A - ENGINEERING SERVICES

The ENGINEER shall furnish engineering services as follows:

1. The ENGINEER will conduct preliminary investigations, prepare preliminary drawings, provide a preliminary itemized list of probable construction costs effective as of the date of the preliminary report, and submit a preliminary engineering report following Rural Development instructions and guides.

2. The ENGINEER will furnish 10 copies of the preliminary engineering report, and layout maps to the OWNER.

3. The ENGINEER will attend conferences with the OWNER, representatives of Rural Development, or other interested parties as may be reasonably necessary.

4. After the preliminary engineering report has been reviewed and approved by the OWNER and by Rural Development and the OWNER directs the ENGINEER to proceed, the ENGINEER will perform the necessary design surveys, accomplish the detailed design of the project, prepare construction drawings, specifications and contract documents, and prepare a final cost estimate based on the final design for the entire system. It is also understood that if subsurface explorations (such as borings, soil tests, rock soundings and the like) are required, the ENGINEER will furnish coordination of said explorations without additional charge, but the costs incident to such explorations shall be paid for by the OWNER as set out in Section D hereof.

5. The contract documents furnished by the ENGINEER under Section A-4 shall utilize Rural Development-endorsed construction contract documents, including Rural Development General Conditions, Contract Change Orders, and partial payment estimates. All of these documents shall be subject to Rural Development approval. Copies of guide contract documents may be obtained from Rural Development.

6. Prior to the advertisement for bids, the ENGINEER will provide for each construction contract, not to exceed 10 copies of detailed drawings, specifications, and contract documents for use by the OWNER, appropriate Federal, State, and local agencies from whom approval of the project must be obtained. The cost of such drawings, specifications, and contract documents shall be included in the basic compensation paid to the ENGINEER.

7. The ENGINEER will furnish additional copies of the drawings, specifications and contract documents as required by prospective bidders, material suppliers, and other interested parties, but may charge them for the reasonable cost of such copies. Upon award of each contract, the ENGINEER will furnish to the OWNER five sets of the drawings, specifications and contract documents for execution. The cost of these sets shall be included in the basic compensation paid to the ENGINEER. Original documents, survey notes, tracings, and the like, except those furnished to the ENGINEER by the OWNER, are and shall remain the property of the ENGINEER.

*Public reporting burden for this collection of information is estimated to average 4 hours per response, including the time for reviewing instructions, searching existing data sources, gathering and maintaining the data needed, and completing and reviewing the collection of information. Send comments regarding this burden estimate or any other aspect of this collection of information, including suggestions for reducing this burden, to U.S. Department of Agriculture, Clearance Officer, STOP 7602, 1400 Independence Avenue, S.W., Washington, D.C. 20250-7602.* **Please DO NOT RETURN this form to this address.** *Forward to the local USDA office only. You are not required to respond to this collection of information unless it displays a currently valid OMB control number.*

Position 6

RD 1942-19 (Rev. 10-96)

**FIGURE 3.4**

Agreement for engineering services.

# Surveyors

Surveyors are needed for practically every development deal. The extent of work done by the surveyors varies. You might need a simple boundary survey, or you might need elevation surveys. Normally, surveyors are on a project several times before their job is complete.

(Section A - continued)

8. The drawings prepared by the ENGINEER under the provisions of Section A-4 above shall be in sufficient detail to permit the actual location of the proposed improvements on the ground. The ENGINEER shall prepare and furnish to the OWNER without any additional compensation, three copies of a map(s) showing the general location of needed construction easements and permanent easements and the land to be acquired. Property surveys, property plats, property descriptions, abstracting and negotiations for land rights shall be accomplished by the OWNER, unless the OWNER requests, and the ENGINEER agrees to provide those services. In the event the ENGINEER is requested to provide such services, the ENGINEER shall be additionally compensated as set out in Section D hereof.

9. The ENGINEER will attend the bid opening and tabulate the bid proposals, make an analysis of the bids, and make recommendations for awarding contracts for construction.

10. The ENGINEER will review and approve, for conformance with the design concept, any necessary shop and working drawings furnished by contractors.

11. The ENGINEER will interpret the intent of the drawings and specifications to protect the OWNER against defects and deficiencies in construction on the part of the contractors. The ENGINEER will not, however, guarantee the performance by any contractor.

12. The ENGINEER will establish baselines for locating the work together with a suitable number of bench marks adjacent to the work as shown in the contract documents.

13. The ENGINEER will provide general engineering review of the work of the contractors as construction progresses to ascertain that the contractor is conforming with the design concept.

14. Unless notified by the OWNER in writing that the OWNER will provide for resident inspection, the ENGINEER will provide resident construction inspection. The ENGINEER'S undertaking hereunder shall not relieve the contractor of contractor's obligation to perform the work in conformity with the drawings and specifications and in a workmanlike manner; shall not make the ENGINEER an insurer of the contractor's performance; and shall not impose upon the ENGINEER any obligation to see that the work is performed in a safe manner.

15. The ENGINEER will cooperate and work closely with Rural Development representatives.

16. The ENGINEER will review the contractor's applications for progress and final payment and, when approved, submit same to the OWNER for payment.

17. The ENGINEER will prepare necessary contract change orders for approval of the OWNER, Rural Development, and others on a timely basis.

18. The ENGINEER will make a final review prior to the issuance of the statement of substantial completion of all construction and submit a written report to the OWNER and Rural Development. Prior to submitting the final pay estimate, the ENGINEER shall submit a statement of completion to and obtain the written acceptance of the facility from the OWNER and Rural Development.

19. The ENGINEER will provide the OWNER with one set of reproducible record (as-built) drawings, and two sets of prints at no additional cost to the OWNER. Such drawings will be based upon construction records provided by the contractor during construction and reviewed by the resident inspector and from the resident inspector's construction data.

20. If State statutes require notices and advertisements of final payment, the ENGINEER shall assist in their preparation.

21. The ENGINEER will be available to furnish engineering services and consultations necessary to correct unforeseen project operation difficulties for a period of one year after the date of statement of substantial completion of the facility. This service will include instruction of the OWNER in initial project operation and maintenance but will not include supervision of normal operation of the system. Such consultation and advice shall be furnished without additional charge except for travel and subsistence costs. The ENGINEER will assist the OWNER in performing a review of the project during the 11th month after the date of the certificate of substantial completion.

22. The ENGINEER further agrees to obtain and maintain, at the ENGINEER'S expense, such insurance as will protect the ENGINEER from claims under the Workman's Compensation Act and such comprehensive general liability insurance as will protect the OWNER and the ENGINEER from all claims for bodily injury, death, or property damage which may arise from the performance by the ENGINEER or by the ENGINEER'S employees of the ENGINEER'S functions and services required under this Agreement.

**FIGURE 3.4**

**Agreement for engineering services.** (*Continued*)

## Other Experts

Other experts who may be needed are soil scientists, geologists, and environmental experts, to name a few. You might need an urban planner, a land planner, or even an interior designer. The experts needed will be determined by your personal needs. It is best to sit down and

(Section A - continued)

23. The services called for in the Section A-1 and A-2 of this Agreement shall be completed and the report submitted within _____ calendar days from the date of authorization to proceed. After acceptance by the OWNER and Rural Development of the Preliminary Engineering Report and upon written authorization from the OWNER, the ENGINEER will complete final plans, specifications and contract documents and submit for approval of the OWNER, Rural Development and all State regulatory

agencies within _____ calendar days from the date of authorization unless otherwise agreed to by both parties.

If the above is not accomplished within the time period specified, this Agreement may be terminated by the OWNER. The time for completion will be extended by the OWNER for a reasonable time if completion is delayed due to unforeseeable causes beyond the control and without the fault or negligence of the ENGINEER.

### SECTION B - COMPENSATION FOR ENGINEERING SERVICES

1. The OWNER shall compensate the ENGINEER for preliminary engineering services in the sum of

_____ Dollars ($ _____ )
after the review and approval of the preliminary engineering report by the OWNER and Rural Development.

2. The OWNER shall compensate the ENGINEER for design and contract administration engineering services in the amount of: (Select (a) or (b))

   (a) _____ Dollars ($ _____ ) or

   (b) As shown in Attachment 1

   When Attachment 1 is used to establish compensation for the design and contract administration services, the actual construction costs on which compensation is determined shall exclude legal fees, administrative costs, engineering fees, land rights, acquisition costs, water costs, and interest expense incurred during the construction period.

3. The compensation for preliminary engineering services, design and contract administration services shall be payable as follows:

   (a) A sum which equals seventy percent (70%) of the total compensation payable under Section B-1 and 2, after completion and submission of the construction drawings, specifications, cost estimates, and contract documents, and the acceptance of the same by OWNER and Rural Development.

   (b) A sum which, together with the compensation provided in Section B-3-(a) above, equals eighty percent (80%) of the compensation payable immediately after the construction contracts are awarded.

   (c) A sum equal to fifteen percent (15%) of the compensation will be paid on a monthly basis for general engineering review of the contractor's work during the construction period on percentage ratios identical to those approved by the ENGINEER as a basis upon which to make partial payments to the contractor(s). However, payment under this paragraph and of such additional sums as are due the ENGINEER by reason of any necessary adjustments in the payment computations will be in an amount so that the aggregate of all sums paid to the ENGINEER will equal ninety-five percent (95%) of the compensation. A final payment to equal 100 percent shall be made when it is determined that all services required by this Agreement have been completed except for the services set forth in Section A-21 hereof.

### SECTION C - COMPENSATION FOR RESIDENT INSPECTION
### AS SET FORTH IN SECTION A-14

When the ENGINEER provides resident inspection, the ENGINEER will, prior to the preconstruction conference, submit a resume of the resident inspector's qualifications, anticipated duties and responsibilities for approval by the OWNER and Rural Development. The OWNER agrees to pay the ENGINEER for such services in accordance with the schedule set out in Attachment 1. The ENGINEER will render to OWNER for such services an itemized bill, once each month, for compensation for such services performed hereunder during such period, the same to be due and payable by the OWNER to the ENGINEER on or before the 10th day of the following period.

Under normal construction circumstances, and for the proposed construction period of _____ days, the cost of

resident inspection is estimated to be $ _____ .

**FIGURE 3.4**

**Agreement for engineering services. (*Continued*)**

make a list of every type of expert that you think might be needed. Then you can go about finding the experts and getting to know them before their services are required.

## Finding the Right People

Finding the right people for your project can be frustrating. If you are not connected to the developing industry, you will have to start from ground zero. Builders have a little advantage in that they often come into contact with various experts during their building chores. A quick

---

### SECTION D - ADDITIONAL ENGINEERING SERVICES

In addition to the foregoing being performed, the following services may be provided UPON PRIOR WRITTEN AUTHORIZATION OF THE OWNER and written approval of Rural Development.

1. Site surveys for water treatment plants, sewage treatment works, dams, reservoirs, and other similar special surveys as may be required.

2. Laboratory tests, well tests, borings, specialized geological, soils, hydraulic, or other studies recommended by the ENGINEER.

3. Property surveys, detailed description of sites, maps, drawings, or estimates related thereto; assistance in negotiating for land and easement rights.

4. Necessary data and filing maps for water rights, water adjudication, and litigation.

5. Redesigns ordered by the OWNER after final plans have been accepted by the OWNER and Rural Development, except redesigns to reduce the project cost to within the funds available.

6. Appearances before courts or boards on matters of litigation or hearings related to the project.

7. Preparation of environment impact assessments or environmental impact statements.

8. Performance of detailed staking necessary for construction of the project in excess of the control staking set forth in Section A-12.

9. The ENGINEER further agrees to provide the operation and maintenance manual for facilities when required for

   $ _____ .

   Payment for the services specified in this Section D shall be as agreed in writing between the OWNER and approved by Rural Development prior to commencement of the work. Barring unforeseen circumstances, such payment is estimated not to exceed

   $ _____ . The ENGINEER will render to OWNER for such services an itemized bill, separate from any other billing, once each month, for compensation for services performed hereunder during such period, the same to be due and payable by OWNER to the ENGINEER on or before the 10th day of the following period.

### SECTION E - INTEREST ON UNPAID SUMS

If OWNER fails to make any payment due ENGINEER within 60 days for services and expenses and funds are available for the

project then the ENGINEER shall be entitled to interest at the rate of _____ percent per annum from said 60th day, not to exceed an annual rate of 12 percent.

### SECTION F - SPECIAL PROVISIONS

**FIGURE 3.4**

---

**Agreement for engineering services. (*Continued*)**

skim of a phone directory will get you started, but hopefully, you can find a better way to find the best people with less effort. If you know people who work with the types of experts that you will need, talk to your acquaintances. Word-of-mouth referrals are generally the best way to find good talent. If you don't have many connections in your community, consider joining some clubs. A lot of networking goes on during club meetings.

---

### SECTION G - APPROVAL BY RURAL DEVELOPMENT

This Agreement shall not become effective until approved by Rural Development. Such approval shall be evidenced by the signature of a duly authorized representative of Rural Development in the space provided at the end of this Agreement. The approval so evidenced by Rural Development shall in no way commit Rural Development to render financial assistance to the OWNER and is without liability for any payment hereunder, but in the event such assistance is provided, approval shall signify that the provisions of this Agreement are consistent with the requirements of Rural Development.

IN WITNESS WHEREOF, the parties hereto have executed, or caused to be executed by their duly authorized officials, this Agreement in duplicate on the respective dates indicated below.

(SEAL)

OWNER:

By _____

ATTEST _____

Type Name _____

Type Name _____

Title _____

Title _____

Date _____

(SEAL)

ENGINEER:

ATTEST _____

By _____

Type Name _____

Type Name _____

Title _____

Title _____

Date _____

APPROVED:

RURAL DEVELOPMENT

By _____

Type Name _____

Title _____

Date _____

**FIGURE 3.4**

**Agreement for engineering services.** (*Continued*)

It's been my personal experience that people in the building and developing businesses are willing to share information on people whom they have done business with. Asking a fellow builder who you should talk to for a fast soils test is not threatening. If you were asking about the builder's plans for next year's home designs, you'd probably get stared down, but this is unlikely to happen when you are asking for leads on development talent. Unlike subcontractors, who builders may keep quiet about to keep from losing them, the experts used for developing land fall into a different category for builders. Joining a local builders' association can be a fast way to get some good information on whom to talk to.

When you make a good contact, work it. For example, assume that you already have a CPA whom you are comfortable with. Ask that CPA for the names of some good tax attorneys. Use every contact to create another contact. The snowball effect of this procedure can fill your phone files quickly with names and numbers. If worst comes to worst

---

**INTERIM AGREEMENT**

(For use only when OWNER is not legally organized on the date the Agreement for Engineering Services is executed.)

In lieu of the execution of the foregoing Agreement for Engineering Services dated the _____ day of

_____ , 19 ___ , by the party designated as OWNER therein, the undersigned, hereinafter referred to as INTERIM PARTIES, have executed this Interim Agreement in consideration of the services described in Section A-1 through A-3, inclusive, of said Agreement for Engineering Services to be performed by the ENGINEER, and the ENGINEER agrees to accept this Interim Agreement as evidenced by ENGINEER'S execution hereof contemporaneously with the execution of the Agreement for Engineering Services. The ENGINEER also agrees to perform the services set forth in Section A-1 through A-3, inclusive, of said Agreement in consideration of the sum stated in Section B-1 of said Agreement be paid in the manner set forth therein.

It is anticipated that the OWNER shall promptly become a legal entity with full authority to accept and execute said Agreement for Engineering Services and that the OWNER, after becoming so qualified, shall promptly take such action necessary to adopt, ratify, execute, and become bound by the Agreement for Engineering Services. The ENGINEER agrees that upon such due execution of the Agreement for Engineering Services by the OWNER, the INTERIM PARTIES automatically will be relieved of any responsibility or of liability assumed by their execution of this Interim Agreement, and that the ENGINEER will hold the OWNER solely responsible for performance of the terms and conditions imposed upon the OWNER by the Agreement for Engineering Services, including the payment of all sums specified in Section B-1 of said Agreement.

If the OWNER is not legally organized, or if after being duly organized it fails or refuses to adopt, ratify, and execute the Agreement for Engineering Services within 30 days from the date it becomes legally organized and qualified to do so, or if for any other reason the project fails to proceed beyond the preliminary stage described in Section A-1 through A-3 inclusive, of said Agreement, the INTERIM PARTIES agree to pay ENGINEER for such preliminary engineering services, an amount not to exceed the sum specified therefor in Section B-1 of said Agreement.

IN WITNESS WHEREOF, the parties hereto have executed, or caused to be executed by their duly authorized officials, this Agreement

in duplicate this _____ day of _____ , 19 ___ .

_____        _____
        OWNER                                  ENGINEER

**FIGURE 3.4**

**Agreement for engineering services. (*Continued*)**

and you are forced to cold-call from a phone book, take the time to meet with potential experts. Face-to-face meetings are very important in establishing how you feel about working with someone.

## Questions to Ask

When you are meeting with experts to interview them for your project, go prepared with a list of questions to ask. You may not be given a lot of time to talk with the experts, so be well prepared. Don't be intimidated by the experts. Remember, they will be working for you. Some rookie developers go into relationships with experts and feel in awe of them. The experts should be respected, but the developer is the one in control and who will be signing the checks. Don't forget this.

When you interview potential experts, don't be shy. Ask for their credentials. Inquire about previous projects that they have done. If they will give you one, get a list of their clients. At the very least, get some names of references to contact for more information on the experts. Ask about projects that are presently in development that you can go and see. Be willing to talk about fees and terms. It will be a waste of everyone's time if you just sit in an office and nod your head a lot as the expert tells you how great the firm is.

## A Rough Plan

Once you have found a group of experts whom you believe will be comfortable to work with, you should come up with a rough plan. I'm not talking about a site plan or blueprints. The plan that I'm referring to is your preference for a project to undertake. How big will the project be? Are you going to do something within a city or out in the country? Is it your intention to develop a piece of land and then sell it as a whole project, or will you cut it up and sell it in parcels? Start asking yourself these types of questions.

Once you begin to flesh out your overall intent for a project, you will know more about which experts will be needed. For example, if you will be developing land where private sewage disposal systems will be required, you will need someone to do soil testing. This type of testing will not be needed if you are going to develop in an area where city sewer hookups are available. Define your rough plan as much as you can and then figure out what types of experts will be needed.

Once you have a list of experts and a good idea of the type of project that you plan to do, it's time to make some phone calls to your experts. Explain to them what your thoughts are. Give them a brief rundown of how you see things going and ask for their advice. Find out how much time is likely to be needed for each expert to complete the work needed on such a project. This will allow you to begin building a framework of what to expect when you find the land that you wish to develop. Confirm, as best you can, that you have covered all of the bases on the list of experts needed. Not all experts will be willing to help you double-check yourself, but some of them will. This part of the planning process will give you a fair example of how each of your experts will be to work with when the real project comes in.

## Lenders

Lenders are almost always used in development deals. Most developers must borrow money to do their developing work. Many developers wait until they find a piece of land to talk to a banker. It's better if you have already established a relationship with a lender when you find land to purchase. I strongly suggest that you get out and meet lenders well in advance of needing money. Wait until you have your list of experts to take with you. If you have chosen well, the names of your experts can help to put a lender's mind at ease. Knowing that seasoned, successful professionals will be working with you may make a banker a bit more agreeable to doing business with you.

Not all lenders offer loans for land development. Many lenders consider the business too risky. Call around and see which lenders in your area are willing to talk about loans for land developing. Make appointments to meet with various loan officers. Take a current balance sheet in with you when you meet with your lenders (Fig. 3.5). It makes sense to start with lenders that you already do business with, but don't limit yourself to your favorite bank. Get out and meet as many loan officers as time will allow for. Once you start rolling, you will probably want to borrow from more than one bank at a time.

Don't expect loan officers to be too quick to give you answers about the odds of a loan approval. Most lenders take each deal on an individual basis. A developer's personal credit, assets, and reputation are important in borrowing money for a development, but there's more to it than just that. Good development plans sell themselves to bankers.

If a development can carry itself strongly on paper, less importance is placed on the financial worth of a developer. Therefore, lenders are reluctant to preapprove anything without full facts.

| | Position 3 | | FORM APPROVED OMB No. 0575-0015 |
|---|---|---|---|

Form RD 442-3
(Rev. 3-97)

**BALANCE SHEET**

Name _____

Address _____

| | Month Day Year<br>*Current Year* | Month Day Year<br>*Prior Year* |
|---|---|---|
| **ASSETS** | | |
| CURRENT ASSETS | | |
| 1. Cash on hand in Banks ......................... | | |
| 2. Time deposits and short-term investments ......... | | |
| 3. Accounts receiveable ............................ | | |
| 4. Less: Allowance for doubtful accounts .......... | ( ) | ( ) |
| 5. Inventories .................................... | | |
| 6. Prepayments ................................... | | |
| 7. _____ ........ | | |
| 8. _____ ........ | | |
| 9. Total Current Assets (Add 1 through 8)........... | | |
| FIXED ASSETS | | |
| 10. Land .......................................... | | |
| 11. Buildings ..................................... | | |
| 12 Furniture and equipment ....................... | | |
| 13. _____ ........ | | |
| 14. Less: Accumulated depreciation ............... | ( ) | ( ) |
| 15. Net Total Fixed Assets (Add 10 through 14) ...... | | |
| OTHER ASSETS | | |
| 16. _____ ........ | | |
| 17. _____ ........ | | |
| 18. Total Assets (Add 9, 15, 16 and 17) ............ | | |
| **LIABILITIES AND EQUITIES** | | |
| CURRENT LIABILITIES | | |
| 19. Accounts payable .............................. | | |
| 20. Notes payable ................................. | | |
| 21. Current portion of USDA note .................. | | |
| 22. Customer deposits ............................. | | |
| 23. Taxes payable ................................. | | |
| 24. Interest payable .............................. | | |
| 25. _____ ........ | | |
| 26. _____ ........ | | |
| 27. Total Current Liabilities (Add 19 through 26) .... | | |
| LONG-TERM LIABILITIES | | |
| 28. Notes payable USDA ........................... | | |
| 29. _____ ........ | | |
| 30. _____ ........ | | |
| 31. Total Long-Term Liabilities (Add 28 through 30) .. | | |
| 32. Total Liabilities (Add 27 and 31).............. | | |
| EQUITY | | |
| 33. Retained earnings ............................. | | |
| 34. Memberships .................................. | | |
| 35. Total Equity (Add lines 33 and 34)............. | | |
| 36. Total Liabilities and Equity (Add lines 32 and 35)... | | |

| **CERTIFIED CORRECT** | Date | Appropriate Official (*Signature*) |
|---|---|---|

*According to the Paperwork Reduction Act of 1995, no persons are required to respond to a collection of information unless it displays a valid OMB control number. The valid OMB control number for this information collection is 0570-0015. The time required to complete this information is estimated to average 1 hour per response, including the time for reviewing instructions, searching existing data sources, gathering and maintaining the data needed, and completing and reviewing the collection of information.*

RD 442-3 (Rev. 3-97)

**FIGURE 3.5**

Balance sheet.

The goal in the early stages with lenders is to get to know them and to let them get comfortable with you. This will help immensely when you make formal application for a loan. By meeting with various

---

## INSTRUCTIONS

### Present Borrowers

This form may be used as a year end Balance Sheet by Rural Development Community Program and Farm Service Agency Group Farm Loan Program borrowers who do not have an independent audit. Submit two copies within 60 days following year's end to the Agency Official. An independently audited balance sheet will substitute for this form.

### Applicants

In preparing this form when the application for financing is for a facility which is a unit of your overall operation, two balance sheets are to be submitted: one for the facility being financed and one for the entire operation. Examples: (a) application to finance a sewage system which is a part of a water-sewage system or municipality, (b) application to finance a nursing home which is part of a larger health care facility.

### Preparation of this Form

1. Enter data where appropriate for the current and prior year.

2. Line 35, Total Equity, of this form will be the same as line 26, on Form RD 442-2, "Statement of Budget, Income and Equity", when using the form.

3. The term Equity is used interchangeably with Net Worth, Fund Balance, etc.

### BALANCE SHEET ITEMS

#### Current Assets

1. **Cash on hand and in Banks**
   Includes undeposited cash and demand deposits.

2. **Time Deposits and Short Term Investments**
   Funds in savings accounts and certificates of deposit maturing within one year.

3. **Accounts Receivable**
   Amounts billed but not paid by customers, users, etc. This is the gross amount before any allowances in item 4.

4. **Allowance for Doubtful Accounts**
   Amounts included in item 3 which are estimated to be uncollectible.

5. **Inventories**
   The total of all materials, supplies and finished goods on hand.

6. **Prepayments**
   Payments made in advance of receipt of goods or utilization of services. Examples: rent, insurance.

7 - 8. List other current assets not included above.

#### Fixed Assets

10 - 12. List land, buildings, furniture and equipment separately by gross value.

13. List other fixed assets.

14. **Accumulated Depreciation**
Indicate total accumulated depreciation for items 10-13.

#### Other Assets

16 - 17. List other assets not previously accounted for.

#### Current Liabilities

19. **Accounts Payable**
    Amounts due to creditors for goods delivered or services completed.

20. **Notes Payable**
    Amounts due to banks and other creditors for which a promissory note has been signed.

21. **Current Portion USDA Note**
    Amount due USDA for principal payment during the next 12 months. Includes any payments which are in arrears.

22. **Customer Deposits**
    Funds of various kinds held for others.

23. **Taxes Payable**

24. **Interest Payable USDA**
    Interest applicable to principal amount in line 21.

25 - 26. List other payables and accruals not shown above.

#### Long Term Liabilities

28. **Notes Payable USDA**
    List total principal payments to USDA which mature after one year and are not included in line 21.

29 - 30. List all other long term liabilities such as bonds, bank loans, etc. which are due after one year.

#### Equity

33. **Retained Earnings**
    Net income which has been accumulated from the beginning of the operation and not distributed to members, users, etc.

34. **Memberships**
    The total of funds collected from persons of membership type facilities, i.e., water and sewer systems.

RD 442-3                    Page 2 of 2

**FIGURE 3.5**

**Balance Sheet.** (*Continued*)

lenders you will also determine which ones seem the easiest to get along with. Developers usually spend a good deal of time working with lenders, so it's important to have a good working relationship. Once you are comfortable with your team, you can begin to search for land. The next chapter will get you started in that direction.

# The Search for Land Begins

When the search for land begins, you may find yourself over-whelmed with choices. Or you may feel that there is no suitable land available that you can afford. These two extremes are common. Many developers who don't have a lot of experience fall into the traps of wanting to buy everything that they see or not wanting to buy any-thing at all. If you don't purchase any land, your career as a developer will be difficult to pursue. Buying too much land or buying land under the wrong conditions can end your career quickly. Knowing what to buy, when to buy it, and how to buy it is very important to your over-all success as a developer.

Some developers rely heavily on real estate agents to find land for development projects. Brokers can be a big help to a developer, but leaving all property searches to brokers means missing some good deals. There are sellers who simply refuse to work with brokers. These sellers may have prime properties for sale. Developers who don't explore the world of private sales are sure to miss some good deals from time to time.

Developers sometimes hire private individuals to research avail-able land. The researchers may be paid an hourly wage or may be paid on the basis of performance. People who don't hold suitable real estate licenses cannot broker deals between a buyer and seller. This doesn't mean that an unlicensed person can't do some digging to turn up prospective properties. If potential properties are located, the researcher can inform the developer of their existence. Then, the developer can negotiate directly with the owner of the property.

Some land owners simply don't like to be bothered by real estate agents and brokers. These same land owners might be very willing to talk to a developer or someone researching land for a developer. The use of a researcher is fine, but the extent of what the researcher can do without violating a state's real estate law varies. Ideally, the researcher should be a licensed broker who is representing the developer. This clears up a lot of potential legal issues. However, if the researchers confine their efforts to locating property and don't become involved in any way with negotiating a transaction, they don't need to be licensed real estate professionals.

Some developers prefer to do all of their own prospecting for potential properties. This approach has its advantages. But it takes a lot of time out of a developer's day. Running down leads on properties can be very time-consuming. Developers who do their own research work have the advantage of knowing moment by moment how their searches are going. Effort is not wasted on property that a developer is not interested in, as could be the case if a researcher was being used to look for land. Most developers employ a multipronged approach to finding land. They look themselves when time allows, have arrangements with various brokers to always be on the lookout for land, and may have researchers doing some digging into private sales. Any of the methods can be effective.

## An Abundance

There may be an abundance of land available for possible development. Most of it will not be for sale or will not be suitable for a developer's desires. Ruling out land that is not right may be the first step in finding land. A lot of time can be spent chasing every parcel of land in sight. To conserve time and effort, some developers prefer to nail down exactly what they want and then look for it. Generally, having predefined parameters of what will be acceptable for development is more time-efficient and more cost-effective.

Developers who wish to work in areas where development is already booming may be faced with a shortage of available land. When this is the case, developers may have to expand the radius in which they are willing to work or to alter their requirements for a piece of land. For example, a developer may have to look at what land is available and determine a way to make it profitable to develop, rather than have a preconceived development plan that will not fit the land available. Depending on circumstances, developers may have to alter their plans to fit whatever land they can buy. Doing this can be more risky than having a good plan that financial numbers support. Trying to mold a plan to a piece of land can lead to compromises that may result in less profit.

Where there is an abundance of land, it can be tempting to try to control much of it. A developer might try to tie up several parcels of land with options instead of concentrating closely on one piece of property. There are times when controlling a lot of surrounding land is a sound move, but it is usually safer to pick the best piece of land available and concentrate heavily on it.

Small developers should not diversify too much in their land control. Keeping all available funds available for a specific project makes more sense than spreading the money out among many potential projects. Entering into multiple projects at once is distracting for seasoned developers, and it can be destructive for new or small developers. Unless several pieces of property are being optioned as part of a single development deal, avoid the temptation to gobble up all of the land in sight.

## Defining Your Needs

Defining your needs for development is an important step in the search for land. You could look for land and then decide what to do with it, but having a plan to follow during your search should prove more efficient and more effective. If you already have a rough idea of what you want to do, and you should, then refining the plan to better identify your land needs shouldn't be too difficult.

The needs for some projects are easier to define than others. For example, if you plan to build a facility where elderly people will be housed and cared for, you probably need a location that is convenient to medical facilities, stores, and the general population of an area. Building such a facility 20 miles from the nearest hospital would not be a good idea.

If you want to develop building lots to build log cabins from kit packages, city lots probably will not sell as well as rural land. The style of the homes indicates a need for more rural land. It would, of course, be possible to build log cabins in a city, but the people who would be interested in buying log cabins probably wouldn't want city lights and noises in their backyards.

Let's say that you want to create a development for professional office space. It is your intent to build a facility and lease space to medical professionals, such as dentists and optometrists, and so forth. Do you want to look for land in the heart of the city? Would land on the fringes of the city serve your needs better? Is country land worth considering?

Country land is pretty much out of the question. Inner-city land is feasible, but will people want to fight city traffic, or would they prefer a fringe location? Many developers have found that fringe locations sell and lease better than inner-city developments. To make a reasonable determination of choosing between inner-city land and fringe land there is much to consider. Let's look at some of the considerations:

- What is the availability of land in each location?

- How do land prices compare between the two locations?

- Are there any zoning problems with either location?

- How populated are outlying areas?

- What does historical data show on the success of other fringe developments?

- Will city dwellers drive out to the fringe areas?

- What do demographics show about income of the population?

- Will you be able to provide adequate parking in both locations?

You could go on and on with the type of questioning that I've just described, and you should. Ask yourself questions daily. Don't assume that one brainstorming session is going to be enough to make a well-rounded decision. Think, think, and then think some more. Before you make an offer to buy land you had better have a solid plan for what you are going to do with it.

## Setting a Budget

Once you know the type of land that you want and where you want it to be located, you have to arrive at a maximum price that you can afford to pay for the land. Don't skip this step on the planning process. If you go out looking for land without an established budget you may get caught up in an emotional rush that traps you into paying too much for a piece of land. Having a price limit preset will help you to stay within your profit zone.

Determining what you can afford to pay for a piece of land can be a complicated process. Many home builders try not to pay more than 20 percent of a completed project's total appraised value for land. I have used the 20 percent rule of thumb for many years and it has worked for me. But, the builders are paying 20 percent for a buildable lot, not raw land that must be developed. As a developer, you must factor in all of your costs to get the land developed to a point where it can be built on.

The costs incurred to develop land can be varied and substantial. Depending on your individual project, you have to estimate all of the development costs before you can arrive at a reasonable price to pay for raw land. These costs may include, but not be limited to:

- Survey expenses
- Soils studies
- Loan origination fees and interest expenses
- Engineering fees
- Permit costs
- The development and drawing of site plans
- Site work
- Legal fees
- And many more potential expenses

To expand on this, let's look at an example of a simple development deal. Assume that you are buying a one-acre tract of land that has a lot of road frontage. Your plan is to cut the land in half to create two building lots. Since the land has road frontage for its entire width and there are no zoning complications, development costs should be low. After some research, you have found that basically all that you have to do is to have a survey crew divide the lot and draw a site plan for each lot that is created. There will be some legal fees and some permit costs, but both will be minimal. Financing costs will be low on this deal. After pushing your pencil around for a while, you estimate that all development costs will not exceed $5000. So, now what do you need to know?

How much will the finished lots be worth? Can you estimate what the total appraised value for a house and lot will be? Assume that research shows a price range of between $150,000 and $165,000. You want to be conservative, so you work with the lower number. Twenty percent of $150,00 is $30,000. You will have two lots for a total value of $60,000. If your development expenses are $5000 you will be left with $55,000.

How much profit do you need to make on the deal? Because of the type of deal that you are working with, very little effort or time is required of you. If you want a 20-percent profit of the gross sales price, you will be looking to make $12,000. Will you have to pay brokerage fees to have the lots sold? Did you factor this expense into the development costs? Are you going to build the homes yourself? There are always more questions to ask and answer. For the sake of our example, let's assume that you anticipate paying a 10 percent real estate commission to have both lots sold. This amounts to $6000. So, you have $55,000 less $6000, which gives you $49,000. You want $12,000 for yourself, so the number drops to $37,000. Basically, you could pay up to $37,000 for the raw land. But, things could go wrong. Maybe you should factor in some percentage for mistakes.

Many developers would try to pay no more than $30,000 for the raw land. It is common for developers to attempt to keep their land acquisition cost at half of what they hope the finished value will be. It's not always possible to maintain this type of spread, but it is desirable when feasible. Maybe you have so much confidence in the project that you will pay up to $35,000 for the raw land. The amount you are willing to pay is up to you. Deciding on values and profit percentages is a personal process. In some way, however, you need to peg a number as the most that you are willing to pay for raw land, and you should do this before you ever begin to look at land. Once you start shopping, you may get carried away with excitement and pay more for property than you should.

## Working with Brokers

Working with brokers is easy if you can tell the brokers what your buying requirements are. Since you are a buyer, you should be working with brokers who are buyers' brokers. This type of broker works for you, but can be paid a commission by the seller or the seller's agent. If you deal with sellers' brokers you are not represented as well as you should be with a buyers' broker. Many brokerages specialize in having only buyers' brokers in their company. Other brokerages specialize in being sellers' agents, and then there are brokerages that offer both types of representation. You should make arrangements to deal with a buyers' broker. Even with a buyers' broker, you should also retain a good real estate attorney to look after your best interest in all of your dealings.

If you retain a good buyers' broker you should be able to leave most of the land searching to the broker. This doesn't mean that you should close your eyes to the market and wait for the broker to bring you a top-drawer deal. Doing your own research can pay big dividends. Depending on how you structure your arrangement with the buyers' broker, you may not be obligated to compensate the broker for deals that you make directly with sellers when the seller's land is not listed with a brokerage. Don't make this assumption, though; have your full arrangement with the buyer's broker in writing and make sure that you understand the agreement completely.

Some investors and developers prefer to work with sellers' agents in order to get more leads on land. When you commit to a buyers' broker, the broker does all the work with listed properties. If you prefer to have several brokers bringing you potential properties, it might be worth the trade-off of not having full representation by a buyers' broker. If you decide to work with sellers' brokers, you can send out a property description of what you are looking for to several brokerages and hope that some agent or broker will bring you a deal to consider. As long as you have good legal representation to review all of your commitments before they are made, this procedure is fine. A really good buyers' broker will probably prove to be your best bet, but the shotgun approach with sellers' agents will prove more effective if the buyers' broker with whom you are working is not aggressive in seeking out properties for your consideration.

## The Do-It-Yourself Approach

The do-it-yourself approach to finding land is a proved technique among successful developers. You can contact numerous brokerages and make your desire known. If the brokerages have listings that fit your criteria, you will hear about them. You can search out land and contact owners directly to see if the land can be purchased. A trip to the tax assessor's office or the hall of records is all that is needed to obtain the name of property owners. Since you are doing all of the prospecting yourself, you are assured of working toward the goal that you have set. Brokers sometimes try to slip in properties that are close to matching a developer's criteria without being a complete match. This is done in hopes of making a sale. You don't have to worry about this type of substitution when you do your own land search.

Time is one of the biggest drawbacks to the do-it-yourself approach. It can take a lot of time to chase down leads. You can go to a brokerage office and sit down with an agent to look through land listings. Most brokerages participate in some form of multiple listing service, which allows you to view the listings of all participating brokerages while going to only one brokerage. Newspaper advertisements can produce decent land deals. As more and more brokerages advertise on the Internet, you can surf your way to listings on the World Wide Web. If you have the time and determination, you can find solid land deals without the help of a broker. However, most developers find that working with brokers, in conjunction with personal searches, is the best way to find land quickly.

## Appraisers

Real estate appraisers are often thought of as professionals who are not needed in a land deal prior to land being found. Developers who think this way are missing out on a great resource. Many appraisers are willing to work with developers in a variety of ways. The appraisers can help you determine what the finished value of a project will be. By looking at development plans and drawings, appraisers can get a good idea of what to expect for market value when a project is completed. Basic reports from appraisers can give you much insight into a project (Fig. 4.1). Equally important is the fact that many appraisers will work as consultants to builders and developers. This is the resource value that is often overlooked.

As a builder and developer, I have retained appraisers as consultants on many occasions. Their help has proved to be extremely valuable in my planning phases. Appraisers are in a perfect position to help a developer determine all sorts of information that may have an economic impact on a project. If you need to know the market values of homes in a certain neighborhood, an appraiser who works the area can tell you quickly what you need to know. Are you curious about the vacancy rate of professional office buildings in the fringe areas of a city? The right appraisers can provide you with dependable numbers on vacancy rates. When it comes to assessing property values, appraisers are the place to turn for answers. Don't wait until you have bought land to find out what its market potential is; consult with appraisers in advance and know that your plans make economic sense.

In order for a development to be successful, you need to start with a piece of land that has viable potential. Sorting out properties can be confusing. Personal research and consultations with appraisers are both good ways to put the odds in your favor. To learn how to choose the best properties for your needs, turn to the next chapter.

Freddie Mac **LoanProspector®** Quantitative Analysis Appraisal Report File No.

THIS SUMMARY APPRAISAL REPORT IS INTENDED FOR USE BY THE LENDER/CLIENT FOR A MORTGAGE FINANCE TRANSACTION ONLY.

**SUBJECT**

Property Address City State Zip Code
Legal Description County
Assessor's Parcel No. Tax Year R.E. Taxes $ Special Assessments $
Borrower Current Owner Occupant: ☐ Owner ☐ Tenant ☐ Vacant
Neighborhood or Project Name Project Type: ☐ PUD ☐ Condominium HOA $ /Mo.
Sales Price $ Date of Sale Description / $ amount of loan charges/concessions to be paid by seller
Property rights appraised ☐ Fee Simple ☐ Leasehold Map Reference Census Tract

**NEIGHBORHOOD**

Note: Race and the racial composition of the neighborhood are not appraisal factors.

| | | | | | | | | Single family housing | Condominium housing |
|---|---|---|---|---|---|---|---|---|---|
| Location | ☐ Urban | ☐ Suburban | ☐ Rural | Property values | ☐ Increasing | ☐ Stable | ☐ Declining | PRICE $ (000) AGE (Yrs) | PRICE (if applic.) $ (000) AGE (Yrs) |
| Built up | ☐ Over 75% | ☐ 25–75% | ☐ Under 25% | Demand/supply | ☐ Shortage | ☐ In balance | ☐ Over supply | Low | Low |
| Growth rate | ☐ Rapid | ☐ Stable | ☐ Slow | Marketing time | ☐ Under 3 mos. | ☐ 3–6 mos. | ☐ Over 6 mos. | High | High |
| Neighborhood boundaries | | | | | | | | Predominant | Predominant |

**SITE**

Dimensions Site area Shape
Specific zoning classification and description
Zoning compliance: ☐ Legal ☐ Legal nonconforming (Grandfathered use) ☐ Illegal, attach description ☐ No zoning
Highest and best use of subject property as improved (or as proposed per plans and specifications): ☐ Present use ☐ Other use, attach description.

| Utilities | Public | Other | | Public | Other | Off-site Improvements | Type | Public | Private |
|---|---|---|---|---|---|---|---|---|---|
| Electricity | ☐ | ☐ | Water | ☐ | ☐ | Street | | ☐ | ☐ |
| Gas | ☐ | ☐ | Sanitary sewer | ☐ | ☐ | Alley | | ☐ | ☐ |

Are there any apparent adverse site conditions (easements, encroachments, special assessments, slide areas, etc.)? ☐ Yes ☐ No If Yes, attach description.

**IMPROVEMENTS**

Source(s) used for physical characteristics of property: ☐ Interior and exterior inspection ☐ Exterior inspection from street ☐ Previous appraisal files ☐ MLS ☐ Assessment and tax records ☐ Prior inspection ☐ Property owner ☐ Other (Describe):
No. of Stories Type (Det./Att.) Exterior Walls Roof Surface Manufactured Housing ☐ Yes ☐ No
Does the property generally conform to the neighborhood in terms of style, condition, and construction materials? ☐ Yes ☐ No If No, attach description.
Are there any apparent physical deficiencies or conditions that would affect the soundness or structural integrity of the improvements or the livability of the property? ☐ Yes ☐ No If Yes, attach description.
Are there any apparent adverse environmental conditions (hazardous wastes, toxic substances, etc.) present in the improvements, on the site, or in the immediate vicinity of the subject property? ☐ Yes ☐ No If Yes, attach description.

**QUANTITATIVE SALES COMPARISON ANALYSIS**

I researched the subject market area for comparable listings and sales that are the most similar and proximate to the subject property.
My research revealed a total of ______ sales ranging in sales price from $______ to $______.
My research revealed a total of ______ listings ranging in list price from $______ to $______.
The analysis of the comparable sales below reflects market reaction to significant variations between the sales and the subject property.

| FEATURE | SUBJECT | SALE 1 | | SALE 2 | | SALE 3 | |
|---|---|---|---|---|---|---|---|
| Address | | | | | | | |
| Proximity to Subject | | | | | | | |
| Sales Price | $ | | $ | | $ | | $ |
| Price/Gross Liv. Area | $ ☐ | $ ☐ | | $ ☐ | | $ ☐ | |
| Data & Verification Sources | | | | | | | |
| VALUE ADJUSTMENTS | DESCRIPTION | DESCRIPTION | +(-) $ Adjustment | DESCRIPTION | +(-) $ Adjustment | DESCRIPTION | +(-) $ Adjustment |
| Sales or Financing Concessions | | | | | | | |
| Date of Sale/Time | | | | | | | |
| Location | | | | | | | |
| Site | | | | | | | |
| View | | | | | | | |
| Design (Style) | | | | | | | |
| Actual Age (Yrs.) | | | | | | | |
| Condition | | | | | | | |
| Above Grade Room Count | Total Bdrms Baths | Total Bdrms Baths | | Total Bdrms Baths | | Total Bdrms Baths | |
| Gross Living Area | Sq. Ft. | Sq. Ft. | | Sq. Ft. | | Sq. Ft. | |
| Basement & Finished Rooms Below Grade | | | | | | | |
| Garage/Carport | | | | | | | |
| | | | | | | | |
| | | | | | | | |
| Net Adj. (Total) | | ☐ + ☐ – | $ | ☐ + ☐ – | $ | ☐ + ☐ – | $ |
| Adjusted Sales Price of Comparables | | | $ | | $ | | $ |
| Date of Prior Sale | | | | | | | |
| Price of Prior Sale | $ | $ | | $ | | $ | |

Analysis of any current agreement of sale, option, or listing of the subject property and analysis of the prior sales of subject and comparables:

Summary of sales comparison and value conclusion:

This appraisal is made ☐ "as-is", ☐ subject to completion per plans and specifications on the basis of a hypothetical condition that the improvements have been completed, or ☐ subject to the following repairs, alterations or conditions:

BASED ON AN ☐ EXTERIOR INSPECTION FROM THE STREET OR AN ☐ INTERIOR AND EXTERIOR INSPECTION, I ESTIMATE THE MARKET VALUE, AS DEFINED, OF THE REAL PROPERTY THAT IS THE SUBJECT OF THIS REPORT TO BE $______, AS OF ______.

Freddie Mac Form 2055 Page 1 of 3 11/97

**FIGURE 4.1**

**Appraisal form.**

---

**Loan Prospector®** — Freddie Mac — **Quantitative Analysis Appraisal Report** — File No. _____

**Project Information for PUDs** (If applicable) — Is the developer/builder in control of the homeowners' association (HOA)? ☐ Yes ☐ No

Provide the following information for PUDs only if the developer/builder is in control of the HOA and the subject property is an attached dwelling unit:

Total number of phases _____ Total number of units _____ Total number of units sold _____

Total number of units rented _____ Total number of units for sale _____ Data Source(s) _____

Was the project created by the conversion of existing buildings into a PUD? ☐ Yes ☐ No If Yes, date of conversion: _____

Does the project contain any multi-dwelling units? ☐ Yes ☐ No Data Source: _____

Are the common elements completed? ☐ Yes ☐ No If No, describe status of completion: _____

Are any common elements leased to or by the homeowners' association? ☐ Yes ☐ No If Yes, attach addendum describing rental terms and options.

Describe common elements and recreational facilities: _____

**Project Information for Condominiums** (If applicable) — Is the developer/builder in control of the homeowners' association (HOA)? ☐ Yes ☐ No

Provide the following information for all Condominium Projects:

Total number of phases _____ Total number of units _____ Total number of units sold _____

Total number of units rented _____ Total number of units for sale _____ Data Source(s) _____

Was the project created by the conversion of existing buildings into a condominium? ☐ Yes ☐ No If Yes, date of conversion: _____

Project Type: ☐ Primary Residence ☐ Second Home or Recreational ☐ Row or Townhouse ☐ Garden ☐ Midrise ☐ Highrise ☐ _____

Condition of the project, quality of construction, unit mix, etc.: _____

Are the common elements completed? ☐ Yes ☐ No If No, describe status of completion: _____

Are any common elements leased to or by the homeowners' association? ☐ Yes ☐ No If Yes, attach addendum describing rental terms and options.

Describe common elements and recreational facilities: _____

**PURPOSE OF APPRAISAL:** The purpose of this appraisal is to estimate the market value of the real property that is the subject of this report based on a quantitative sales comparison analysis for use in a mortgage finance transaction.

**DEFINITION OF MARKET VALUE:** The most probable price which a property should bring in a competitive and open market under all conditions requisite to a fair sale, the buyer and seller, each acting prudently, knowledgeably and assuming the price is not affected by undue stimulus. Implicit in this definition is the consummation of a sale as of a specified date and the passing of title from seller to buyer under conditions whereby: (1) buyer and seller are typically motivated; (2) both parties are well informed or well advised, and each acting in what he considers his own best interest; (3) a reasonable time is allowed for exposure in the open market; (4) payment is made in terms of cash in U.S. dollars or in terms of financial arrangements comparable thereto; and (5) the price represents the normal consideration for the property sold unaffected by special or creative financing or sales concessions* granted by anyone associated with the sale.

*Adjustments to the comparables must be made for special or creative financing or sales concessions. No adjustments are necessary for those costs which are normally paid by sellers as a result of tradition or law in a market area; these costs are readily identifiable since the seller pays these costs in virtually all sales transactions. Special or creative financing adjustments can be made to the comparable property by comparisons to financing terms offered by a third party institutional lender that is not already involved in the property or transaction. Any adjustment should not be calculated on a mechanical dollar for dollar cost of the financing or concession but the dollar amount of any adjustment should approximate the market's reaction to the financing or concessions based on the appraiser's judgment.

### STATEMENT OF LIMITING CONDITIONS AND APPRAISER'S CERTIFICATION

**CONTINGENT AND LIMITING CONDITIONS:** The appraiser's certification that appears in the appraisal report is subject to the following conditions:

1. The appraiser will not be responsible for matters of a legal nature that affect either the property being appraised or the title to it. The appraiser assumes that the title is good and marketable and, therefore, will not render any opinions about the title. The property is appraised on the basis of it being under responsible ownership.

2. The appraiser has provided any required sketch in the appraisal report to show approximate dimensions of the improvements and the sketch is included only to assist the reader of the report in visualizing the property and understanding the appraiser's determination of its size.

3. The appraiser will not give testimony or appear in court because he or she made an appraisal of the property in question, unless specific arrangements to do so have been made beforehand.

4. The appraiser has noted in the appraisal report any adverse conditions (such as, but not limited to, needed repairs, the presence of hazardous wastes, toxic substances, etc.) observed during the inspection of the subject property or that he or she became aware of during the normal research involved in performing the appraisal. Unless otherwise stated in the appraisal report, the appraiser has no knowledge of any hidden or unapparent conditions of the property or adverse environmental conditions (including the presence of hazardous wastes, toxic substances, etc.) that would make the property more or less valuable, and has assumed that there are no such conditions and makes no guarantees or warranties, expressed or implied, regarding the condition of the property. The appraiser will not be responsible for any such conditions that do exist or for any engineering or testing that might be required to discover whether such conditions exist. Because the appraiser is not an expert in the field of environmental hazards, the appraisal report must not be considered as an environmental assessment of the property.

5. The appraiser obtained the information, estimates, and opinions that were expressed in the appraisal report from sources that he or she considers to be reliable and believes them to be true and correct. The appraiser does not assume responsibility for the accuracy of such items that were furnished by other parties.

6. The appraiser will not disclose the contents of the appraisal report except as provided for in the Uniform Standards of Professional Appraisal Practice.

7. The appraiser must provide his or her prior written consent before the lender/client specified in the appraisal report can distribute the appraisal report (including conclusions about the property value, the appraiser's identity and professional designations, and references to any professional appraisal organizations or the firm with which the appraiser is associated) to anyone other than the borrower; the mortgagee or its successors and assigns; the mortgage insurer; consultants; professional appraisal organizations; any state or federally approved financial institution; or any department, agency, or instrumentality of the United States or any state or the District of Columbia; except that the lender/client may distribute the report to data collection or reporting service(s) without having to obtain the appraiser's prior written consent. The appraiser's written consent and approval must also be obtained before the appraisal can be conveyed by anyone to the public through advertising, public relations, news, sales, or other media.

8. The appraiser has based his or her appraisal report and valuation conclusion for an appraisal that is subject to completion per plans and specifications on the basis of a hypothetical condition that the improvements have been completed.

9. The appraiser has based his or her appraisal report and valuation conclusion for an appraisal that is subject to completion, repairs, or alterations on the assumption that completion of the improvements will be performed in a workmanlike manner.

Freddie Mac Form 2055 — Page 2 of 3 — 11/97

**FIGURE 4.1**

**Appraisal form.** (*Continued*)

Freddie Mac | **Loan** *Prospector®* | **Quantitative Analysis Appraisal Report** | File No.

**APPRAISER'S CERTIFICATION:** The Appraiser certifies and agrees that:

1. I performed this appraisal by (1) personally inspecting from the street the subject property and neighborhood and each of the comparable sales (unless I have otherwise indicated in this report) that I also inspected the interior of the subject property); (2) collecting, confirming, and analyzing data from reliable public and/or private sources; and (3) reporting the results of my inspection and analysis in this summary appraisal report. I further certify that I have adequate information about the physical characteristics of the subject property and the comparable sales to develop this appraisal.

2. I have researched and analyzed the comparable sales and offerings/listings in the subject market area and have reported the comparable sales in this report that are the best available for the subject property. I further certify that adequate comparable market data exists in the general market area to develop a reliable sales comparison analysis for the subject property.

3. I have taken into consideration the factors that have an impact on value in my development of the estimate of market value in the appraisal report. I further certify that I have noted any apparent or known adverse conditions in the subject improvements, on the subject site, or on any site within the immediate vicinity of the subject property of which I am aware, have considered these adverse conditions in my analysis of the property value to the extent that I had market evidence to support them, and have commented about the effect of the adverse conditions on the marketability of the subject property. I have not knowingly withheld any significant information from the appraisal report and I believe, to the best of my knowledge, that all statements and information in the appraisal report are true and correct.

4. I stated in the appraisal report only my own personal, unbiased, and professional analysis, opinions, and conclusions, which are subject only to the contingent and limiting conditions specified in this form.

5. I have no present or prospective interest in the property that is the subject of this report, and I have no present or prospective personal interest or bias with respect to the participants in the transaction. I did not base, either partially or completely, my analysis and/or the estimate of market value in the appraisal report on the race, color, religion, sex, age, marital status, handicap, familial status, or national origin of either the prospective owners or occupants of the subject property or of the present owners or occupants of the properties in the vicinity of the subject property or on any other basis prohibited by law.

6. I have no present or contemplated future interest in the subject property, and neither my current or future employment nor my compensation for performing this appraisal is contingent on the appraised value of the property.

7. I was not required to report a predetermined value or direction in value that favors the cause of the client or any related party, the amount of the value estimate, the attainment of a specific result, or the occurrence of a subsequent event in order to receive my compensation and/or employment for performing the appraisal. I did not base the appraisal report on a requested minimum valuation, a specific valuation, or the need to approve a specific mortgage loan.

8. I estimated the market value of the real property that is the subject of this report based on the sales comparison approach to value. I further certify that I considered the cost and income approaches to value, but, through mutual agreement with the client, did not develop them, unless I have noted otherwise in this report.

9. I performed this appraisal as a limited appraisal, subject to the Departure Provision of the Uniform Standards of Professional Appraisal Practice that were adopted and promulgated by the Appraisal Standards Board of The Appraisal Foundation and that were in place as of the effective date of the appraisal (unless I have otherwise indicated in this report that the appraisal is a complete appraisal, in which case, the Departure Provision does not apply).

10. I acknowledge that an estimate of a reasonable exposure time in the open market is a condition in the definition of market value. The exposure time associated with the estimate of market value for the subject property is consistent with the marketing time noted in the Neighborhood section of this report. The marketing period concluded for the subject property at the estimated market value is also consistent with the marketing time noted in the Neighborhood section.

11. I personally prepared all conclusions and opinions about the real estate that were set forth in the appraisal report. I further certify that no one provided significant professional assistance to me in the development of this appraisal.

**SUPERVISORY APPRAISER'S CERTIFICATION:** If a supervisory appraiser signed the appraisal report, he or she certifies and agrees that: I directly supervise the appraiser who prepared the appraisal report, have examined the appraisal report for compliance with the Uniform Standards of Professional Appraisal Practice, agree with the statements and conclusions of the appraiser, agree to be bound by the appraiser's certifications numbered 5 through 7 above, and am taking full responsibility for the appraisal and the appraisal report.

| **APPRAISER:** | **SUPERVISORY APPRAISER (ONLY IF REQUIRED):** |
|---|---|
| Signature _____ | Signature _____ |
| Name _____ | Name _____ |
| Company Name _____ | Company Name _____ |
| Company Address _____ | Company Address _____ |
| Date of Report/Signature _____ | Date of Report/Signature _____ |
| State Certification # _____ | State Certification # _____ |
| or State License # _____ | or State License # _____ |
| State _____ | State _____ |
| Expiration Date of Certification or License _____ | Expiration Date of Certification or License _____ |
| **ADDRESS OF PROPERTY APPRAISED:** | **SUPERVISORY APPRAISER:** |

**SUBJECT PROPERTY:**
☐ Did not inspect subject property
☐ Did inspect exterior of subject property from street
☐ Did inspect interior and exterior of subject property

**APPRAISED VALUE OF SUBJECT PROPERTY $** _____
**EFFECTIVE DATE OF APPRAISAL/INSPECTION** _____
**LENDER/CLIENT:**

**COMPARABLE SALES:**
☐ Did not inspect exterior of comparable sales from street
☐ Did inspect exterior of comparable sales from street

Name _____
Company Name _____
Company Address _____

Freddie Mac Form 2055      Page 3 of 3      11/97

**FIGURE 4.1**

**Appraisal form.** (*Continued*)

# Selecting Viable Projects

Selecting viable projects for development comes naturally to some developers. The process can be as simple as a gut feeling, but acting with so little to base a decision on is risky. Most investors and developers require extensive documentation on a property before a purchase offer is made. Once a developer begins searching for land, there is a good chance that the developer will have so many parcels to choose from that confusion will run rampant. If there are a number of real estate brokers submitting properties for review, developers can fall even further behind in their decision-making roles.

There is no particular rule that dictates how a buying decision must be made. Some investors do operate almost entirely on gut feelings. Most investors have some type of system that they utilize to evaluate various properties. A few investors have strict guidelines that they will not stray from in the selection of real estate. Where do you fit in? Unless you have a very special gift of seeing into the future, you should require yourself to come up with a system for ranking potential properties. Flying by the seat of your pants will probably cause you to crash and burn at some point. Proved systems tend to produce more consistent results.

# Hard Sells

The first step to take in choosing viable projects is to resist the hard sells that some real estate brokers will throw at you. Some real estate agents have a flair for making a mundane property sound fantastic. With some salesmanship, these agents can talk a lot of people into buying almost anything. Be careful of this type of situation. You are the developer and the decision of what to buy is yours. Don't let brokers or sellers try to convince you of something that you are not already sure of. Never jump on any deal just to get it before the next developer does. Some deals do require fast action to secure, but most of them will be waiting for you after you have done your homework on the property. It is better to miss a good deal than it is to buy into a bad deal.

Avoid deals that look too good to be true. Most opportunities that look like a steal have hooks in them. They are worth exploring, but don't make the mistake of entering into a purchase agreement without plenty of provisions for contingency clauses to protect yourself. Developers are good targets for people selling land. Since land can be difficult to sell, sellers love the idea of selling a lot of land in one quick sale to a developer. You have to protect yourself.

Developers are entrepreneurs and dreamers. They see visions of the future and get caught up in how they will change the world around them. These qualities set the stage for land sharks to feast on developers. If a salesperson can paint a pretty picture, some developer might just grab the deal without looking beyond the image that the developer wants to see. Sometimes the truth is much darker than the glorified vision of a land hustler or starry-eyed developer. The key is to avoid acting until you are convinced, with proper research, that a deal is viable.

# Competition

There is competition among land developers. They try to beat each other to the best parcels of land. To make your projects viable and less risky, you should avoid this type of competition. Compete against yourself. Force yourself to buy into only deals that will pan out well.

If you are racing to beat a fellow developer to a deal, you are much more likely to make a mistake. The true competition between developers is settled when the projects are over and the outcome is weighed. If you have a great-looking project that was profitable, you are a winner.

Over the years, I've seen developers buy land just to keep it out of the hands of their competitors. On rare occasions, this type action can be justified. For example, assume that I had a new subdivision nearly ready to build on. My plans called for building a complete subdivision of Victorian homes. If I found out that a competitor was about to buy adjoining land to develop for some purpose that would lower the value of my subdivision, I might be well justified in taking control of the property to keep the other developer from having an adverse effect on my development. Generally speaking though, racing to a bank to buy land in order to keep competitors from getting it will result in losses rather than profits.

## Average Deals

Average deals are offered for sale on a daily basis. These are deals that offer some possibility of profits, but the profit range is usually limited. Two ways exist to turn average deals into great deals. The first way is to buy land at a price below market value. This can be done, but it is seldom easy to accomplish. A better way, if you are creative enough, is to find a use for land being offered that others have not yet thought of. Basically, you are looking for the highest and best use of the land. If land is being offered as a large building lot, see if it can be subdivided into two building lots. When land is being offered for single-family use, see if local zoning laws will allow the construction of a duplex, triplex, or four-unit building. Turn every average deal around as many times as you can to see all of the facets of a land opportunity.

Average deals are abundant. They are rarely very profitable. If you have to pay full market value for land and then use it for the purpose for which it was sold, you will not make much money as a developer. The key is seeing below the surface and spotting opportunities that others have yet to see. Don't ignore average deals, but don't accept them on their face value. Find a way to make the land more valuable.

# The Mass Market

The mass market offers a lot of land for sale. Pick up a newspaper and read the classified ads. Look in the little booklets sold in convenience stores to see what land offerings exist. I have found some very nice properties in the weekly classified booklets that fill countless shelves in grocery stores and convenience stores. Check out the Internet; there are listings there to cover nearly any need or desire. Spend some time driving around, looking for "For Sale" signs. Flip through a multiple-listing book with a real estate agent. Everywhere you look there is land being offered for sale. The mass marketing of real estate opens the doors of opportunity to almost anyone interested in seeking rich rewards in real estate.

Are the mass offerings worth considering? Would you be better off searching out the unknown parcels of land that are not so obviously for sale? There are pieces of land that could classify as hidden treasure, and they are well worth finding. However, we will dig deeply into this topic in the next chapter. As for mass offerings, yes, they are well worth investigating. You will run through many listings that are not of interest, but you may stumble on some that are right up your alley. For many investors and developers, it takes only one good find to make all of the effort worthwhile.

Real estate that is advertised aggressively can receive a lot of attention. Potential buyers scour advertisements in search of the one property that they hope to find. The competition associated with mass offerings is substantial. Finding a prime listing among the many mundane listings can take months, if you find one at all. Time is spent looking from listing to listing. Is the time well spent? As soon as you find something that fits your needs the wasted time on other properties will be forgotten.

Dealing with the maze of mass listings is easier if you have a formula for success. Developers who know what they are looking for and who can stay focused don't lose much time in skimming over the mass offerings. However, developers who are not committed to their game-plan can waste a huge amount of time in weighing various offerings and considering a change in plans.

Much of what is offered for sale has some potential. If you spend all of your time trying to shift with the land available, you may never get into the development stage. Being committed to a particular plan makes weeding through hundreds of offerings easy. Let me give you a quick example of what I'm talking about.

Assume that you want to develop a small subdivision of about 20 house lots. You want each home to have enough land to feel comfortable, and you need room for roads. After designing your development on paper, you have decided that you need a minimum of 18 acres of land to work with. Most of the land will be turned into house lots, but some of it will be consumed by roads, utilities, and possibly a community picnic area. You know that you want land outside of the city limits, but within a 5-mile range of the city. According to your plan, you want the building lots to be wooded sites. Access to the land must be from a good road that is near a major road leading into the city. You know that within the distance that you are limiting your search that municipal water and sewer systems will be available. The criteria of your plan will hone your search results.

Given the example above, you can eliminate many of the land offerings that you may come into contact with through mass marketing channels. As long as you stay committed to your buying criteria, sorting through the mounds of paperwork on properties for sale will not be a major task. As you skim through the pile you can disregard properties as soon as some aspect of their details fall outside of your buying criteria. If you have a secretary or assistant, the screening process can be done for you. What you will be left with is a handful of potential properties that all fall within the limits that you have set for potential properties to meet.

By having a defined list of requirements for any parcel to meet, you can quickly eliminate most of the mass offerings. The more defined your buying criteria is, the easier it will be to rule out properties. Spending a little time planning on what you are looking for can save you hours upon hours of time in the searching process. Once the basic stack of mass offerings is reduced to a manageable group of prospective properties, you can start taking the smaller stack apart, piece by piece.

## Fine Tuning

Fine tuning your selection can be fairly simple. If you are resolute in your decision about the requirements you have established for a piece of property, it's simple to sort through properties. Unfortunately, finding property that meets every need you have can be very difficult. Most developers are willing to bend a little. If there are only minor discrepancies, you may be able to adjust your plans, without restructuring your entire program, to make a piece of land work for your needs. Developers who are willing to be a bit flexible have more trouble sorting through properties. Which group will you be in?

Sticking to your guns is a solid plan. As soon as you are willing to make exceptions, you expose yourself. But, you also open more opportunities. You have to weigh the risk and decide how flexible you are willing to be. If you are going to stand firm on your land requirements, you don't need any help in learning how to sort out properties. When you find a property that meets all of your criteria, you buy it. But, if you are going to consider properties that don't fit your needs exactly, you may have a lot to consider, so let's talk more about this issue.

How far outside of the parameters that you have set are you willing to go when considering properties? Can you be flexible on price? If you have decided that you want to buy property for half of what you expect to sell it for, you may be able to accept a property that is priced higher than you would like. The question becomes one of how much additional money you are willing to pay.

Money is not the only issue that you might be willing to negotiate on. Suppose you were looking for 18 acres and found a parcel that was perfect in every way, except it has only 16 acres. Can you live with less acreage? What would you do if you wanted wooded acreage and found a prime parcel that fit all of your needs, with the exception of trees? Any of these circumstances could be worked around for most projects.

If you are going to alter your plans, you have to factor in the changes and how they will affect your profit. For example, wooded lots would probably sell better and for a higher price than lots that don't have trees. A reduction in acreage is sure to affect your final income. How much a change affects your plans will depend on the type of change that you are dealing with. Before you agree to alter your plan, make sure what the end result is likely to be.

## Going around in Circles

Going around in circles is not productive. If you vacillate too much, the confusion will tear you up. Some developers change their minds so often that they might spend months accomplishing nothing. Viable properties are available. You have to know them when you see them. The best way to reduce the time you spend searching for properties is to define your needs closely and then stick to them. It can take a lot of self-discipline to adhere to your own rules. If you do, your odds of success are better. And, if you can do this, you might be able to dig out some hidden treasure that is being overlooked by other developers. Let's move to the next chapter to discuss this further.

# Finding Hidden Treasure

I s finding hidden treasure in real estate still possible? Absolutely! There is plenty of land waiting for some aspiring developer to grab it and turn it into powerful profits. Times have changed over the years. I remember riding around with my grandfather when I was a young child. My grandfather was retired and enjoyed working with real estate. He was not a big-league developer, but he did plenty of deals, many of which he made from either the front seat of his car or in a rocking chair on a porch. Riding around from farm to farm with my grandfather was my introduction to real estate dealing. As it turned out, it was an education that I still use and that has done well for me financially.

Over 35 years ago, when I was basically going door to door with my grandfather, I learned the value of prospecting. My grandfather's name was Paul, but I called him Amos. He was a very special man in my life and the lessons I learned with him close to four decades ago still pay off today. Back then, the game was to carry a large roll of cash around to flash on farmers who might be willing to sell off part of their land. When Amos would see a piece of land he liked, he would drive up to houses and start talking to people. Sometimes they owned the land, sometimes they didn't. But, they almost always knew who owned the land. This was the first step in mining out the gold from raw land.

I can still see the old farmers in their bib-overalls. Sometimes they were working their fields, feeding their cattle, or rocking on their porches. We would pull into their driveways and blow the horn on the old Chevy. Dogs would come out barking and then someone would amble over to the car. Occasionally, we would be invited to the porch for lemonade or iced tea. More often than not, negotiations started right at the car window. After basic greetings, Amos would get right to the point and start talking business. If the farmer showed any interest in selling some land, Amos would whip out his roll of cash and flash it. Hard cash always got the attention of the landowners. The visual impact of greenbacks was much stronger than a cashier's check would have been, even if it had been in a larger amount.

My grandfather's buying strategies were sound. He would ride around and find property that he felt had potential. Then he would canvas an area to find the owner and ask the owner if the land could be purchased. There were plenty of rejections, but there were a lot of deals made, too. The land that Amos went after was never listed with brokers or advertised in newspapers. Finding land that was not known to be for sale made it easier to get a good deal—there was no competition. This type of approach still works today.

## Dealing Directly

Dealing directly with landowners is one of the most efficient ways to acquire quality properties, if you can locate the land and the owners without too much effort. Sellers will often sell for less if they don't have to pay a brokerage commission out of their sale proceeds. Sellers who don't have to pay commissions or advertising costs can sell for less and still net the same amount of income. Some sellers are extremely willing to work directly with buyers. But, if you plan to search out properties on your own and to go directly to landowners, you also have to be prepared for a lot of rejection.

People who make their living selling things know very well what cold calling is. It is one of the worst parts of selling for most salespeople who have to do it. Cold calling is a numbers game. I remember one company that I used to work with that tracked the results of cold calling. Their formula was that it took 10 calls to get one appointment to meet with a prospect. Company requirements were to get eight appointments a day. This could mean making 80, or more, cold calls daily. It was no fun. Going door to door to buy land is not much different from calling people and asking them to change their long-distance phone service. Many people hang up on cold callers, and some landowners are not much more amiable to prospecting developers. I don't tell you this to turn you off on the idea of making phone calls and knocking on doors, but you have to know that you will meet with a lot of rejection as a roaming prospector.

Some developers get lucky and make a deal almost as soon as they begin talking to landowners. This is the exception, rather than the rule. If you are not comfortable with calling people whom you don't know or knocking on their doors, you can use a letter to introduce yourself. I prefer direct mail over cold calling and door knocking. Letters are not as effective, but they are faster and if you have enough land to go after, the odds are in your favor. Let me give you a case-history example of how I've done my prospecting in the past.

I moved from Virginia to Maine about 12 years ago. Maine is a state that sees a lot of vacationers. It is common for Maine land to be owned by people who live outside of the state. As both a broker and an investor, I have used this to my advantage. I have gone to the tax assessor's office and gotten the names and addresses of all landowners within a tax district. A quick skim of the list shows which owners live out of state. These people become my first target. A well-written letter mailed to the out-of-state owners can result in some fast action.

I've done mass mailings to out-of-state owners and received responses in less than a week. Since the owners are not in Maine, they sometimes tire of owning property and paying taxes on it when they can't use or enjoy it. This makes the sellers anxious to entertain offers. In many cases, the tax offices have supplied me with pressure-sensitive labels for the mailing addresses of landowners. This makes a mailing campaign easy. I have used direct mail successfully for many years. You can too.

Ownership records of real estate are public knowledge. This means that you have access to the information. The local tax assessor's office is the first place to start when seeking the name of an owner. If you have a property address, getting the name and address of the owner is simple; you just look it up in the tax records. If you want more information, you can take the data you get from the tax office and research the deed on the property. Nearly all real estate deeds are recorded. Once the deeds are recorded, they become open to the public. Deeds will tell you how large a parcel of land is, what easements exist, what liens are filed against the property, any covenants and restrictions that may exist, and so forth.

Deeds are usually kept in local courthouses. Some regions keep their deeds in what is called a hall of records. A phone call to the local tax office will put you on the right track for finding where deeds are kept. Normally, deeds are kept at the county seat, not in local town offices. Check with you local authorities to find out where you should go to look for deeds. Whether you knock on doors, make telephones ring, or do your prospecting by mail, private owners can be a great source of outstanding land deals.

## Back Taxes

Back taxes can be a serious problems for some landowners. Since raw land doesn't usually produce income, it can be hard for owners to justify keeping the property. Sometimes owners become delinquent in their tax bills. If tax bills go unpaid for long enough, the taxing jurisdiction may take the land and sell it to collect the unpaid taxes. Buying land from tax sales is one way of getting low prices, but finding owners who are in trouble with taxes and making deals with them before a tax auction may be a better way to cash in on the opportunity.

If you find and contact people who are behind on their land taxes they may be happy to sell their land to you. In some cases, you might be able to buy the land with excellent owner financing. For instance, you might pay the back taxes as your down payment and then make periodic interest-only payments on the land until you are ready to begin the developing process. Reviewing records in the tax assessor's office should reveal properties that have outstanding tax bills due.

## Auctions

I have never found auctions to be very good in terms of land sales for development. If you are looking for houses, apartment buildings, commercial space, or even farms, auctions can produce good results. However, finding the right land for development at an auction is a crap shoot. Another problem with properties sold at auction is that payment is expected for the full purchase price in a short period of time. This usually is not compatible with the needs of a developer. Some real estate investors do very well by working auctions, so you may want to check this option out. My personal experience has not shown this method to be effective enough to concentrate on, but you may encounter different results.

# Foreclosures

Foreclosures, like auctions, have not proved fruitful for me as a developer. Buying property that is in foreclosure is a good way to get a low price, but finding property that you want to develop that just happens to be in foreclosure is difficult and time-consuming. Like tax auctions, waiting for a foreclosure auction is not the best way to deal in foreclosures. It is often possible to become known by lenders as an investor who is always interested in foreclosure properties. Getting to know the people at lending institutions who are responsible for liquidating foreclosed properties could pay off big for you.

Any lender who loans money on land is sure to handle some foreclosures. Generally, there is a special officer within a lending institution who is in charge of properties that are in default of loan payments. Sometimes these people have the title of work-out officers. The term comes from the job description of working something out with someone to protect the lender's financial interest in real estate. You could call lenders and ask to speak to the person in charge of foreclosures. This procedure will work, but there may be a better way.

My approach to foreclosures has been to go in a side door. Normally, I meet with loan officers first. I explain to the loan officers what I do and investigate the opportunities of borrowing money for my ventures. As these talks progress, I ask the loan officers about how foreclosures are handled at their institute. Once a relationship is formed with the loan officers, getting to the work-out officers is easy. A side benefit of my way is that a path is already made for financing when I find a foreclosure property that I'm interested in.

You may find that the effort required to turn up foreclosures is not rewarded often enough with prime development properties. This has been my experience. But, you might walk into a bank on just the right day and find a diamond in the rough. Also, depending on the type of developing that you are doing, you might be interested in dilapidated buildings. If your development plans call for small lots, you might find rundown, abandoned buildings that can be torn down to give you new use of the land. When this is your angle, foreclosures and auctions can both be very productive. Each developer must create an individual system that works on a personal basis, so consider every option once you define your development plans.

## Lawyers

Lawyers can be excellent sources of leads for land. When estates have to be settled, lawyers are usually involved in the process. If you become known as someone to call when there is land to be sold, you may have your phone ringing regularly with lawyers on the other end who have land to sell for their clients. Seasoned investors work with lawyers frequently, and once you are in the loop, there can be a lot of opportunities coming your way. Properties bought in this manner are sometimes less expensive because of the savings on marketing and brokerage fees.

Some investors who are not familiar with working with lawyers concentrate on real estate attorneys. However, estate attorneys are the ones to go after. Use real estate lawyers to represent you when buying and selling real estate, but look to estate lawyers for good land deals. A simple letter of introduction mailed to all of the lawyers in your area can be enough to get the ball rolling for estate sales.

## Accountants

Accountants are another source of potential hidden treasures in real estate. Landowners frequently consult their accountants for advice on the tax advantages and benefits of selling real estate. If you have yourself listed with a number of accountants as a potential buyer of real estate you can be one of the first people called when a landowner is thinking of selling. Not all accountants or attorneys are willing to give their clients the names of potential buyers, but many will. The process is not like insider trading or some other form of questionable conduct. There is nothing wrong with professionals providing a list of potential buyers to clients who have real estate to sell. If a professional, such as an accountant, were giving out only your name, that might raise some ethical issues, but it doesn't hurt to get your name on the list of potential buyers with professionals who do offer such information to their clients.

## Benefits

There are benefits of getting to sellers before they list with brokerages and before they begin advertising their properties for sale. If property is not on the open market, the level of competition between buyers is much lower. Sellers who don't have to pay real estate commissions or marketing expenses can sell for less and still be happy. Your work will be more extensive if you seek out private sales, but the benefits may be strong enough to warrant the extra time and effort. Once you find property that you are interested in, getting control of it is the next step. Chapter 7 is right around the corner, and it will guide you in ways to protect yourself as you enter into purchase agreements.

# Tying up Land without a Full Commitment

Learning how to control land without a full purchase commitment is very important to most developers. Land that seems to be ideal can turn into a disaster. To avoid costly errors in judgment, many investors and developers shield themselves with contingency clauses in their purchase offers. The clauses give buyers certain rights and remedies for getting out of contracts that they enter into. Most contracts have some contingency clauses in them. A familiar one is that a sale is subject to a purchaser obtaining financing to buy a property. This particular contingency is in most real estate contracts, but it is only one example of the many contingencies that might be employed in the drafting or a contract.

Control of a property can be done in various ways. A buyer doesn't have to enter into a purchase agreement to gain control and an insurable interest in real property. An option, for example, can give a developer control of a property without making a full commitment to purchase the real estate. Many developers use options to gain control of land that they are interested in. However, the money set forth for an option is usually forfeited if the option is not exercised—meaning that the property is not purchased.

Take-down schedules are normally used between builders and developers. In a sense, a take-down schedule is a purchase agreement that extends the period of time in which a buyer will acquire property. Most take-down schedules are a form of a purchase agreement. Developers use purchase agreements and options as their normal way of doing business, but a take-down schedule might be used in special cases. All three methods allow developers to gain control of real estate, and each method has its place in the business. Knowing when to use what and knowing how to use it can mean the difference between success and failure as a developer.

Options give developers a lot of power, usually with a small cash gamble. Contingency contracts offer the same power and sometimes with less risk than options carry. Take-down schedules are rare in terms of buying land for development, but they are an essential tool for developers to use as they create developments. Let's open our discussion with options, since they have built-in escapes for developers who decide that a property is not right for them.

## Options

Options (Fig. 7.1) are often used by developers. By using options, developers can control large amounts of land with very little money. There is do direct commitment to purchase property involved in an option. However, most options require the developer to either buy the property that is under option or to forfeit the option money to the seller. Options are not a free ride, but they are a good tool for developers to use.

An option can be used on any type of real estate. Not all sellers will agree to options, but many will, especially if the term of the option is not unreasonable. The amount of money needed to bind an option can range from nearly nothing to several thousand dollars. The amount is determined by the seller. If a seller is not aggressively marketing a piece of property the amount of money required to tie up the real estate could be very low. But, if a seller has high hopes of a fast sale, an option may be refused or, at the least, a substantial option fee might be required by the seller. Once a property is under option, the seller's hands are tied for the term of the option. If a cash buyer comes along while an option is in place, the seller must refuse to sell the real estate.

Because of this risk, sellers of prime property may make the requirements for option money quite high. They want to be compensated if they should lose a sale to another prospective buyer.

---

Form RD 440-34
(Rev. 6-97)

*Position 5*

UNITED STATES DEPARTMENT OF AGRICULTURE
RURAL DEVELOPMENT
FARM SERVICE AGENCY

FORM APPROVED
OMB NO. 0575-0172

### OPTION TO PURCHASE REAL PROPERTY

1.   In consideration of the sum of $ _____ in hand paid and other valuable consideration, the receipt and sufficiency of which are hereby acknowledged, the undersigned (hereinafter called the "Seller"), who covenants to be the owner thereof, hereby, for the Seller and the Seller's heirs, executors, administrators, successors and assigns, offers and agrees to sell and convey to

_____

*(Name and Address)*

(hereinafter called the "Buyer"), and hereby grants to the said Buyer the exclusive and irrevocable option and right to purchase, under

the conditions hereinafter provided, the following-described property, located in _____

County, State of _____ :
(Insert here full and complete legal description, including volume and page where recorded, of the property including any water rights and water stock being purchased.)

RD 440-34 (Rev. 6-97)

**FIGURE 7.1**

Option to purchase form.

## The Mechanics

The mechanics of an option are simple. A developer offers a seller an amount of money to lock up a piece of property for a period of time. The amount of time might be a month or a year, or any other term agreed to by both parties. An option agreement is drafted, usually by

The title to said property is to be conveyed free and clear of all encumbrances except for the following reservations, exceptions and leases, and no others:
(Insert here a full statement of all reservations, exceptions and leases, including in the case of leases, the date of the termination of the lease, the correct name(s) and address(es) of the lessee(s) and, if recorded, the place of recordation)

2.   The option is given to enable the Buyer to obtain a loan made by the United States of America, acting through the ☐ Rural Housing Service; ☐ Rural Utilities Service; ☐ Rural Business-Cooperative Service; ☐ Farm Service Agency, hereinafter called the "Government" for the purchase of said property. It is agreed that the Buyer's efforts to obtain a loan constitute a part of the consideration for this option and any downpayment will be refunded if the loan cannot be processed by the Government.

3.   The total purchase price for said property is $ _____ ; said amount

☐ includes  ☐ excludes  the $ _____mentioned in paragraph 1.

4.   The Seller agrees to pay all expenses of title clearance including, if required, abstract or certificate of title or policy of title insurance, continued down to the date of acceptance of this option and thereafter continued down to and including date of recordation of the deed from the Seller to the Buyer, costs of survey, if required, and attorney's fees; and the Seller agrees that, except as herein provided, all taxes, liens, encumbrances or other interests in third persons will be satisfied discharged, or paid by the Seller including stamp taxes and other expenses incident to the preparation and execution of the deed and other evidences of title. Title evidences will be obtained from persons and be in such form as the Government shall approve.

  (Strike inapplicable language above or insert herein any different agreement regarding the paying of title clearance charges)

5.   The Seller also agrees to secure for the Buyer, from the records of the Farm Service Agency, aerial surveys of the property when available, all obtainable information relating to allotments and production history and any other information needed in connection with the consideration of the proposed purchase of the property.

6.   The Seller further agrees to convey said property to the Buyer by general warranty deed (except where the law provides otherwise for conveyances by trustees, officers of courts, etc.) in the form, manner and at the time required by the Government, conveying to the Buyer a valid, unencumbered, indefeasible fee-simple title to said property meeting all requirements of the Government; that the purchase price shall be paid at the time of recording such deed; and that said lands, including improvements, shall be delivered in the same condition as they now are, customary use and wear excepted.

7.   Taxes, water assessments and other general and special assessments of whatsoever nature for the year in which the closing of the transaction takes place shall be prorated as of the date of the closing of the transaction, it being expressly agreed that for the purpose of such proration the tax year shall be deemed to be the calendar year. If the closing of the transaction shall occur before the tax rate is fixed, the apportionment of taxes shall be on the basis of the tax rate for the next preceding year applied to the latest assessed valuation.

  (Insert here any different tax agreement)

**FIGURE 7.1**

Option to purchase form. (*Continued*)

an attorney, that details all elements of the option agreement. Money given to the seller as option money is held by the seller. If the property is purchased, the option money is usually applied to the purchase price. When a developer decides not to exercise an option, the seller keeps the option money in return for having kept the property secured for the developer during the option term.

8. This option may be exercised by the Buyer, at any time while the offer herein shall remain in force, by mailing, telegraphing or delivering in person a written notice of acceptance of the offer herein to _____ ,

at _____ , in the city of _____ ,

County of _____ , State of _____ ,

The offer herein shall remain irrevocable for a period of _____ months from the date hereof and shall remain in force thereafter until one (1) year from the date hereof unless earlier terminated by the Seller. The Seller may terminate this offer at any time after the _____ months irrevocable period provided herein by giving to the Buyer ten (10) days written notice of intention to terminate at the address of the Buyer. Acceptance of this option by the Buyer within ten (10) days after such notice is received by the Buyer shall constitute a valid acceptance of the option.

9. Loss or damage to the property by fire or from an act of God shall be at the risk of the Seller until the deed to the Buyer has been recorded, and in the event that such loss or damage occurs, the Buyer may, without liability, refuse to accept conveyance of title, or may elect to accept conveyance of title, in which case there shall be an equitable adjustment of the purchase price.

10. The Seller agrees that, irrespective of any other provision in this option, the Buyer, or the Buyer's assignees, may, if the option is accepted, without any liability therefore refuse to accept conveyance of the property described herein if the foresaid loan cannot be made or insured because of defects in the title to other land now owned by, or being purchased by, the buyer.

11. The Seller agrees to furnish, at Seller's expense, to the Buyer a certificate from a reliable firm certifying that the following described building(s) covered by this option (a) is now free of termite infestation and (b) either is now free of unrepaired termite damage or has suffered unrepaired termite damage which is specifically described in the certificate.

12. The Seller agrees to furnish, at the Seller's expense, to the Buyer evidence from the Health Department or a reliable and competent source that the waste disposal system for the dwelling is functioning properly, and the water supply for domestic use meets State Health Department requirements. This evidence must be in the Agency Office before a loan will be approved.

13. The Seller hereby gives the Government or its agents consent to enter on said property at reasonable times for the purpose of inspecting or appraising it, in connection with the making of a loan to purchase the property.

_____

14. Insert here conditions peculiar to this particular transaction.      *(Sellers Telephone Number)*

IN WITNESS WHEREOF, the Seller and the Buyer have set their hands and seals this _____ day

of _____ , 19 ___ .

WITNESSESS:

_____  _____

_____  _____ *(Seller)\**

_____  _____ *(Seller)\**

_____  _____ *(Buyer)\**

_____  _____ *(Buyer)\**

_____  _____

_____  _____

_____  _____

*\*(Indicate marital status of Seller as "married", "legally separated", "unmarried", after signature)*
*(over)*

**FIGURE 7.1**

**Option to purchase form. (*Continued*)**

Some options don't require more than a single sheet of paper, while others may run on for a dozen pages, or more. It is wise to outline every aspect of a deal in writing. The more documentation you have in a written agreement, the less likely you are to have confusion and problems with the other party. The reasons for using options are numerous.

*(For use if Seller is a corporation)*

IN WITNESS WHEREOF, the Seller has caused its corporate name to be hereunto subscribed by its _____

President, and its duly attested corporate seal to be hereunto affixed by its _____

Secretary, at _____ , State of _____

on the _____ day of _____ , 19____ .

(CORPORATE SEAL)                        _____
                                                                    *(Name of Corporation)*

*ATTEST:* _____        By _____

_____ *Secretary.*        _____ *President.*

ACKNOWLEDGMENT

**FIGURE 7.1**

**Option to purchase form.** (*Continued*)

## Why Options?

Why options are desirable depends on individual developers. There are any number of good reasons to use options to control land. Options are good in that they don't require a developer to complete a purchase transaction. The most a developer has to lose is the option money.

| FORMS MANUAL INSERT | FORM RD 440-34 |
|---|---|

Used by the applicant/
borrower to obtain
option on real property
to be purchased.

(see reverse)

| PROCEDURE FOR PREPARATION | : | RD HB-1-3550 and RD HB-2-3550. FSA transferred Instructions 1943-A and 1943-B. |
|---|---|---|
| PREPARED BY | : | Applicant. |
| NUMBER OF COPIES | : | Original and two copies. *(Original and three - Extra copy will be prepared for Attorney when the Agency so desires).* |
| SIGNATURES REQUIRED | : | Original and one copy by seller and applicant. |
| DISTRIBUTION OF COPIES | : | Original to applicant's loan docket; signed copy to seller; copy to applicant and copy to Attorney, if prepared. |

**FIGURE 7.1**

Option to purchase form. *(Continued)*

Developers can buy time with options, and this makes them desirable. To expand on this issue, let's look at some examples where options might be used.

Assume that you are very interested in building a large subdivision, but you are not completely sure that the area that you wish to build in will support massive housing. The deal is one that you really want to do, but you don't want to buy up all of the land needed if you can't sell the finished lots. What can you do? Buy part of the land and use it for the first phase of the subdivision. Option the surrounding land so that you can buy it at a set price if you see that the first phase of your project is selling well. When you are near a sellout on phase one, buy the second piece of land and leave the rest under option. Continue this process until you either build out or reach the saturation level. By doing this, you are buying only what you need when you need it. If the project doesn't bloom fully, you lose your option money but are not stuck with a lot of land that you can't develop profitably.

Let's say that you find a piece of land that shows a lot of promise for use as a parking garage in a city. You could make a purchase offer for the land with contingencies in it to secure the land and to still have time to investigate the costs of tearing down existing buildings and putting up the parking garage. Assume that you go this route but the seller refuses your offer, because of the amount of time you need for research to clear the contingencies. If you counter back with the offer of an option, the seller might take the deal, since there will be some money made by the seller whether you go through with the purchase or not.

Options can fill voids left by purchase offers. Developers often need extensive time to complete their preliminary planning in determining the viability of a project. When sellers won't accept contingency contracts, because of the time lag, options can be the answer. Remember, though, that if you don't follow through on an option, the sellers will usually be entitled to keep any money you offered to bind the option agreement.

## Contingency Contracts

Contingency contracts (Fig. 7.2) are extremely common in real estate transactions. Nearly all purchase offers have some provisions for contingencies. Such contingencies might range from termite inspections, to water tests, to obtaining financing. Developers can use contingency contracts to secure properties and hold them off the market while research is being done. Of course, sellers must agree to the terms of the offer, and this can sometimes be a problem if a lot of time is needed to remove the contingencies.

Form RD 1955-45
(Rev. 6-97)

FORM APPROVED
OMB NO. 0575-0172

UNITED STATES DEPARTMENT OF AGRICULTURE
RURAL DEVELOPMENT
FARM SERVICE AGENCY

Advice No.

**STANDARD SALES CONTRACT**
**SALE OF REAL PROPERTY BY THE UNITED STATES**

1. THE OFFER DATE OF THIS CONTRACT (THE DATE SIGNED BY THE PURCHASER) IS _____ 19____.

2. THE UNITED STATS OF AMERICA, acting through the ☐ Rural Housing Service; ☐ Rural Utilities Service; ☐ Rural Business-Cooperative Service; ☐ Farm Service Agency, hereinafter referred to as the "Agency", as SELLER, agrees to sell to the PURCHASER named below, and said purchaser agrees to buy, the property identified hereinafter, subject to the CONDITIONS OF SALE on pages 3 and 4 hereof which are incorporated and made part hereof.

3. PROPERTY IDENTIFICATION. Street address, including ZIP code and county:

   Brief Legal Description:

   together with the appurtenances thereunto belonging.

4. EARNEST MONEY DEPOSIT, $ _____, (TO BE REFUNDED TO PURCHASER IF THIS OFFER REJECTED OR IF AGENCY CREDIT SALE IS NOT APPROVED) ☐ TO BE REFUNDED TO PURCHASER AT CLOSING ☐ TO BE APPLIED TO CLOSING COSTS, AT CLOSING, WITH ANY BALANCE REFUNDED TO PURCHASER ☐ TO BE APPLIED TO CLOSING COSTS, AT CLOSING, WITH ANY BALANCE APPLIED TO THE PURCHASE PRICE.

5. PRICE: $ _____ CASH AT CLOSING: $ _____ , WITH BALANCE OF $ _____ BY CREDIT SALE (SECURED BY MORTGAGE OR DEED OF TRUST) ACCEPTED BY AGENCY PROVIDING FOR EQUAL _____ INSTALLMENTS OF PRINCIPAL AND INTEREST AT THE AGENCY INTEREST RATE IN EFFECT AS SET FORTH IN RD INSTRUCTION 440.1 (AVAILABLE IN ANY AGENCY OFFICE) AT THE TIME THE APPLICANT IS NOTIFIED THE CREDIT SALE IS APPROVED ☐ WITH ANY BALANCE OF THE LOAN TO BE PAID IN FULL NOT LATER THAN THE _____ ANNIVERSARY OF THE LOAN.

6. CONTINGENCY. If a credit sale is indicated in paragraph 5 above, this contract is contingent upon the Agency approving a credit sale, satisfactory to and in the name of the following party(ies):

7. CONVEYANCE. Title is to be taken in the following name and style:

8. SIGNATURE. This contract is signed by one or more of those personally named in paragraph 6 or an authorized party or official of the legal entity named in paragraph 6 (called the Purchaser).

9. OCCUPANCY. Purchaser will close with property ☐ vacant; subject to ☐ Purchaser's own occupancy only; ☐ occupancy by other(s).

10. THE PROPERTY DESCRIBED IN THIS CONTRACT ☐ is ☐ is not subject to taxation while owned by the Government. Taxes will be ☐ paid in full ☐ prorated in accordance with Item H, page 3 of form.

11. DEED RESTRICTION. The property ☐ is ☐ is not subject to deed restrictions in accordance with Item O, page 3 of form.

12. SPECIAL STIPULATIONS:

13. The sale shall be closed at _____ within thirty (30) days after indication by the Seller of readiness to close, unless the parties otherwise agree in writing.

   **Purchaser has signed this contract on the date shown in paragraph 1, above.**

_____
*Purchaser's Signature*

_____
Type or Print Purchaser's Name

_____
*Purchaser's Signature*

_____
Type of Print Purchaser's Name

_____
*Co-Signer's Signature*

_____
Type or Print Co-Signer's Name

**ACCEPTED BY THE UNITED STATES OF AMERICA**

BY _____
*(Signature)*

_____
*(Type Name and Title of Official)*

_____
*(Agency)*

**UNITED STATES DEPARTMENT OF AGRICULTURE**

Date Accepted _____

According to the Paperwork Reduction Act of 1995, no persons are required to respond to a collection of information unless it displays a valid OMB control number. The valid OMB control number for this information collection is 0575-0172. The time required to complete this information collection is estimated to average 30 minutes per response, including the time for reviewing instructions, searching existing data sources, gathering and maintaining the data needed, and completing and reviewing the collection of information.

**FIGURE 7.2**

**Standard sales contract.**

Contingencies in purchase offers are usually legitimate and done with good cause. However, they can be tricky, effective loopholes for developers to use when breaking off a deal. I used to know a developer who had perfected the art of masterful contingency clauses that were more like escape clauses than legitimate contingencies. One of the developer's favorite clauses gave him the right to void an offer if he was not "satisfied" with the survey and engineering studies. On the surface and to an untrained eye, the clause looked okay, but it was a tricky little back door for getting out of the contract. Let me explain.

When the developer used the word "satisfied" and stated that he must be satisfied with the results of the studies, he had complete control. There was no language that dealt with what would make the studies satisfactory or what would make them unsatisfactory. While a clause pertaining to survey and engineering studies is common, most clauses are fairer to both parties than the clause used by my old competitor. In essence, the developer would break any deal he wanted to simply by not being "satisfied" with the findings of a study. Most sellers and many brokers wouldn't pick up on such tricky wording, and the developer got many purchase offers accepted with the clause in place. He did buy some of the land, but he also walked away from many deals. His prowess for using carefully worded contingencies gave him a lot of power in controlling property that he may have had no intention of ever purchasing. For him, this was better than an

---

**BROKER'S CERTIFICATION (IF SOLD THROUGH A REAL ESTATE BROKER)**

The undersigned Broker certifies that neither he/she nor anyone authorized to act for him/her has declined to sell the property described herein to or to make it available for inspection or consideration by a prospective purchaser because of race, color, religion, sex, age, handicap, national origin or marital status. The undersigned further acknowledges that no commission, as stated on the notice of real property for sale shall be due or earned until and unless this contract is closed and title has passed to the purchaser herein. Earned commissions will be paid in cash at closing and passing of title only where sufficient cash to cover the commission is paid by purchaser; otherwise commission is paid by the Agency in approximately four weeks after closing.

**NOTE: The broker must sign this certification.**

_____
*(Broker's Signature)*

_____        _____
Broker's Social Security or Employer Identification No.        *(Type or Print Name of Broker)*

_____
*(Co-Broker Signature, if applicable)*

_____        _____
Co-Broker's Social Security or Employer Identification No.        *(Type or Print Name of any Co-Broker)*

**FIGURE 7.2**

Standard sales contract. *(Continued)*

option, because any earnest-money deposit given had to be returned to him if the studies were not satisfactory.

## Time Limits

Time limits are set when contingencies are used in purchase contracts. For example, if you are requiring a contingency to have a soils study done, you might have two weeks within which to have the study completed. Once the study is done and meets the requirements of the con-

---

**THE FOLLOWING CONDITIONS OF SALE ARE AGREED TO BY PURCHASER AND SELLER BEING THE CONDITIONS OF SALE REFERRED TO IN PARAGRAPH 2, PAGE 1**

**GENERAL - APPLICABLE TO ALL CONTRACTS EXCEPT AS MODIFIED BY PRIOR PARAGRAPHS**

A. Earnest Money Deposit. The earnest money deposit, shall be in the amount set forth in Agency regulations (7 CFR, Part 1955, Subpart C or 7 CFR Part 3550, as appropriate).

B. Deed to the Property. Within thirty (30) days after acceptance of the contract or removal of the contingency of Paragraph 6, page 1 (if applicable), whichever occurs last, the Government shall prepare for the purchaser a quitclaim deed to the property for delivery at the closing. The closing shall occur within thirty (30) days after the Government notifies the purchaser that the sale is ready to be closed. If a credit sale has been approved, the Government will also provide the required promissory note and security instruments. The purchaser shall deliver the executed promissory note and security instruments to the Government at the closing. If the contingency in Paragraph 6 is applicable and the Government disapproves the purchaser's credit, the purchaser shall be notified of the disapproval of credit and the contract shall terminate.

C. Encumbrances or Defects. If the purchaser, before receiving a deed and within thirty (30) days after the Government's acceptance of the bid, submits proof of any encumbrances or title defects, the Government may take any necessary remedial action. If the Government does not elect to exercise the right, the purchaser may, if the encumbrance or title defect affects the marketability of the title, rescind purchaser's purchase obligation and recover all amounts paid by purchaser to the Government on account of the purchase price. However, neither the purchaser nor parties claiming under purchaser shall be entitled, under any circumstances, to recover from the Government any damages, interest, or costs on account of any encumbrance or defect affecting the title of the property. Unless proof of encumbrances or defects, other than any enumerated on Exhibit A, is submitted by the purchaser within the time specified above, any and all encumbrances and defects shall be conclusively presumed waived, and the purchaser and any parties claiming under purchaser shall be forever barred from asserting them against the Government.

D. Abstracts or Title Evidence. The Government is not obligated to furnish any abstracts or other title evidence but will permit purchaser to inspect its title papers at a place selected by, and at no expense to, the Government.

E. Accepting the Property. The purchaser agrees to accept the property as is, in its present condition. No warranty is given on the condition of the property.

F. Loss or Damage to Property. If, through no fault of either party, the property is lost or damaged as a result of fire, vandalism or an act of God between the time of acceptance of the offer and the time the title of the property is conveyed by the Agency, the Agency will reappraise the property. The reappraised value of the property will serve as the amount the Agency will accept from the purchaser. However, if the actual loss, based on reduction in market value as determined by the Agency is less than $500, payment of the full purchase price is required. In the event the two parties cannot agree upon an adjusted price, either party, by mailing notice in writing to the other, may terminate the contract of sale, and the earnest money will be returned to the offeror.

G. Possession Rights. The purchaser will accept the property subject to the rights of any person or persons in possession of or presently occupying the property or claiming a right to occupy the property as indicated in Paragraph 9, page 1.

H. Payment of Taxes. If the property while in Government inventory is subject to taxation, the taxes will be prorated between the Government and the purchaser as of the date title is conveyed. If the property is not subject to taxation while in Government inventory, the purchaser will pay all taxes on the property which become due and payable on or after the date the title of the property is conveyed by the Government.

I. Mineral Rights. The Government will convey to the purchaser all mineral rights to which it has title.

J. Liquidated Damages. If the purchaser fails to comply with any of the terms or conditions hereof, the Government, by mailing notice in writing, may terminate the contract for sale. The earnest money deposit shall be retained by the Government as full liquidated damages except where failure to close is due to non-approval of credit.

K. Representation Regarding Property. Representations or statements regarding the property made by any representative of the Government shall not be binding on the Government or considered as grounds for any claim for adjustment in or rescission of any resulting contract. The purchaser expressly waives any claim for adjustment or rescission based upon any representation or statement not expressly included herein. The Government makes no warranties or representations not set forth in writing herein concerning the condition of title or the permissible uses of the property.

L. Member of Congress. No Member of or Delegate to Congress or Resident Commissioner shall be admitted to any share or part of the contract of which these conditions form a part, or to any benefit that may arise therefrom.

M. Subject to Agency Regulations. All offers and resulting contracts shall be subject to the regulations of the Agency, now or hereafter in effect.

N. Documentary Stamps. The purchaser will be required to purchase and place upon the deed the necessary documentary stamps.

**FIGURE 7.2**

**Standard sales contract.** (*Continued*)

tingency, the contingency is removed. If the study is not done on time, you are exposed, since the time that you had to void the contract has passed. Any knowledgeable seller or broker is going to require you to provide a time limit within which you must remove a contingency or void the contract.

Developers can be faced with a lot of contingencies to work out. The time needed to compile all of the research needed can be substantial. Some sellers will not be willing to wait several months while you remove contingencies. When this is the case, you may have to offer the seller an option to hold the property for you while research is done. If you have a strong development team who can work quickly, you should be able to use contingencies with most sellers, especially sellers who have anticipated doing business with developers.

## Types of Contingencies

How many types of contingencies are there? It depends on your imagination. Almost anything that you can think of could become a contingency in a purchase offer. You could stipulate that you would buy a piece of land only after determining that it had the ability to grow spruce trees for a Christmas tree farm. Another contingency might be

O. Deed Restrictions *(If Applicable)*. This property contains a dwelling unit or units which the Agency has deemed to be inadequate for residential occupancy. The quitclaim deed by which this property will be conveyed to the purchaser will contain a covenant binding the purchasers and the property which will restrict the residential unit(s) on the property from being used for residential occupancy until such time as the dwelling unit(s) is (are) structurally sound and habitable, has a potable water supply, has functionally adequate, safe, and operable heating, plumbing, electrical and sewage disposal systems, and meets the Thermal Performance Standards as outlined in Exhibit D, 7 CFR Part 1924, Subpart A, which are the Agency requirements for a residential unit(s) to meet decent, safe, and sanitary standards. This restriction is required by Section 510(e) of the Housing Act of 1949, as amended, 42 U.S.C. § 1480(e).

P. Entire Agreement. This contract contains the final and entire agreement between the parties hereto and they shall not be bound by any terms, conditions, statements, or representations, oral or written, not herein contained.

**APPLICABLE TO CREDIT SALES (LOANS BY THE AGENCY) ONLY**

Q. Purchaser Financial Information. The purchaser will submit financial information upon request of the Government within 30 days of such request.

R. Security Instruments. Upon closing all deeds and mortgages or other security instruments incident to the sale shall be on Agency forms and shall immediately be filed for record by the Agency at the expense of purchaser.

S. Insurance. To protect the Government's security in any buildings and appurtenances, the purchaser shall carry insurance against loss by fire, windstorm, flood and any other hazards required by the Government. The insurance shall be in an amount and form, and with an insurer, satisfactory to the Government. The original policy with evidence of premium payment shall be delivered to the Government at the time of delivery of the quitclaim deed to the purchaser.

T. Prepayment. The purchaser may pay at any time all or part of the unpaid balance of the purchase price with no prepayment penalty. *(For Multiple Family Housing sales only, the purchaser may be subject to prepayment restrictions of Section 502(c) of the Housing Act of 1949, 42 U.S.C. §1472(c)*

**FIGURE 7.2**

Standard sales contract. (*Continued*)

that you would buy land only after proving that it could support a population of pickerel frogs. Most contingencies are a bit more normal than the two examples given. But the point is, you can insert any contingency you like when preparing a purchase offer. Sellers may not accept your contingencies, but you can certainly ask for them. Now, let's talk about more common contingencies that are used by developers.

## Zoning

Zoning regulations can make or break a development deal. A contingency in a purchase offer that allows you to confirm current zoning requirements should be considered standard procedure. If you want to extend the contingency to include time to see if you can change zoning rules, you can ask for the privilege. Zoning changes can take several months to complete, and some sellers simply will not tie a property up for long periods of time without something more than a contingency contract.

## Deed Inspections

Deed inspections are needed for many reasons. Reviewing a deed can tell you about the chain of title in ownership, covenants, restrictions, easements, and related information that is vital to making a buying decision. This is a contingency that should be allowed for in a purchase contract. It doesn't take very long to run down a title and inspect a deed, so if you can buy yourself 30 days to complete this work you should be in good shape.

## Surveys

Surveys are normally needed in development deals. Depending on your local survey companies, this work could take anywhere from a few days to months to complete. However, you should be able to get what you need within 30 days. Most sellers are willing to gamble on contingency contracts where all contingencies will be removed within 30 days. You may be able to extend the time to 45 to 60 days, or longer.

## Soil Tests

If you will be having soil tests done, this is another reason for a contingency in a purchase offer. You will have to check with local sources to see how long to expect to wait for these tests. Once you get the right people on the site to do the tests, it doesn't usually take too long to get results back.

### Engineering Studies

Engineering studies can cover a lot of topics and they can take months to complete. A preliminary report can sometimes be done quickly and with enough accuracy to give a developer a comfort level for moving ahead with a purchase. Having a contingency in your offer to cover engineering studies will not be unusual, but not all deals require this type of study.

### Environmental Studies

Depending upon the issues at hand, environmental studies can take from 2 weeks to several months. You have to talk with the proper authorities in your area to get an estimate of how much time might be needed to receive a full report on a property that you are considering.

### Demolition

Demolition cost estimates can usually be obtained in less than 30 days. If you are buying land that has existing buildings on it, this might be a needed contingency in your purchase offer.

### Utilities

Finding out what utilities are available to a parcel of land and what the cost of the service installations will be can be an important issue. This is another example of a typical contingency. Look for any easement agreements that may affect the use and value of a property (Fig. 7.3).

### Financing

Most developers require some form of financing for their projects. It is common to include a contingency clause in a contract offer that allows you to void the agreement if financing cannot be obtained. You could use the "satisfactory" line insomuch as you must be able to obtain satisfactory financing or the deal is off. But savvy sellers will require you to pinpoint exactly what the upper limits of your requirements are. For example, you may have to dictate the terms that you are willing to accept for financing and agree to apply for that financing by a set date.

## Access

Access to land sometimes has to be verified. This element of research usually comes out of the deed research, but it is a topic that deserves a contingency clause.

Form RD 442-20 (Rev. 10-96)

UNITED STATES DEPARTMENT OF AGRICULTURE
RURAL DEVELOPMENT

FORM APPROVED
OMB NO. 0575-0015

### RIGHT-OF-WAY EASEMENT

KNOW ALL MEN BY THESE PRESENTS:

That in consideration of One Dollar ($1.00) and other good and valuable consideration paid to

_____and _____,

hereinafter referred to as GRANTOR, by _____
hereinafter referred to as GRANTEE, the receipt of which is hereby acknowledged, the GRANTOR does hereby grant, bargain, sell, transfer, and convey unto the GRANTEE, its successor and assigns, a perpetual easement with the right to erect, construct, install, and lay, and thereafter use, operate, inspect, repair, maintain, replace, and remove

_____

_____

_____

over, across, and through the land of the GRANTOR situate in _____ County,

State of _____, said land being described as follows:

_____

_____

_____

together with the right of ingress and egress over the adjacent lands of the GRANTOR, his successors and assigns, for the purposes of this easement.

The easement shall be _____ feet in width, the center line of which is described as follows:

_____

_____

_____

The consideration hereinabove recited shall constitute payment in full for any damages to the land of the GRANTOR, his successors and assigns, by reason of the installation, operation, and maintenance of the structures or improvements referred to herein. The GRANTEE covenants to maintain the easement in good repair so that no unreasonable damage will result from its use to the adjacent land of the GRANTOR, his successors and assigns.

The grant and other provisions of this easement shall constitute a covenant running with the land for the benefit of the GRANTEE, its successors and assigns.

IN WITNESS WHEREOF, the GRANTORS have executed this instrument this _____ day of _____

19 _____ .

_____ (SEAL)

_____ (SEAL)

RD 442-20 (Rev. 10-96)

**FIGURE 7.3**

**Easement agreement.**

### Insurance

If the property that you are making an offer on might be subject to special insurance needs, such as flood or earthquake insurance, you should have a contingency clause that allows you to confirm if this type of insurance is needed, available, and acceptable to you.

Depending on the type of development you are getting involved in, the list of potential contingencies could grow to a long length. Essentially, any aspect of a deal that might cause you concern should be addressed as a contingency. Your attorney can help you word various contingency clauses to protect youself.

## Take-down Schedules

Take-down schedules are normally given by developers to builders, but they are sometimes given to developers by landowners. We talked earlier about using options to expand a project as production-warranted expansion. A take-down schedule would work in a similar way, except that the take-down schedule usually requires the purchase of property, unlike an option. As a developer, I would prefer to use options over take-down schedules. Once a project is developed and ready to market, offering builders a take-down schedule is very sensible.

The two main tools to use in controlling land are options and contingency contracts. Once you have land locked up, you have to begin your work at removing contingencies or in deciding whether or not to exercise your options. Chapter 8 deals with getting a development team working, so let's turn the page and see what to expect when the wheels of developing go into motion.

# Having Your Experts Do Preliminary Checks

aving your experts do preliminary checks is a critical part of the development process. There are times when mobilizing the teams will be similar to deployment of troops by a general. Large development plans can require a small army of experts to confirm the viability of a project. Even small developments often require several types of experts to be involved in the preliminary development work. As the developer, you are likely to be the person in charge of all of the experts. You might have a project manager handle the work for you, but most small developers do most of their own project management.

Timing can be a major consideration when you activate your troops. If you are working against deadlines to remove contingencies, you may have to keep steady pressure on the people you have researching your project for you. Developers who do not develop a voice and a level of professional performance with their development teams often suffer the consequences. The old saying about squeaky wheels getting the grease often proves to be true. However, being a pest can make matters worse for you. If you did your screening of experts properly, you should know the people on whom you are depending. Hopefully, you established a working relationship in advance and know basically what to expect from your people.

Once you put a property under option or contract, it is time to roll out the experts. Your attorney is usually the first expert to be called into service. Normally, a lawyer is retained to review legal agreements before they are entered into. After getting control of a property, you must then call on the various people you need to make verifications for you. The types of people that you need will depend on your skills and the type of development that you are doing. While it is not feasible for me to guess what your needs will be, I can give you a good overview of how the preliminary process might work for a development project. With this in mind, let's go through some of the steps that you might require on your job.

## Your Lawyer

Your lawyer should be involved during the process when you are gaining control of a property. Once you have a property locked up, the lawyer should move into a research mode. This would include doing a title search and checking out the deed of the property for any potential problems. Some developers do this work themselves, but unless you are very comfortable with your expertise to catch minor items that could amount to major problems, having a top-notch real estate attorney do the research is a good idea. If your lawyer works fast, you might want to have this work done before you start sending the rest of your team into action. There is no point in running up expensive bills with other experts if your lawyer shoots the deal down in the first day or two.

## A Survey Crew

A survey crew should normally be dispatched quickly to confirm what it is that you think you are buying. A simple boundary survey in developed areas doesn't take long to complete. In rural areas, the same type of survey can be time-consuming, as benchmarks and other reference points may be difficult to locate. You will probably want the survey crew to do an elevation survey, in addition to the boundary survey. An elevation survey makes it easy to see how building placement and drainage issues will come into play with a development.

The slope of land can affect many aspects of a development. For example, there are recommended slope percentages that are normally used in developing land. In the case of a lawn, a slope of up to 3 percent would be considered good. A lawn that has a 5 percent slope would be considered too steep by many developers. Road areas, on the other hand, may have a slope of up to 8 percent. Elevation surveys and topographical (topo) maps make it possible to read the slope of land. Topo maps are readily available from many sources, which range from the U.S. government to local sporting goods stores. Many map companies now offer topo maps on CD ROMs for computer use. Surveyors will create site plans in conjunction with engineers (Fig. 8.1).

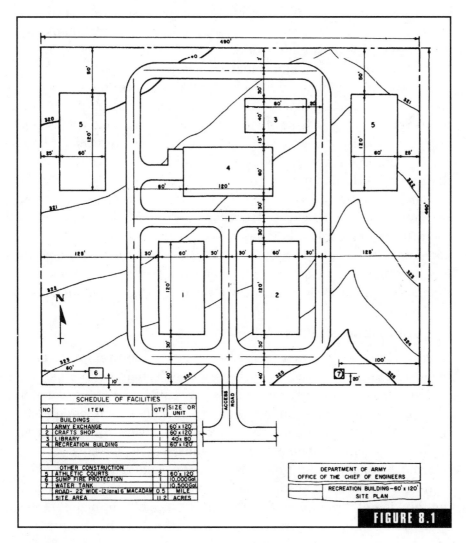

**Typical site plan.**

## Soil Tests

Soil tests are used to confirm that land where a private septic system will be installed can perk sufficiently. The soil test can dictate the type of septic system that may be used and how it must be installed. Additionally, soil studies can reveal facts about how well land will compact during development. Drainage issues can also be addressed when soils are tested. Independent engineers are usually retained to perform soil tests.

Soil engineers will review soil maps for the area being researched. Government maps are available to the engineers and local maps may also be available. If you are working with an engineer who works in the site area often, the engineer may have in-house maps to work with. Studies will be conducted for such conditions as underground waterways, potential earthquake risks, compaction, absorption, and so forth. Seismic maps, also available from the government, are used to evaluate the risk of earthquakes. Topo maps are used to check for flood plains and flood zones. Hydrology maps are used to determine drainage patterns and needs.

Small developments may not require much, if any, soil testing. However, drainage issues and similar needs must be addressed by someone. In some areas, builders make their own assessments. Local code officers may render opinions on the needs for drainage control. Engineering work is expensive and can take a considerable amount of time to complete, but it is generally needed on larger developments.

## Environmental Studies

Environmental studies may be needed to obtain approval for development. The increased awareness of preserving wetlands and other natural features can destroy a developer's plans quickly. Having water on a site can make the development more valuable. People often enjoy living and working around lakes, streams, and rivers. But, aside from flood issues, environmental concerns must be evaluated. It doesn't take much water for a section of land to be considered wetlands. Vegetation is one measuring stick used by environmental agencies. If you are thinking of developing land that shows any hint of potential wet spots, you had better insist on an environmental study, and this is a good thing to require on all properties.

There are state and federal standards that must be observed in terms of environmental issues. Normally, a phone call to your local environmental agency will get an inspector to your site for a free inspection. This may not always be the case, but it has proved to be true during my development projects. Violating an environmental law can be extremely costly, so don't take any chances on this detail of development.

## Zoning

Zoning is a key issue in any development. Without the proper zoning, obtaining permits to develop land will not be possible. The legal elements of zoning laws are such that this is an area where you should have your attorney look into the zoning requirements for you. Some of the elements that your attorney should be checking will include:

- Permitted uses
- Density regulations
- Special uses
- Design standards
- Conditional uses
- Contiguous property restrictions

## Building Codes

You, your builder, or your project manager should look into the requirements of local building codes. Issues here could run from permits for street entrances to drainage for storm water. Fire codes should also be considered. You may be required to provide fire hydrants that you were not counting on, or some other similarly expensive proposition.

## Utilities

Utilities are often taken for granted—they shouldn't be. Just because a subdivision at the other end of the street has city water and sewer doesn't mean that your piece of land has the necessary utilities running in front of it. You might be required to pay for an extension of a sewer line or water main, and this can be very expensive. An existing sewer may be too small to handle the increased demands that your project will put on it, and upgrading the sewer could be your responsibility. Building streets and sidewalks might turn out to be a lot more than you bargained for. These improvements may be required and you might be required to build them to state standards, which could cost much more than a private type of installation. Your land planner and engineers should be able to steer you safely around these potential obstacles.

As you can see, there is no shortage of work for a lot of people to do in a typical development project. If you are going to be your own project manager, you will have to arrange for the needed services, coordinate them, and keep all of your information organized. This is not a small task, but it is one that most people can manage.

## Managing Your Experts

Managing your experts and their reports is a responsibility that you should not take lightly. Most people like to think that, when they hire professionals, they can leave all the work to them and wait for their results. Sometimes this is true, but more often than not, some prodding is needed to keep everything on track. Calling and scheduling a survey should be all that is needed to get a survey done. It probably is enough to get the job done, but getting the job done when it is promised to you is another matter altogether.

Developers who have years of experience know what to expect from their development teams. The odds are that over the years a good working relationship has evolved. Rookie developers don't have this luxury. Even established developers have to keep their fingers in the pies to make sure that everything turns out correctly and on time. Some phases of the developing process require more attention from a developer than others. But all aspects of the work should be tracked and managed by the developer or the project manager. If a project manager is used, the developer should manage the project manager.

Land developing is not a business that is well suited to hands-off people. Getting involved is what makes the business both fun and successful. Taking an active role in all phases of development will also make you a better developer. You will learn from start to finish what is required to turn a piece of raw land into a sparkling development. Learning how to motivate, push, manage, and manipulate your experts may take some time, and you are sure to make some mistakes along the way. If you don't go around with a chip on your shoulder and don't pretend to be a know-it-all, you shouldn't have many bad encounters. The players on a development team are usually willing to work together and to work with the developer of a project. So, let's take a step-by-step tour of how you might go about managing your experts for faster turnaround, high-quality work, and bigger profits.

## Develop a System

Your first step should be to develop a system for keeping track of what is going on with your project. A lot of developers use computers to organize their management duties. Computers are great, but not everyone likes to work with them. Using a combination system might work best for you. What is a combination system? It is a system that used computerized files and old-fashioned paper trails. Personally, I favor a combination system and I have one that has worked very well for me over the years.

My system involves corkboards and a computer. I do my day-to-day tracking on cork boards and maintain an ongoing record of activities on my computer. There are people who would say that my system is too simple, but simple systems are sometimes the best systems. Let me give you a brief overview of how I operate.

I use multiple corkboards in my office. One of the boards has headings for days of the week. Under each of these headings I keep small pieces of paper that tell me what I'm required to do on a particular day. When I complete a task, I remove the piece of paper. This not only keeps me organized but gives me a sense of accomplishment as each piece of paper comes off the board.

Another board that I use has headings with expert specialty areas listed, such as: surveyors, soils tests, zoning, and so forth. The pieces of paper under these headings may duplicate what is on my daily board, but each piece of paper keeps me informed of what I need to accomplish.

A third board that I maintain is my "think-tank" board. This is where I post pieces of paper with my ideas on them. Whenever I think of something that is or might be of value during the development of a project I jot down a note and post it on the think-tank board. When I have time, I review the notes and think more about them. Sometimes I look at them while I'm talking on the telephone. By keeping the ideas in front of me I can digest them day by day. This, I believe, is an edge for me, and it is something that would be more difficult if I had all of my information on a computer.

The computerized version of my organizational procedure is a weekly recap of what I've done and what I need to do. Of course, there are spreadsheets on the computer that keep me in touch with my development budget. It's common for me to print reports from the computer and pin them to my office walls. I find that the more often I see what I'm doing, the better prepared I am to accomplish my goals. To some people, my system is clumsy, but it has worked well for me over the years. You have to define your own system, and it can be anything that you are comfortable with and that works. But you must have a system for tracing your efforts and your requirements.

## Tickler Files

Most developers have some version of tickler files. These are files that remind the developers to do something at a specific time. A tickler file can be as simple as a stack of index cards and a small box to hold them. The important aspect of the files is to make sure that nothing of importance is forgotten or not followed up on. For example, if a survey is due in on Wednesday, the tickler file should alert you to check for it on Thursday. If the survey has not arrived, you will know to call the survey firm and find out what the delay is. Tickler files are invaluable when it comes to staying on top of a development project.

## Phone Calls

Phone calls can keep your project on time. Unfortunately, it is usually necessary to follow up on work that you have scheduled. This can take a big bite out of your workday, but it is essential if you want to keep your project on schedule. Don't wait days to follow up on work that should be done. Every day you lose is costing you money. Be aggressive. Avoid being a pest, but don't hesitate to make polite inquiries pertaining to the status of work that you have requested. If you are timid on the phone, get over it. You have to learn to call people and push them to make your project come out on time.

## Files

Office files must be kept as projects are developed. Plan on making a lot of photocopies of documents. Some developers make copies of every check that they write and receive. Maintaining copies of all correspondence is essential. Written records are indispensable if you ever have to go to court to resolve differences with others. Not only are the records important during litigation, they make doing business much easier. There is so much involved in a development project that keeping your thoughts clear can be very difficult. If you can turn to a file and find your answers, you are way ahead in the game.

## Personal Involvement

Personal involvement is instrumental in making a project profitable. You can have an associate perform many of the tasks for you, but someone close to you must be willing to stay on top of all aspects of your work. Leaving your fate in the hands of subcontractors and vendors is risky business. You have to rely on outside help, but it is up to you to make sure that the people working with and for you are doing their jobs properly and on time. There is no substitute for first-hand management. If you don't already possess good organizational and management skills, work on them. Consider going to some seminars. Read more books and develop the skills as quickly as you can. The sooner you learn to run your business well, the better the business will do.

# Going over the Ground, from Top to Bottom

A piece of land can give many different impressions to various people. If four people look at the same piece of property they may see four different images for development. One person might see a golf course while another developer might see a prime site for a shopping mall. A third investor could conjure up an idea for a town house development while the fourth person might see a wonderful opportunity for an office park. Some parcels of land cry out for a particular treatment. Others are more versatile and stimulate creative minds. Every piece of property is unique in some way. Successful developers learn to find the highest and best use of land.

Some developers depend on land planners to evaluate land. This is not a bad idea, but many developers prefer to be more personally involved. Most builders like to pick their own parcels for development. Learning to see various aspects of land is a key factor in making wise purchases. Even if your perception of a parcel of land is only the first step in a buying decision, it is extremely helpful to have an ability to spot the differences between prime properties and problem properties.

Average people don't have the education and experience needed to make a full assessment of land. This is not to say that you can't make a reasonable assessment of land that you may wish to develop. Going on a gut reaction is dangerous as a developer, but it is often the first impression that a developer has that proves to be accurate. How do you feel about your ability to look at a piece of raw land and to see it as a developed project? Are you nervous? If you don't have confidence in yourself, you should hire a professional to do your assessments for you. Don't be concerned. As you work in the business you will gain a better understanding of what to look for. If you have strong feelings and a sense of seeing into the future, you are better prepared than many developers.

## Rock

A major consideration to developers is the presence and depth of bedrock. This type of rock is solid and can have a tremendous impact on the cost of development. In some regions bedrock is referred to as ledge. Living in Maine, I run into a lot of ledge when seeking buildable land. Bedrock runs deeper in some regions than it does in others. Many places can be developed without ever having to deal with bedrock. But some parcels of land have exposed bedrock. If the bedrock is exposed, you should see it when you walk a piece of land. Looking at the lay of the land can indicate the presence of bedrock close to the surface.

Even if you can't see bedrock, you can test for it with simple tools. One way of testing for the depth of bedrock is to drive a pointed steel rod into the ground. If the rod hits rock frequently in different locations, there is a good chance that it is hitting bedrock. I've gone to many sites with steel rods, a stepladder, and a sledgehammer to test for ledge. This method can be time-consuming and it is not sure proof of what's below the soil, but it's not a bad way to get a good read on a piece of land.

Another way to explore bedrock is to use a backhoe to dig test holes. This is something that should be addressed as a contingency clause in a purchase contract. By having a backhoe dig holes in random locations you can determine if bedrock will be a problem for you. Geology maps can also be used to predict what the bedrock conditions are on a project site. These maps are available from the U.S. Geological Survey. Local county engineering offices often have these maps available for your review on the premises.

The problems that may arise from bedrock can be numerous. For example, if you wanted to build homes with basements and found that there was bedrock 2 feet below the ground's surface, you would have a serious problem. You would either have to scrap your plans for basements or do a lot of blasting, which would be cost-prohibitive. Burying sewer and water pipes can be a big problem if bedrock is too close to the earth's surface. Roads built over solid bedrock can be less expensive to build, since compaction is not needed as much as it would be without the bedrock. However, fractured bedrock made of limestone can collect water and collapse downward. If this happens under a road, sinkholes develop. This could also happen under a footing for a building. Before you do a deal, you will need an engineer to evaluate your site and create a plan for it, but if you find things on your own that blow a deal out of the water, you save yourself the cost of an engineer.

## Soil Conditions

Soil conditions can have a strong influence on the cost of a project. For example, trying to build in sandy soil that runs deep can get expensive. Footings for construction must be taken down to solid ground, and this can make for some very expensive foundation walls. If your development plans call for private sewage disposal, the perk rate of soil in the septic area will be critical. Not all soils will perk well enough to permit the installation of a septic field. While there are ways of working around most types of problems with soils, the cost of doing so can be prohibitive.

The U.S. Department of Agriculture Soil Conservation Service and the U.S. Geological Survey for your region can be of great help in determining soil types and conditions. Digging test holes is a way for you to do your own on-site soils test. Augers can be used to create deep holes with small diameters. You will need to see the layers of the soil. A shallow test pit might show a sandy soil that would indicate good drainage. Digging a deeper pit may reveal that there is a layer of clay below the sandy soil. The clay would slow the absorption rate considerably. Without an extended knowledge of soils, you will not be able to avoid having a soils expert on your development team for larger properties. But, you can do some preliminary tests yourself before calling in the expert, and this could save you some money.

# Drainage Conditions

Drainage conditions are always a factor in land developing. Some drainage features can be seen easily. Others are not so easy to spot and require the use of elevation maps for evaluation. Developers can, and do, alter elevations. Dirt hauled into some sites can be cut out of other sites. But finding a site that requires a minimum amount of dirt movement is advantageous, both in time and money. When you walk a piece of land you can get a good feel for the drainage issues that may come into play.

If you are considering the purchase of riverfront property for development you must determine if the construction area will be in a floodplain of a flood zone. This may seem like a simple task, but don't be lulled into a false sense of security. Sites that appear to be well away and above a flood risk may not be rated as being out of the danger zone. Local county engineering offices usually have flood maps that you can review. Take advantage of this research opportunity. Buying land that winds up being in a floodplain can be a very costly mistake.

When you are walking land, look for gullies that might fill with water during hard rains, hills that might erode, and depressions that may hold water for long periods of time. Think as you walk and look over the land. Pay attention to what you are seeing. Make sketches if it will help you to maintain a focused view of the lay of the land. Picture where your buildings will be, where your roads will run, and where other elements may be located. Don't hesitate to walk the land more than once. Go over the land time and time again, until you are sure of your feelings about it.

# Hazardous Materials

Hazardous materials that are discovered on a piece of land can create a major expense when it comes to cleanup costs. It can be difficult to tell just by looking that a piece of land is affected by hazardous materials. However, the signs of trouble can sometimes be seen if you look hard enough. It would probably be obvious if you saw dozens of 55-gallon drums strewed around a piece of land that you might be in for some trouble. Of course, it would depend on what was in the drums.

Dump sites are not uncommon as large parcels of land. And remember, small pieces of land started out as large parcels. When raw land is used as an open dump, any number of substances might be discarded on the land. Finding a dump site doesn't mean that you should run in the opposite direction. The site might be mostly harmless, but any dump site is reason for concern.

Underground storage tanks can be expensive to remove. These tanks could be found nearly anywhere. An apartment building might have had underground oil tanks for many years and then converted to aboveground tanks. If the underground tanks are still buried, they are a risk. I've run into this type of situation before. Fortunately, I was able to spot enough evidence to arouse suspicion before the building was purchased. What tipped me off? When I inspected the basement walls of the building I saw some patch marks that were about the right size to hide the removal of oil pipes.

When I looked in the basement there were no oil tanks in it. A quick inspection would not have revealed the evidence of what looked like old piping that had been removed. I followed up on my suspicions by going over the lawn with a metal detector. I found a large metal object with the detector. Then I did some probing with a pointed steel rod. Sure enough, there were two buried oil tanks in the ground. Since I found them early, the seller had to pay for their removal. If I had purchased the property and found the tank later, I'd have been paying the big bucks for the tank removal work.

Farmers may have underground tanks that store gasoline or diesel fuel. If you buy a farm to develop and then stumble on the underground tanks, you have an added expense, and it can be quite costly. Modern regulations are fairly tight for anyone having underground storage tanks, but the regulations were not always so strict. Older properties can pose quite a risk of underground tanks and other types of hazardous materials. Land that looks perfectly normal could be an expensive nightmare for any developer who buys it. Have all land screened for environmental risks prior to a full commitment to purchasing the land.

## Looking to the Past

Looking to the past is wise when you are researching a piece of land. Can you imagine buying a large tract of land for development and finding out that it was protected from development because of its historical value? Well, it could happen. Make sure that any land that you are planning to develop will not be frozen with red tape. Don't think that you are safe just because other developments have been completed nearby. Each piece of land, and even portions of a piece of land, can fall into a protected status. Getting into a legal battle over the right to develop a piece of land that appears to be protected is not something that many developers would ever wish to do.

## Old Wells

If you are not familiar with country property, you might not think to keep an eye out for open, abandoned water wells. Falling into an old well could be fatal. I've run across dozens of abandoned wells over the years. Sometimes they have a rotted cover on them, and sometimes there is no cover. One wrong step could send you some 30 feet down, into cold water, with little chance of escape. If you see evidence of an old foundation, turn on your well radar—there's probably a well close by. If you can't see clearly where you will be placing your feet, use a staff to probe the ground before you walk. It's wise to take someone with you when you are walking land, and this is even more essential if you suspect risks, such as water wells.

## Other Things

There are many other things that you should pay attention to when you are going over a piece of land. Perhaps one of the most important is the location of the property. Location is always a prime consideration when dealing with real estate. The size of a parcel is also of interest. Of course, location, size, and price are all issues that you will probably have considered prior to walking a piece of property.

When you walk a piece of land you should study the vegetation. If you have a good understanding of vegetation, the plants growing on a piece of land can speak volumes to you. It's easy to see if trees are on a piece of land. But smaller vegetation can be very informative. For example, ferns indicate moisture. An abundance of ferns could indicate wetlands or at the least, land that will not drain well. It's not unusual for developers to study books on vegetation to learn what the various types of growth can tell them about a piece of land.

Access to land is not always what it seems. You must make sure that the parcel of land that you are considering has suitable access. Finding this out will take some paper research, but you should note site conditions to refer to when you do your deed research. While you are looking around, take notes about the existence of utilities. Do you see fire hydrants? How far away are electrical and telephone wires? Do you see any sewer manhole covers in the road in front of the property? Do surrounding properties have water wells in plain view? Make mental and written notes regarding utilities. These notes will be appreciated when you, or your experts, begin to look into the feasibility and cost of getting utilities to the property for your development plans.

Carry a camera with you on site inspections and take lots of pictures. Photograph surrounding properties, as well as the subject property. The photos can prove very helpful when you research the property values of surrounding parcels. When you leave the land, note the mileage on your odometer. You should pay attention to how far the land you are looking at is from various amenities, such as hospitals, schools, and stores.

There is much more to walking a piece of property than just moving across it. A camera and a notebook should be considered required equipment for all site visits. Once you are satisfied with your site visit, it's time to start putting some plans on paper. Chapter 10 will give you some tips on how to plan your development.

# Planning on Paper

Planning on paper is a sure way of making a project more likely to succeed. The benefits of a solid, written plan are numerous. Yet, some developers don't have much patience for paperwork. They think of the planning as boring, and some developers see it as a waste of time. Well, it is not a waste of time. It can be boring, but it doesn't have to be. Many developers find the planning stage to be one of the most enjoyable aspects of developing land. There is some risk that you will find the planning so fascinating that you will spend too much time on it. You have to know when to accept a plan as being as good as it needs to be. Some perfectionists keep tinkering with their plans for too long. It's possible that a developer who is unsure might use planning as an excuse to postpone the commencement of a project.

Many factors must be assessed as a plan is made for a development. Before a project goes into production there will usually be a plan that has been created by experts. But developers need to create their own plans to give the experts a direction to move in. Not all developers do their own planning, and you don't have to. It's possible to hire people to do the planning for you. But doing it yourself can be quite reward-ing. Even if you are not comfortable with doing a complete plan on your own, you can complete many of the components within a plan.

The more direction that you can offer your experts, the more likely you are to get a project plan that you like.

## The Components

The components of a master plan tend to be consistent. However, different types of projects can call for different types of planning elements. Site features are a prime consideration. Both natural features and constraints of land must be considered. Location may be one of the biggest factors to look at. In terms of location, you might be concerned about how close a property is to schools, shopping, and medical care. You will also want to think about comparable properties in the area that you intend to develop.

After working on a plan that deals with existing features, you must create a plan for the development. For example, if you are building a residential subdivision, what house style will you allow in the development? Are you going to have play areas throughout the development for children? Should you plan on paved bike paths? Will open areas provide recreational opportunities? Do you plan to build swimming pools and tennis courts? Will you be creating a high-density development? Would residents appreciate a community meeting hall within the development? Good developers ask themselves hundreds of questions during the planning of a development.

People who don't have experience in land development generally have no idea how much effort is required to create a working plan. Anyone who has not developed land may not realize that someone has to think of everything from a name for the development to how the streets will be lighted. The amount of thought that goes into a development is tremendous. Minor details can have a major effect on a development. And failure to recognize a need can be extremely costly.

Demographics and psychographics both need to be considered when defining a neighborhood. The age, income, and family status of people can have a major influence on the type of development required. Developers must consider as many factors as possible to determine how to structure a development. For example, recreational needs vary with age. This could affect the need for walking paths or racquetball courts. Knowing your target market is the only way to build a development that can be sold at maximum profit (Fig. 10.1).

## U.S. Census Bureau

### Housing Vacancies and Homeownership
### Historical Tables

Table 8.    Quarterly Estimates of Total Housing Inventory for the
                 United States:  1965 - Present

(Numbers in Thousands)

|  | 1965 | | | |
|---|---|---|---|---|
|  | 1st Qtr | 2nd Qtr | 3rd Qtr | 4th Qtr |
| All Housing Units | 63668 | 63993 | 64459 | 64730 |
| Vacant | 6821 | 6534 | 6613 | 6880 |
| Year-Round Vacant | 4825 | 4769 | 4813 | 5003 |
| For Rent | 1766 | 1736 | 1680 | 1781 |
| For Sale Only | 539 | 499 | 542 | 509 |
| Rented or Sold | 242 | 350 | 379 | 314 |
| Held off Market | 1843 | 1764 | 1789 | 1950 |
| Occ'l Use | 454 | 442 | 463 | 507 |
| URE | 372 | 341 | 343 | 433 |
| Other | 1017 | 981 | 983 | 1010 |
| Seasonal | 1996 | 1766 | 1799 | 1877 |
| Total Occupied | 56848 | 57459 | 57846 | 57850 |
| Owner | 35728 | 36113 | 36380 | 36700 |
| Renter | 21119 | 21346 | 21467 | 21150 |

|  | 1966 | | | |
|---|---|---|---|---|
| All Housing Units | 64564 | 65378 | 65653 | 65252 |
| Vacant | 6888 | 6731 | 6728 | 6556 |
| Year-Round Vacant | 5030 | 4874 | 4911 | 4821 |
| For Rent | 1712 | 1583 | 1587 | 1623 |
| For Sale Only | 509 | 525 | 509 | 448 |
| Rented or Sold | 312 | 360 | 407 | 276 |
| Held off Market | 2050 | 1950 | 1964 | 2051 |
| Occ'l Use | 527 | 472 | 498 | 559 |
| URE | 452 | 393 | 382 | 473 |
| Other | 1071 | 1085 | 1083 | 1019 |
| Seasonal | 1858 | 1857 | 1816 | 1735 |
| Total Occupied | 57676 | 58646 | 58925 | 58696 |
| Owner | 36624 | 37064 | 37300 | 37448 |
| Renter | 21052 | 21582 | 21625 | 21248 |

|  | 1967 | | | |
|---|---|---|---|---|
|  | 1st Qtr | 2nd Qtr | 3rd Qtr | 4th Qtr |
| All Housing Units | 65227 | 65732 | 66731 | 66364 |
| Vacant | 6734 | 6589 | 6598 | 6231 |
| Year-Round Vacant | 4962 | 4840 | 4832 | 4414 |
| For Rent | 1522 | 1444 | 1495 | 1303 |

**FIGURE 10.1**

U.S. housing inventory.

| | | | | |
|---|---|---|---|---|
| For Sale Only | 494 | 476 | 491 | 458 |
| Rented or Sold | 284 | 352 | 400 | 319 |
| Held off Market | 2223 | 2130 | 2023 | 1905 |
| Occ'l Use | 557 | 521 | 536 | 525 |
| URE | 514 | 449 | 414 | 426 |
| Other | 1152 | 1160 | 1073 | 954 |
| Seasonal | 1772 | 1749 | 1766 | 1817 |
| | | | | |
| Total Occupied | 58493 | 59143 | 60133 | 60133 |
| Owner | 37026 | 37792 | 38365 | 38184 |
| Renter | 21467 | 21351 | 21768 | 21949 |

| | 1968 | | | |
|---|---|---|---|---|
| | 1st Qtr | 2nd Qtr | 3rd Qtr | 4th Qtr |
| All Housing Units | 66803 | 67119 | 67357 | 67403 |
| | | | | |
| Vacant | 6352 | 6380 | 6161 | 5980 |
| Year-Round Vacant | 4487 | 4558 | 4411 | 4329 |
| For Rent | 1297 | 1324 | 1272 | 1170 |
| For Sale Only | 396 | 386 | 429 | 430 |
| Rented or Sold | 324 | 373 | 450 | 363 |
| Held off Market | 1981 | 2029 | 1861 | 1944 |
| Occ'l Use | 515 | 503 | 500 | 546 |
| URE | 448 | 466 | 394 | 406 |
| Other | 1018 | 1060 | 967 | 992 |
| Seasonal | 1865 | 1822 | 1749 | 1651 |
| | | | | |
| Total Occupied | 60451 | 60739 | 61196 | 61423 |
| Owner | 38447 | 38934 | 39227 | 39065 |
| Renter | 22004 | 21805 | 21969 | 22358 |

| | 1969 | | | |
|---|---|---|---|---|
| | 1st Qtr | 2nd Qtr | 3rd Qtr | 4th Qtr |
| All Housing Units | 67987 | 68362 | 68740 | 68825 |
| | | | | |
| Vacant | 6228 | 6221 | 6328 | 6095 |
| Year-Round Vacant | 4490 | 4423 | 4520 | 4314 |
| For Rent | 1184 | 1190 | 1188 | 1120 |
| For Sale Only | 362 | 358 | 404 | 402 |
| Rented or Sold | 346 | 395 | 458 | 356 |
| Held of Market | 2154 | 2028 | 2065 | 2051 |
| Occ'l Use | 599 | 551 | 584 | 580 |
| URE | 498 | 433 | 413 | 434 |
| Other | 1057 | 1044 | 1068 | 1037 |
| Seasonal | 1739 | 1798 | 1808 | 1781 |
| | | | | |
| Total Occupied | 61759 | 62141 | 62412 | 62730 |
| Owner | 39587 | 40019 | 40193 | 40398 |
| Renter | 22172 | 22122 | 22219 | 22332 |

| | 1970 | | | |
|---|---|---|---|---|
| | 1st Qtr | 2nd Qtr | 3rd Qtr | 4th Qtr |
| All Housing Units | 69026 | 69553 | 70247 | 70283 |
| | | | | |
| Vacant | 6196 | 6075 | 6229 | 6049 |
| Year-Round Vacant | 4416 | 4418 | 4475 | 4255 |
| For Rent | 1192 | 1211 | 1197 | 1168 |
| For Sale Only | 396 | 386 | 415 | 420 |

**FIGURE 10.1**

U.S. housing inventory. (*Continued*)

|  | 1st Qtr | 2nd Qtr | 3rd Qtr | 4th Qtr |
|---|---|---|---|---|
| Rented or Sold | 349 | 428 | 490 | 387 |
| Held off Market | 2073 | 2018 | 2016 | 1902 |
| Occ'l Use | 560 | 589 | 579 | 561 |
| URE | 450 | 415 | 418 | 410 |
| Other | 1063 | 1014 | 1019 | 931 |
| Seasonal | 1780 | 1657 | 1754 | 1794 |
| | | | | |
| Total Occupied | 62830 | 63478 | 64018 | 64234 |
| Owner | 40399 | 40600 | 41228 | 41110 |
| Renter | 22431 | 22878 | 22790 | 23124 |

|  | 1971 | | | |
|---|---|---|---|---|
|  | 1st Qtr | 2nd Qtr | 3rd Qtr | 4th Qtr |
| All Housing Units | 70522 | 71159 | 71505 | 72092 |
| | | | | |
| Vacant | 6160 | 6246 | 6241 | 6306 |
| Year-Round Vacant | 4460 | 4540 | 4630 | 4605 |
| For Rent | 1208 | 1223 | 1325 | 1308 |
| For Sale Only | 407 | 379 | 396 | 400 |
| Rented or Sold | 392 | 475 | 544 | 446 |
| Held off Market | 2064 | 2110 | 2031 | 2083 |
| Occ'l Use | 611 | 612 | 588 | 614 |
| URE | 436 | 401 | 360 | 444 |
| Other | 1017 | 1097 | 1083 | 1025 |
| Seasonal | 1700 | 1706 | 1611 | 1701 |
| | | | | |
| Total Occupied | 64362 | 64913 | 65264 | 65786 |
| Owner | 41192 | 41609 | 42030 | 42432 |
| Renter | 23170 | 23304 | 23234 | 23354 |

|  | 1972 | | | |
|---|---|---|---|---|
|  | 1st Qtr | 2nd Qtr | 3rd Qtr | 4th Qtr |
| All Housing Units | 72867 | 73500 | 73609 | 73274 |
| | | | | |
| Vacant | 6272 | 6389 | 6309 | 6502 |
| Year-Round Vacant | 4535 | 4611 | 4708 | 4806 |
| For Rent | 1333 | 1410 | 1514 | 1427 |
| For Sale Only | 434 | 434 | 399 | 461 |
| Rented or Sold | 430 | 542 | 609 | 481 |
| Held off Market | 2338 | 2225 | 2186 | 2437 |
| Occ'l Use | 682 | 627 | 295 | 662 |
| URE | 466 | 389 | 369 | 450 |
| Other | 1190 | 1209 | 1222 | 1325 |
| Seasonal | 1737 | 1778 | 1601 | 1696 |
| | | | | |
| Total Occupied | 66595 | 67111 | 67300 | 66772 |
| Owner | 42821 | 43286 | 43274 | 43001 |
| Renter | 23774 | 23825 | 24026 | 23771 |

|  | 1973 | | | |
|---|---|---|---|---|
|  | 1st Qtr | 2nd Qtr | 3rd Qtr | 4th Qtr |
| All Housing Units | 74676 | 75055 | 75751 | 76144 |
| | | | | |
| Vacant | 6361 | 6605 | 6629 | 6635 |
| Year-Round Vacant | 4679 | 4902 | 4934 | 4890 |
| For Rent | 1463 | 1529 | 1538 | 1552 |
| For Sale Only | 445 | 419 | 479 | 525 |
| Rented or Sold | 452 | 560 | 598 | 484 |

**FIGURE 10.1**

**U.S. housing inventory.** (*Continued*)

| | 1st Qtr | 2nd Qtr | 3rd Qtr | 4th Qtr |
|---|---|---|---|---|
| Held off Market | 2319 | 2394 | 2319 | 2329 |
| Occ'l Use | 591 | 586 | 571 | 602 |
| URE | 433 | 433 | 433 | 432 |
| Other | 1295 | 1375 | 1315 | 1294 |
| Seasonal | 1682 | 1703 | 1695 | 1745 |
| | | | | |
| Total Occupied | 68315 | 68450 | 69122 | 69509 |
| Owner | 44336 | 44082 | 44515 | 44763 |
| Renter | 23979 | 24368 | 24607 | 24745 |

**1974**

| | 1st Qtr | 2nd Qtr | 3rd Qtr | 4th Qtr |
|---|---|---|---|---|
| All Housing Units | 76644 | 77576 | 77632 | 77996 |
| | | | | |
| Vacant | 6930 | 7159 | 6833 | 6695 |
| Year-Round Vacant | 5094 | 5339 | 5130 | 5055 |
| For Rent | 1639 | 1691 | 1687 | 1628 |
| For Sale Only | 534 | 519 | 569 | 605 |
| Rented or Sold | 459 | 598 | 627 | 489 |
| Held off Market | 2462 | 2531 | 2247 | 2333 |
| Occ'l Use | 631 | 609 | 604 | 625 |
| URE | 470 | 499 | 413 | 424 |
| Other | 1361 | 1423 | 1230 | 1284 |
| Seasonal | 1836 | 1820 | 1703 | 1640 |
| | | | | |
| Total Occupied | 69714 | 70417 | 70799 | 71301 |
| Owner | 45175 | 45630 | 45736 | 45918 |
| Renter | 24539 | 24787 | 25063 | 25383 |

**1975**

| | 1st Qtr | 2nd Qtr | 3rd Qtr | 4th Qtr |
|---|---|---|---|---|
| All Housing Units | 78212 | 78611 | 79208 | 79251 |
| | | | | |
| Vacant | 6956 | 7005 | 7058 | 6564 |
| Year-Round Vacant | 5196 | 5227 | 5356 | 5030 |
| For Rent | 1667 | 1724 | 1708 | 1489 |
| For Sale Only | 575 | 556 | 655 | 577 |
| Rented or Sold | 432 | 559 | 638 | 514 |
| Held off Market | 2522 | 2388 | 2355 | 2450 |
| Occ'l Use | 650 | 617 | 633 | 697 |
| URE | 514 | 473 | 462 | 432 |
| Other | 1358 | 1298 | 1260 | 1321 |
| Seasonal | 1760 | 1778 | 1702 | 1534 |
| | | | | |
| Total Occupied | 71256 | 71606 | 72150 | 72687 |
| Owner | 45889 | 46472 | 46609 | 46883 |
| Renter | 25367 | 25134 | 25541 | 25804 |

**1976**

| | 1st Qtr | 2nd Qtr | 3rd Qtr | 4th Qtr |
|---|---|---|---|---|
| All Housing Units | 79771 | 80049 | 80418 | 80517 |
| | | | | |
| Vacant | 6813 | 6925 | 6829 | 6528 |
| Year-Round Vacant | 5197 | 5282 | 5238 | 5042 |
| For Rent | 1519 | 1619 | 1580 | 1466 |
| For Sale Only | 577 | 597 | 630 | 586 |
| Rented or Sold | 516 | 600 | 629 | 512 |
| Held off Market | 2585 | 2466 | 2399 | 2478 |

**FIGURE 10.1**

U.S. housing inventory. (*Continued*)

| | 1st Qtr | 2nd Qtr | 3rd Qtr | 4th Qtr |
|---|---|---|---|---|
| Occ'l Use | 710 | 714 | 666 | 731 |
| URE | 497 | 455 | 465 | 451 |
| Other | 1378 | 1297 | 1268 | 1296 |
| Seasonal | 1616 | 1643 | 1591 | 1486 |
| | | | | |
| Total Occupied | 72958 | 73124 | 73589 | 73989 |
| Owner | 47131 | 47238 | 47759 | 47945 |
| Renter | 25827 | 25886 | 25830 | 26044 |

**1977**

| | 1st Qtr | 2nd Qtr | 3rd Qtr | 4th Qtr |
|---|---|---|---|---|
| All Housing Units | 81142 | 81379 | 81828 | 82232 |
| | | | | |
| Vacant | 6843 | 6992 | 6848 | 6762 |
| Year-Round Vacant | 5237 | 5271 | 5250 | 5138 |
| For Rent | 1433 | 1491 | 1530 | 1434 |
| For Sale Only | 638 | 618 | 525 | 513 |
| Rented or Sold | 542 | 695 | 732 | 633 |
| Held off Market | 2624 | 2467 | 2463 | 2558 |
| Occ'l USE | 771 | 670 | 671 | 714 |
| URE | 494 | 410 | 408 | 441 |
| Other | 1359 | 1387 | 1384 | 1403 |
| Seasonal | 1606 | 1721 | 1598 | 1624 |
| | | | | |
| Total Occupied | 74299 | 74387 | 74980 | 75470 |
| Owner | 48146 | 47979 | 48737 | 48980 |
| Renter | 26153 | 26408 | 26243 | 26490 |

**1978**

| | 1st Qtr | 2nd Qtr | 3rd Qtr | 4th Qtr |
|---|---|---|---|---|
| All Housing Units | 82932 | 83402 | 83630 | 84019 |
| | | | | |
| Vacant | 7000 | 7043 | 6891 | 6856 |
| Year-Round Vacant | 5207 | 5317 | 5301 | 5214 |
| For Rent | 1425 | 1470 | 1413 | 1422 |
| For Sale Only | 525 | 470 | 527 | 574 |
| Rented or Sold | 531 | 672 | 794 | 603 |
| Held off Market | 2726 | 2705 | 2567 | 2615 |
| Occ'l Use | 689 | 723 | 663 | 681 |
| URE | 494 | 435 | 435 | 502 |
| Other | 1543 | 1547 | 1469 | 1432 |
| Seasonal | 1793 | 1726 | 1590 | 1642 |
| | | | | |
| Total Occupied | 75932 | 76359 | 76739 | 77163 |
| Owner | 49280 | 49175 | 50034 | 50465 |
| Renter | 26652 | 27184 | 26705 | 26698 |

**1979**

| | 1st Qtr | 2nd Qtr | 3rd Qtr | 4th Qtr |
|---|---|---|---|---|
| All Housing Units | 84267 | 85141 | 85227 | 85609 |
| | | | | |
| Vacant | 7028 | 7204 | 7178 | 7104 |
| Year-Round Vacant | 5251 | 5503 | 5512 | 5393 |
| For Rent | 1371 | 1455 | 1478 | 1421 |
| For Sale Only | 523 | 551 | 591 | 599 |
| Rented or Sold | 585 | 697 | 704 | 572 |
| Held off Market | 2772 | 2800 | 2739 | 2801 |
| Occ'l Use | 686 | 725 | 694 | 733 |

**FIGURE 10.1**

U.S. housing inventory. (*Continued*)

| | | | | |
|---|---|---|---|---|
| URE | 552 | 538 | 535 | 537 |
| Other | 1534 | 1537 | 1510 | 1531 |
| Seasonal | 1777 | 1701 | 1666 | 1711 |
| | | | | |
| Total Occupied | 77239 | 77937 | 78048 | 78505 |
| Owner | 50437 | 50737 | 51512 | 51656 |
| Renter | 26802 | 27200 | 26536 | 26849 |

|  | **1979/r** | | | |
|---|---|---|---|---|
|  | 1st Qtr | 2nd Qtr | 3rd Qtr | 4th Qtr |
| All Housing Units | 84865 | 85839 | 85877 | 86359 |
| | | | | |
| Vacant | 7413 | 7714 | 7645 | 7586 |
| Year-Round Vacant | 5631 | 6051 | 5990 | 5899 |
| For Rent | 1486 | 1607 | 1641 | 1579 |
| For Sale Only | 551 | 589 | 626 | 660 |
| Rented or Sold | 639 | 755 | 787 | 637 |
| Held off Market | 2954 | 3100 | 2937 | 3023 |
| Occ'l Use | 740 | 874 | 765 | 796 |
| URE | 598 | 605 | 591 | 571 |
| Other | 1616 | 1620 | 1581 | 1656 |
| Seasonal | 1782 | 1663 | 1654 | 1686 |
| | | | | |
| Total Occupied | 77452 | 78125 | 78232 | 78773 |
| Owner | 50189 | 50703 | 51477 | 51518 |
| Renter | 27263 | 27422 | 26755 | 27256 |

|  | **1980** | | | |
|---|---|---|---|---|
|  | 1st Qtr | 2nd Qtr | 3rd Qtr | 4th Qtr |
| All Housing Units | 87167 | 87650 | 88080 | 88060 |
| | | | | |
| Vacant | 8054 | 8220 | 8187 | 7945 |
| Year-Round Vacant | 5882 | 6109 | 6178 | 5813 |
| For Rent | 1516 | 1639 | 1682 | 1462 |
| For Sale Only | 703 | 722 | 775 | 737 |
| Rented or Sold | 576 | 617 | 715 | 583 |
| Held off Market | 3088 | 3131 | 3007 | 3031 |
| Occ'l Use | 812 | 835 | 789 | 818 |
| URE | 581 | 579 | 566 | 547 |
| Other | 1694 | 1718 | 1652 | 1666 |
| Seasonal | 2172 | 2111 | 2009 | 2131 |
| | | | | |
| Total Occupied | 79113 | 79431 | 79893 | 80115 |
| Owner | 51819 | 52027 | 52570 | 52476 |
| Renter | 27294 | 27404 | 27324 | 27640 |

|  | **1981** | | | |
|---|---|---|---|---|
|  | 1st Qtr | 2nd Qtr | 3rd Qtr | 4th Qtr |
| All Housing Units | 90598 | 90880 | 90911 | 91059 |
| | | | | |
| Vacant | 8243 | 8201 | 8028 | 7806 |
| Year-Round Vacant | 6061 | 6242 | 6220 | 6020 |
| For Rent | 1545 | 1529 | 1491 | 1529 |
| For Sale Only | 736 | 742 | 798 | 759 |
| Rented or Sold | 513 | 675 | 667 | 523 |
| Held off Market | 3267 | 3297 | 3263 | 3207 |
| Occ'l Use | 885 | 918 | 906 | 925 |
| URE | 656 | 606 | 627 | 569 |

**FIGURE 10.1**

U.S. housing inventory. (*Continued*)

| | | | | |
|---|---|---|---|---|
| Other | 1726 | 1772 | 1730 | 1713 |
| Seasonal | 2182 | 1959 | 1808 | 1787 |
| | | | | |
| Total Occupied | 82355 | 82679 | 82883 | 83253 |
| Owner | 53943 | 53907 | 54288 | 54198 |
| Renter | 28412 | 28772 | 28595 | 29055 |

| | 1982 | | | |
|---|---|---|---|---|
| | 1st Qtr | 2nd Qtr | 3rd Qtr | 4th Qtr |
| All Housing Units | 91829 | 91847 | 91749 | 92078 |
| | | | | |
| Vacant | 8178 | 8283 | 8112 | 8005 |
| Year-Round Vacant | 6336 | 6483 | 6362 | 6294 |
| For Rent | 1654 | 1607 | 1658 | 1762 |
| For Sale Only | 787 | 888 | 839 | 859 |
| Rented or Sold | 525 | 572 | 605 | 512 |
| Held off Market | 3370 | 3416 | 3259 | 3161 |
| Occ'l Use | 929 | 1019 | 952 | 937 |
| URE | 653 | 593 | 569 | 538 |
| Other | 1788 | 1805 | 1737 | 1686 |
| Seasonal | 1842 | 1800 | 1750 | 1711 |
| | | | | |
| Total Occupied | 83651 | 83564 | 83637 | 84073 |
| Owner | 54206 | 54233 | 54280 | 54227 |
| Renter | 29445 | 29331 | 29357 | 29846 |

| | 1983 | | | |
|---|---|---|---|---|
| | 1st Qtr | 2nd Qtr | 3rd Qtr | 4th Qtr |
| All Housing Units | 92518 | 92634 | 93164 | 93859 |
| | | | | |
| Vacant | 8421 | 8438 | 8567 | 8489 |
| Year-Round Vacant | 6585 | 6663 | 6779 | 1798 |
| For rent | 1834 | 1755 | 1851 | 1798 |
| For Sale Only | 774 | 837 | 918 | 919 |
| Rented or Sold | 555 | 652 | 733 | 590 |
| Held off Market | 3422 | 3419 | 3278 | 3436 |
| Occ'l Use | 941 | 975 | 886 | 902 |
| URE | 704 | 646 | 583 | 634 |
| Other | 1777 | 1799 | 1809 | 1900 |
| Seasonal | 1836 | 1776 | 1788 | 1746 |
| | | | | |
| Total Occupied | 84097 | 84196 | 84597 | 85370 |
| Owner | 54411 | 54475 | 54819 | 54978 |
| Renter | 29686 | 29721 | 29778 | 30392 |

| | 1984 | | | |
|---|---|---|---|---|
| | 1st Qtr | 2nd Qtr | 3rd Qtr | 4th Qtr |
| All Housing Units | 94496 | 94969 | 95478 | 96080 |
| | | | | |
| Vacant | 8871 | 8878 | 8822 | 9068 |
| Year-Round Vacant | 6985 | 7022 | 7069 | 7243 |
| For Rent | 1831 | 1798 | 1990 | 2115 |
| For Sale Only | 904 | 946 | 995 | 944 |
| Rented or Sold | 595 | 701 | 719 | 639 |
| Held off Market | 3654 | 3577 | 3365 | 3545 |
| Occ'l Use | 965 | 1040 | 968 | 995 |
| URE | 672 | 628 | 552 | 636 |
| Other | 2016 | 1910 | 1845 | 1914 |

**FIGURE 10.1**

U.S. housing inventory. (*Continued*)

| | | | | |
|---|---|---|---|---|
| Seasonal | 1886 | 1856 | 1753 | 1824 |
| Total Occupied | 85625 | 86091 | 86656 | 87012 |
| Owner | 55314 | 55615 | 55980 | 55774 |
| Renter | 30311 | 30476 | 30676 | 31237 |

| | 1985 | | | |
|---|---|---|---|---|
| | 1st Qtr | 2nd Qtr | 3rd Qtr | 4th Qtr |
| All Housing Units | 96418 | 97142 | 97748 | 98024 |
| Vacant | 9347 | 9456 | 9538 | 9444 |
| Year-Round Vacant | 7314 | 7350 | 7550 | 7386 |
| For Rent | 2109 | 2109 | 2336 | 2328 |
| For Sale Only | 1016 | 1071 | 1014 | 922 |
| Rented or Sold | 584 | 711 | 737 | 622 |
| Held off Market | 3604 | 3459 | 3463 | 3514 |
| Occ'l Use | 1060 | 964 | 897 | 986 |
| URE | 669 | 570 | 681 | 714 |
| Other | 1875 | 1925 | 1885 | 1814 |
| Seasonal | 2033 | 2106 | 1988 | 2058 |
| Total Occupied | 87071 | 87686 | 88211 | 88580 |
| Owner | 55813 | 56207 | 56331 | 56256 |
| Renter | 31259 | 31479 | 31880 | 32325 |

| | 1986 | | | |
|---|---|---|---|---|
| | 1st Qtr | 2nd Qtr | 3rd Qtr | 4th Qtr |
| All Housing Units | 98764 | 99206 | 99415 | 99888 |
| Vacant | 9947 | 10263 | 10220 | 10263 |
| Year-Round Vacant | 7557 | 7895 | 7884 | 7948 |
| For rent | 2423 | 2577 | 2631 | 2719 |
| For Sale Only | 875 | 960 | 957 | 955 |
| Rented or Sold | 569 | 723 | 793 | 648 |
| Held off Market | 3691 | 3635 | 3504 | 3626 |
| Occ'l Use | 1029 | 958 | 934 | 1041 |
| URE | 805 | 712 | 693 | 754 |
| Other | 1857 | 1966 | 1877 | 1831 |
| Seasonal | 2390 | 2368 | 2335 | 2315 |
| Total Occupied | 88817 | 88943 | 89195 | 89625 |
| Owner | 56448 | 56756 | 56944 | 57226 |
| Renter | 32369 | 32187 | 32251 | 32399 |

| | 1987 | | | |
|---|---|---|---|---|
| | 1st Qtr | 2nd Qtr | 3rd Qtr | 4th Qtr |
| All Housing Units | 101204 | 101580 | 102154 | 102304 |
| Vacant | 11176 | 11331 | 11530 | 11138 |
| Year-Round Vacant | 8025 | 8236 | 8536 | 8262 |
| For Rent | 2639 | 2688 | 2879 | 2802 |
| For Sale Only | 979 | 995 | 1003 | 933 |
| Rented or Sold | 578 | 695 | 787 | 690 |
| Held off Market | 3828 | 3859 | 3867 | 3837 |
| Occ'l Use | 1018 | 1005 | 1082 | 1158 |
| URE | 848 | 712 | 783 | 803 |
| Other | 1962 | 2142 | 2002 | 1876 |
| Seasonal | 3151 | 3095 | 2995 | 2876 |

**FIGURE 10.1**

U.S. housing inventory. (*Continued*)

|  | 1st Qtr | 2nd Qtr | 3rd Qtr | 4th Qtr |
|---|---|---|---|---|
| Total Occupied | 90027 | 90249 | 90624 | 91166 |
| Owner | 57429 | 57619 | 58202 | 58411 |
| Renter | 32598 | 32630 | 32422 | 32756 |

**1988**

|  | 1st Qtr | 2nd Qtr | 3rd Qtr | 4th Qtr |
|---|---|---|---|---|
| All Housing Units | 102909 | 103771 | 104018 | 103603 |
| Vacant | 11617 | 11882 | 11750 | 11282 |
| Year-Round Vacant | 8553 | 8723 | 8596 | 8259 |
| For Rent | 2890 | 2821 | 2836 | 2660 |
| For Sale Only | 937 | 982 | 971 | 982 |
| Rented or Sold | 568 | 753 | 793 | 602 |
| Held off Market | 4158 | 4167 | 3996 | 4015 |
| Occ'l Use | 1124 | 1288 | 1221 | 1217 |
| URE | 962 | 873 | 792 | 921 |
| Other | 2072 | 2005 | 1983 | 1878 |
| Seasonal | 3064 | 3159 | 3154 | 3023 |
| Total Occupied | 91292 | 91889 | 92268 | 92321 |
| Owner | 58158 | 58518 | 59055 | 58871 |
| Renter | 33134 | 33371 | 33213 | 33450 |

**1989**

|  | 1st Qtr | 2nd Qtr | 3rd Qtr | 4th Qtr |
|---|---|---|---|---|
| All Housing Units | 104700 | 105073 | 105506 | 105222 |
| Vacant | 11659 | 11742 | 11895 | 11337 |
| Year-Round Vacant | 8612 | 8736 | 8857 | 8253 |
| For Rent | 2677 | 2669 | 2701 | 2505 |
| For Sale Only | 926 | 946 | 1095 | 1001 |
| Rented or Sold | 648 | 657 | 788 | 613 |
| Held off Market | 4361 | 4464 | 4273 | 4133 |
| Occ'l Use | 1232 | 1404 | 1370 | 1256 |
| URE | 992 | 962 | 918 | 977 |
| Other | 2137 | 2098 | 1985 | 1900 |
| Seasonal | 3047 | 3006 | 3038 | 3084 |
| Total Occupied | 93041 | 93331 | 93611 | 93886 |
| Owner | 59455 | 59612 | 59953 | 59782 |
| Renter | 33586 | 33719 | 33658 | 34104 |

**1989/r**

|  | 1st Qtr | 2nd Qtr | 3rd Qtr | 4th Qtr |
|---|---|---|---|---|
| All Housing Units | 105197 | 105691 | 106287 | 105734 |
| Vacant | 12088 | 12221 | 12524 | 12120 |
| Year-Round Vacant | 9245 | 9432 | 9618 | 9099 |
| For Rent | 2763 | 2752 | 2809 | 2632 |
| For Sale Only | 993 | 1052 | 1195 | 1099 |
| Rented or Sold | 673 | 685 | 816 | 652 |
| Held off Market | 4817 | 4942 | 4798 | 4717 |
| Occ'l Use | 1443 | 1646 | 1646 | 1546 |
| URE | 1068 | 1026 | 955 | 1037 |
| Other | 2306 | 2271 | 2198 | 2133 |
| Seasonal | 2843 | 2789 | 2906 | 3021 |

**FIGURE 10.1**

**U.S. housing inventory.** (*Continued*)

|                    | 1st Qtr | 2nd Qtr | 3rd Qtr | 4th Qtr |
|--------------------|---------|---------|---------|---------|
| Total Occupied     | 93109   | 93470   | 93763   | 93613   |
| Owner              | 59519   | 59678   | 60056   | 59766   |
| Renter             | 33590   | 33792   | 33707   | 33847   |

| 1990               | 1st Qtr | 2nd Qtr | 3rd Qtr | 4th Qtr |
|--------------------|---------|---------|---------|---------|
| All Housing Units  | 105883  | 106164  | 106755  | 106328  |
| Vacant             | 12171   | 11963   | 12159   | 11943   |
| Year-Round Vacant  | 9187    | 9009    | 9242    | 9075    |
| For Rent           | 2761    | 2590    | 2664    | 2652    |
| For Sale Only      | 1068    | 1063    | 1072    | 1055    |
| Rented or Sold     | 591     | 700     | 720     | 632     |
| Held off Market    | 4767    | 4656    | 4786    | 4735    |
| Occ'l Use          | 1475    | 1438    | 1489    | 1531    |
| URE                | 1134    | 971     | 1007    | 1175    |
| Other              | 2157    | 2247    | 2290    | 2029    |
| Seasonal           | 2984    | 2954    | 2917    | 2868    |
| Total Occupied     | 93713   | 94201   | 94596   | 94385   |
| Owner              | 60005   | 59985   | 60515   | 60488   |
| Renter             | 33708   | 34217   | 34081   | 33897   |

| 1991               | 1st Qtr | 2nd Qtr | 3rd Qtr | 4th Qtr |
|--------------------|---------|---------|---------|---------|
| All Housing Units  | 107189  | 107329  | 107569  | 107017  |
| Vacant             | 12207   | 12131   | 12114   | 11641   |
| Year-Round Vacant  | 9267    | 9219    | 9201    | 8861    |
| For Rent           | 2802    | 2747    | 2849    | 2722    |
| For Sale Only      | 1066    | 1090    | 1115    | 1009    |
| Rented or Sold     | 566     | 670     | 638     | 531     |
| Held off Market    | 4833    | 4712    | 4599    | 4599    |
| Occ'l Use          | 1449    | 1522    | 1513    | 1495    |
| URE                | 1277    | 1004    | 1007    | 1048    |
| Other              | 2108    | 2186    | 2078    | 2057    |
| Seasonal           | 2940    | 2912    | 2913    | 2780    |
| Total Occupied     | 94982   | 95198   | 95455   | 95376   |
| Owner              | 60685   | 60844   | 61298   | 61214   |
| Renter             | 34297   | 34354   | 34156   | 34162   |

| 1992               | 1st Qtr | 2nd Qtr | 3rd Qtr | 4th Qtr |
|--------------------|---------|---------|---------|---------|
| All Housing Units  | 108002  | 108489  | 108240  | 108533  |
| Vacant             | 12018   | 12039   | 11814   | 11832   |
| Year-Round Vacant  | 9023    | 9080    | 8914    | 8709    |
| For Rent           | 2788    | 2917    | 2735    | 2637    |
| For Sale Only      | 969     | 983     | 1003    | 924     |
| Rented or Sold     | 576     | 661     | 711     | 566     |
| Held off Market    | 4691    | 4519    | 4465    | 4583    |
| Occ'l Use          | 1480    | 1438    | 1422    | 1432    |
| URE                | 1146    | 996     | 900     | 1000    |
| Other              | 2065    | 2084    | 2143    | 2152    |
| Seasonal           | 2995    | 2959    | 2900    | 3123    |

**FIGURE 10.1**

U.S. housing inventory. (*Continued*)

| | 1st Qtr | 2nd Qtr | 3rd Qtr | 4th Qtr |
|---|---|---|---|---|
| Total Occupied | 95984 | 96450 | 96426 | 96702 |
| Owner | 61435 | 61591 | 61959 | 62306 |
| Renter | 34550 | 34859 | 34467 | 34396 |

| **1993** | | | | |
|---|---|---|---|---|
| | 1st Qtr | 2nd Qtr | 3rd Qtr | 4th Qtr |
| All Housing Units | 109251 | 109300 | 109960 | 110351 |
| Vacant | 12193 | 12030 | 11866 | 11864 |
| Year-Round Vacant | 9068 | 8945 | 8793 | 8727 |
| For Rent | 2996 | 2877 | 2682 | 2609 |
| For Sale Only | 879 | 897 | 890 | 882 |
| Rented or Sold | 533 | 649 | 691 | 624 |
| Held off Market | 4660 | 4522 | 4530 | 4612 |
| Occ'l Use | 1535 | 1471 | 1503 | 1533 |
| URE | 1027 | 961 | 942 | 989 |
| Other | 2099 | 2090 | 2084 | 2090 |
| Seasonal | 3125 | 3085 | 3073 | 3137 |
| Total Occupied | 97058 | 97270 | 98094 | 98487 |
| Owner | 62270 | 62633 | 63441 | 63647 |
| Renter | 34789 | 34637 | 34654 | 34840 |

| **1993/r** | | | | |
|---|---|---|---|---|
| | 1st Qtr | 2nd Qtr | 3rd Qtr | 4th Qtr |
| All Housing Units | 109168 | 109186 | 109850 | 110242 |
| Vacant | 12117 | 11937 | 11762 | 11760 |
| Year-Round Vacant | 9145 | 9002 | 8831 | 8771 |
| For Rent | 3026 | 2893 | 2689 | 2629 |
| For Sale Only | 898 | 902 | 891 | 885 |
| Rented or Sold | 531 | 651 | 691 | 627 |
| Held off Market | 4690 | 4557 | 4561 | 4630 |
| Occ'l Use | 1529 | 1474 | 1503 | 1524 |
| URE | 1045 | 972 | 957 | 1004 |
| Other | 2116 | 2111 | 2101 | 2102 |
| Seasonal | 2972 | 2935 | 2931 | 2989 |
| Total Occupied | 97051 | 97249 | 98088 | 98482 |
| Owner | 61784 | 62169 | 62990 | 63189 |
| Renter | 35267 | 35079 | 35098 | 35293 |

| **1994** | | | | |
|---|---|---|---|---|
| | 1st Qtr | 2nd Qtr | 3rd Qtr | 4th Qtr |
| All Housing Units | 110263 | 110470 | 111267 | 111806 |
| Vacant | 12281 | 12200 | 12339 | 12213 |
| Year-Round Vacant | 9237 | 9039 | 9274 | 9368 |
| For Rent | 2915 | 2859 | 2798 | 2864 |
| For Sale Only | 895 | 909 | 933 | 1076 |
| Rented or Sold | 675 | 840 | 848 | 727 |
| Held off Market | 4754 | 4431 | 4696 | 4701 |
| Occ'l Use | 1629 | 1548 | 1631 | 1641 |
| URE | 953 | 627 | 866 | 813 |
| Other | 2172 | 2256 | 2199 | 2247 |
| Seasonal | 3044 | 3161 | 3065 | 2845 |
| Total Occupied | 97982 | 98270 | 98927 | 99593 |

**FIGURE 10.1**

**U.S. housing inventory.** (*Continued*)

| | | | | |
|---|---|---|---|---|
| Owner | 62522 | 62684 | 63391 | 63947 |
| Renter | 35459 | 35586 | 35536 | 35646 |

| | 1995 | | | |
|---|---|---|---|---|
| | 1st Qtr | 2nd Qtr | 3rd Qtr | 4th Qtr |
| All Housing Units | 112359 | 112743 | 112530 | 112987 |
| Vacant | 12587 | 12811 | 12656 | 12624 |
| Year-Round Vacant | 9401 | 9794 | 9557 | 9529 |
| For Rent | 2882 | 2969 | 2966 | 2966 |
| For Sale Only | 1003 | 1046 | 987 | 1050 |
| Rented or Sold | 712 | 865 | 900 | 763 |
| Held off Market | 4804 | 4914 | 4704 | 4750 |
| Occ'l Use | 1643 | 1726 | 1630 | 1671 |
| URE | 869 | 837 | 710 | 786 |
| Other | 2292 | 2351 | 2364 | 2293 |
| Seasonal | 3186 | 3017 | 3099 | 3095 |
| Total Occupied | 99772 | 99932 | 99874 | 100363 |
| Owner | 64050 | 64668 | 64885 | 65355 |
| Renter | 35722 | 35264 | 34989 | 35008 |

| | 1996 | | | |
|---|---|---|---|---|
| | 1st Qtr | 2nd Qtr | 3rd Qtr | 4th Qtr |
| All housing units | 113,258 | 114,207 | 114,534 | 114,555 |
| Vacant | 12,786 | 13,125 | 13,414 | 13,291 |
| Year-round vacant | 9,656 | 9,949 | 10,197 | 9,979 |
| For-rent | 3,026 | 2,975 | 3,080 | 2,950 |
| For-sale-only | 1,066 | 997 | 1,119 | 1,146 |
| Rented or Sold | 723 | 894 | 954 | 763 |
| Held off Market | 4,841 | 5,083 | 5,044 | 5,120 |
| Occ'l use | 1,604 | 1,678 | 1,812 | 1,742 |
| URE | 853 | 883 | 796 | 877 |
| Other | 2,384 | 2,522 | 2,436 | 2,501 |
| Seasonal | 3,130 | 3,176 | 3,217 | 3,312 |
| Total Occupied | 100,472 | 101,082 | 101,120 | 101,264 |
| Owner | 65,453 | 66,147 | 66,288 | 66,277 |
| Renter | 35,019 | 34,935 | 34,832 | 34,987 |

| | 1997 | | | |
|---|---|---|---|---|
| | 1st Qtr | 2nd Qtr | 3rd Qtr | 4th Qtr |
| All housing units | 115,064 | 115,722 | 115,804 | 115,892 |
| Vacant | 13,362 | 13,676 | 13,371 | 13,268 |
| Year-round vacant | 10,007 | 10,356 | 10,031 | 10,078 |
| For-rent | 2,886 | 3,043 | 3,018 | 2,966 |
| For-sale-only | 1,176 | 1,107 | 1,062 | 1,187 |
| Rented or Sold | 807 | 905 | 941 | 813 |
| Held off Market | 5,138 | 5,301 | 4,992 | 5,112 |
| Occ'l use | 1,751 | 1,920 | 1,795 | 1,805 |
| URE | 906 | 960 | 880 | 793 |
| Other | 2,481 | 2,421 | 2,317 | 2,514 |

**FIGURE 10.1**

U.S. housing inventory. (*Continued*)

| | | | | |
|---|---|---|---|---|
| Seasonal | 3,355 | 3,320 | 3,358 | 3,190 |
| Total Occupied | 101,702 | 102,046 | 102,433 | 102,624 |
| Owner | 66,497 | 67,094 | 67,556 | 67,424 |
| Renter | 35,205 | 34,952 | 34,877 | 35,200 |

| | 1998 | | | |
|---|---|---|---|---|
| | 1st Qtr | 2nd Qtr | 3rd Qtr | 4th Qtr |
| All housing units | 116,770 | 117,401 | 117,368 | 117,589 |
| Vacant | 13,684 | 13,880 | 13,876 | 13,544 |
| Year-round vacant | 10,370 | 10,672 | 10,508 | 10,514 |
| For-rent | 2,975 | 3,112 | 3,120 | 2,978 |
| For-sale-only | 1,202 | 1,167 | 1,208 | 1,242 |
| Rented or Sold | 853 | 980 | 964 | 909 |
| Held off Market | 5,340 | 5,413 | 5,216 | 5,385 |
| Occ'l use | 1,727 | 1,818 | 1,758 | 1,868 |
| URE | 919 | 921 | 880 | 920 |
| Other | 2,694 | 2,674 | 2,578 | 2,597 |
| Seasonal | 3,314 | 3,208 | 3,368 | 3,040 |
| Total Occupied | 103,086 | 103,521 | 103,492 | 104,035 |
| Owner | 67,963 | 68,347 | 69,143 | 69,097 |
| Renter | 35,123 | 35,174 | 34,349 | 34,938 |

| | 1999 |
|---|---|
| | 1st Qtr |
| All housing units | 118,445 |
| Vacant | 13,984 |
| Year-round vacant | 10,897 |
| For-rent | 3,132 |
| For-sale-only | 1,296 |
| Rented or Sold | 835 |
| Held off Market | 5,634 |
| Occ'l use | 1,955 |
| URE | 933 |
| Other | 2,746 |
| Seasonal | 3,087 |
| Total Occupied | 104,461 |
| Owner | 69,638 |
| Renter | 34,823 |

/r Revised.

Source:  Current Population Survey/Housing Vacancy Survey, Series H-111,
Bureau of the Census, Washington, DC 20233.

**FIGURE 10.1**

U.S. housing inventory. (*Continued*)

## Small Developments

Small developments have become popular. Residents often prefer a small development since it preserves a feeling of a close community. Developers sometimes feel that small developments are less expensive to develop. In terms of total cost, a small development does cost less than a large one. However, when the development cost is divided by the number of units available for sale, a larger development will often cost less per unit. This is because some development expenses remain essentially the same, regardless of the size of the development.

Extremely small developments don't usually require the same types of expenses that larger developments do. Your budget may influence the size of your projects. But it can be just as easy, if not easier, to finance a large development as it is to finance a small one. Tiny developments can fail since there are so few units to be sold. This is a risk with larger developments, too, but there may be safety in numbers. By this, I mean that if you have 20 building lots and have two that won't sell, you will probably survive holding the two lots. But, if you have four lots to sell and can't sell two of them, you could be in deep trouble.

The appeal to small developments for buyers is the hometown feel of the development. Large developments often come off as being cold and impersonal. If you are going to create small developments, you should plan on putting many personal touches into your planning. For example, the entry to the subdivision and the interior streets should be identifiable with the concept of the development.

## Your Job

Your job as a developer requires you to come up with a plan that is unique. It should be a plan that cries out for attention and offers plenty of appeal to your target market. The size and scale of a development must be planned. When establishing size and scale you should consider whether the scale will be based on vehicular traffic or foot traffic. Development scale should be in proportion to the proper setting. Don't pick one set of criteria and use it throughout the community. It is better to vary and balance size and scale to keep a development more interesting.

Construction materials can have a lot to do with the tone of a development. What type of look will you be hoping to achieve? Are you going to use a stone wall and stone pillars for the entrance to your development? Would a more modern look suit the nature of the development better? Many types of materials can be used to create different moods. Your development could be rustic or contemporary. It could be based on a high-tech motif or a classical setting. You, and your experts, have to decide what image you wish to create and then choose materials that will allow you to recognize your goal.

Land planning is an area for experts to help developers with, but you can start the process on your own. Architectural styles and land planning combine to define a neighborhood. You should strive to create a combination that will not become boring. Yet, you should not diversify to a point where the development loses its overall tone. Let's look at an example of how you might create a unique development.

Assume that you are creating a development on the outskirts of a city. Your land is rural, rolling land that offers a country feeling, even though it is close enough to the city for a reasonable commute. The project is fairly large and will combine different types of living opportunities. There will be detached homes, condos, and duplexes. The natural land conditions make the parcel look perfect to house a development of highly styled farmhouse designs. This design allows for large areas of living space and many options in exterior treatments. The building lots are large enough to accommodate big houses and ample parking.

Your development will be divided into sections for each type of housing to be built. Single-family homes will be in one area, condos will be in another, and duplexes will be in the third section of the development. Since farmhouses are large by tradition, you will be able to build condos and duplexes that will give the appearance of a single-family home. Creative placement of garages and entry doors will make it difficult for people to tell one type of housing from another when driving through the subdivision. You can mix up the look of the development by using porches, varying roof designs, entry ways, attached storage areas, garages, and so forth. All of the housing will be in the theme of farmhouses, but there will be enough variation to keep the subdivision desirable.

As a continuation of the farmhouse theme, you might plan to use rustic appointments in common areas. For example, if there is a stream for a foot bridge to pass over, you might consider making the bridge a covered bridge. Bicycle racks might be built to look like hitching posts.

Water fountains could be encased in small structures that resemble a covered well, where a well bucket hangs from the rafters. The creative possibilities are usually limited only by financial constraints. You can use census data to help you decide what direction to take (Fig. 10.2).

## You Make the Rules

As a developer, you make the rules that must be followed by people buying into your development. It is your decision on how covenants and restrictions will be used to maintain the look of your development. Your work should cover acceptable house designs, minimum square-footage requirements, allowable paint and stain colors, the types and colors or roofing materials, and so forth. Some developers go so far as to dictate the types of mailboxes residents may use. Without strong development guidelines, a development can lose its appeal quickly. You, the developer, are responsible for creating and protecting the development. Of course, you will probably turn to land planners and architects to assist you in the final stages of developing your guidelines.

### Land Use

Guidelines for land use may begin with setback requirements. The setback refers to the distance that a building must be, as a minimum, from some other object, such as a property boundary. There are front, back, and side setbacks. For example, you may stipulate that houses must be at least 35 feet from any community sidewalk or street curb. You could say that no buildings may be erected closer than 15 feet to any side property line. And you might require a rear setback of 25 feet between a building and the back property line.

Another means of land control is to set a standard for how much of a building lot may be consumed by homes, garages, parking areas, and other impervious surfaces. A rule such as this can guarantee a certain minimum amount of green space around all homes. Then you move into regulations for site improvements, such as private sidewalks, patios, and decks.

When you establish the rules that builders and homeowners must live by when in your development, you have to be very specific. For example, how wide can a private sidewalk be? Does your development

## U.S. Census Bureau

### Housing Vacancy Survey
### First Quarter 1999

Table 11.  Percent Distribution by Type of Unit, for the United States and Regions:
First Quarter 1999 and 1998

(Percent distribution may not add to total, due to rounding)

**First quarter 1999**

|  | United States | North-east | Mid-West | South |
|---|---|---|---|---|
| All housing units........................ | 100 | 100 | 100 | 100 |
| Year-round vacant.................... | 9.2 | 6.9 | 6.6 | 9.7 |
| For rent........................... | 2.6 | 2.3 | 2.4 | 3.1 |
| For sale only...................... | 1.1 | 0.8 | 0.9 | 1.4 |
| Rented or sold, awaiting occupancy. | 0.7 | 0.6 | 0.8 | 0.8 |
| Held off market................... | 4.8 | 4.2 | 4.1 | 6.0 |
| For occasional use.............. | 1.7 | 1.3 | 0.9 | 2.4 |
| Temporarily occupied by persons with usual residence elsewhere... | 0.8 | 0.8 | 0.7 | 0.9 |
| For other reasons............... | 2.3 | 2.1 | 2.5 | 2.7 |
| Seasonal vacant...................... | 2.6 | 3.7 | 2.4 | 2.3 |
| Occupied............................ | 88.2 | 88.4 | 89.4 | 86.4 |

**First quarter 1998**

| Type of housing unit | United States | North-east | Mid-West | South |
|---|---|---|---|---|
| All housing units........................ | 100 | 100 | 100 | 100 |
| Year-round vacant.................... | 8.9 | 6.9 | 6.6 | 9.7 |
| For rent........................... | 2.5 | 2.2 | 2.2 | 2.8 |
| For sale only...................... | 1.0 | 1.0 | 0.8 | 1.3 |
| Rented or sold, awaiting occupancy. | 0.7 | 0.6 | 0.7 | 0.9 |
| Held off market................... | 4.6 | 3.8 | 3.8 | 5.9 |
| For occasional use.............. | 1.5 | 1.1 | 0.8 | 2.1 |
| Temporarily occupied by persons with usual residence elsewhere... | 0.8 | 0.8 | 0.6 | 1.0 |
| For other reasons............... | 2.3 | 1.9 | 2.4 | 2.8 |
| Seasonal vacant...................... | 2.8 | 3.9 | 2.5 | 2.6 |
| Occupied............................ | 88.3 | 88.5 | 89.9 | 86.6 |

**FIGURE 10.2**

Housing vacancies.

have minimum and maximum widths on record? Wouldn't it look strange to have most sidewalks 3 feet wide and then to encounter some that were 5 feet wide? Will walkways have to be made of concrete, or will gravel walkways be allowed? Consistency is important in development. Are covered entryways going to be allowed in your development? Perhaps they will be required? You must decide.

Here are some other topics to consider when you are setting up rules and regulations:

- Porches
- Swimming pools
- Lawn care
- Patios
- Storage buildings
- Driveways
- Decks
- RV storage
- Lighting

Developers can dictate all sorts of rules for their developments. Too many restrictions can scare buyers away. But too few restrictions will make buyers nervous that a development may not maintain its standards. Even the smallest details, such as the type and style of house numbers used to display an address should be considered when developing your master plan for a project.

## Building Regulations

Building regulations are common for subdivisions, and they are needed. Depending on the type of development, a developer may prohibit the construction of certain types of houses. You might prohibit the construction on single-level homes or homes built on slab foundations. Your rules might prevent builders from constructing houses that don't follow a specific theme. Rules could cover roof pitches, square footage, exterior trim, paint and stain colors, roofing materials, window designs, and so forth. A developer could require that all homes built in a development have brick foundations. The use of vinyl siding might be prohibited in a development.

# Construction Regulations

Construction regulations must be planned in advance. Once a project is started, the construction requirements become a means of controlling workers and staying on time and on budget. Some builders and developers tend to overlook the planning of construction rules. Don't fail to allow provisions for construction procedures as you build out your master plan. What types of things do you need to be concerned about? Well, let's find out.

## Temporary Roads

You may need to build temporary roads to get workers into a project early. Don't omit this expense from your cost projections. Make arrangements early for allowing workers access to your project. Getting a project ready to begin construction and then realizing that your crews can't get to the job sites is not only embarrassing, it sets you back on your schedule, and this cuts into your profits.

Temporary utilities are likely to be needed for your project. This will not always be the case, but determine if any utilities will be needed during the developing process. It can take several weeks, or more, to get temporary electrical service to a building site. If you think that this is a long time, just imagine how long it might take to provide services to a full development. You probably won't run into major needs for temporary utilities unless you are acting as the building contractor and the developer.

Depending on site location and conditions, you may have to install some type of retention system to control erosion. If construction equipment creates a lot of dust in a populated area, you may have to contract with someone to provide dust-control services, such as sprinkling construction roads. All of these types of needs must be accounted for in your master plan.

## Site Needs

There are certain site needs that may required for your project. For example, portable toilet facilities are needed. Noise control is also a potential concern. Trees that are to be saved should be protected with temporary barriers. Some provisions should be made for the storage of equipment and materials. For material storage, many developers use the trailers that are pulled by 18-wheelers. Construction office space is needed, so a site trailer should be placed on the property. Some developers buy their storage and office trailers while others rent them.

Fenced enclosures help to protect the expensive equipment used in developing land. Not all developers go to this expense, but you might want to consider the option. Provisions must be made to control storm water and erosion during construction and development. A place should be established for the posting of required documents, such as permits and safety posters. Temporary signs will be needed, and you may need some place to post them. Sit down and figure out all that you can about your needs.

## Management

The management of a project is crucial to the success of a development deal. Someone must make sure that all permits are obtained and posted. Keeping active insurance on a project is essential. Any subcontractors used for a project must be screened for insurance and general business compliance. Time schedules must be set. Work hours for contractors must be established. The management needs of a project can be extensive.

You must decide if you will serve as your own project manager or if you will hire one. Good project managers don't work for peanuts. If you are going to hire one, you must factor the overhead cost into your overall budget. Maybe you are not sure if you can do the work yourself. If you have any doubts about your abilities, factor in the cost of a project manager. It's better to have the overhead factored into your budget and not need it than it is to have the expense missing and then find that you need a manager.

The planning stages of a development can be tedious. If you prefer to have it done for you by experts, go that route. Most developers do their preliminary planning on their own, and it's good experience. Once you have a general plan you can turn it over to the experts. Then, as results come in from the experts you can compare the final plan with your rough draft. Look to see how much has changed. When you get to the level where changes are minor or extremely technical, you will know that you have a good handle on what it takes to be a successful developer.

Regardless of how your master plan is completed, you will find yourself working with engineers. This can be a daunting experience.

However, you should not let the work of engineers go over your desk without some form of review. You might not know what you are looking at when you see it. Ask questions if you don't understand an engineering report. You're paying the bills, which entitles you to know what you are buying. Let's move to the next chapter and see what is involved with the engineering process.

# Engineering Evaluations

Engineering evaluations are a part of any major development deal. Most developers consider the reports as a needed part of the process but are not interested in reading or understanding them. It's common for developers to want a report summary that is easy to read and understand. For most developers, a summary is enough. There are, however, some developers who prefer a much more detailed report to study. Many developers hardly do more than scan their engineering reports before they are passed on or filed. Will you be a developer who learns to understand the reports or one who will simply take the advice offered in a summary report?

Working with summary reports is faster than digging through piles of technical terms. But there is something lost in the translation, so to speak. Abridged versions of reports obviously omit certain details. If you are the type of person who wants to know every aspect of your developing process, you will want complete engineering reports to keep tabs on. However, if you are like most developers, you will be very busy with other requirements and will appreciate the simplicity of a summary.

# Site Engineering

Site engineering can become extremely expensive. The work is needed in most cases, but with proper management, costs can usually be controlled. What types of issues are covered in the engineering of a site? Many factors are considered when engineering a site for development. Elements of the work cover everything from grading to site utilities. Roads, drainage, erosion, and other issues are looked at. Proper engineering, while expensive to pay for, can save you a great deal of money during the course of a development.

Grading and drainage are key issues in site engineering. Your experts have to design a plan that will ensure proper drainage and suitable control of storm water. This can involve anything from huge storm drains to simple gutters on a house that empty into a subsurface drain. A development that is graded poorly and that has drainage problems is going to be a pain in the neck for the developer for many years to come.

Unless you are an engineer you can't reasonably do your own engineering studies. You can look at topo maps, review surveys, and eyeball your land, but you don't have the specific education or experience to make your own decisions for large projects. If you are developing only a couple of house lots you might well be able to avoid the cost of site engineering. Common sense should tell you when a site is complex enough to warrant the services of an engineer.

The purpose behind site engineering is to create a development that is problem-free. While that is a lofty goal, it is possible to design sites that will contain few flaws on completion. An engineer will determine what the best means of providing access to a site is. Factors affecting access will be safety, costs, topography, access permits, and general site design. Shaping the earth is part of land development. Filling in low spots, cutting out high spots, and grading for a uniform flow are all expected in most developing jobs. Developers will look for ways to limit the amount of fill that must be trucked into a site. By using natural land characteristics and building to suit them, developers can reduce the cost of earthwork. Maintaining the existing lay of the land is often beneficial, in terms of both limited disruption to the region and cost savings.

Any risk of erosion or sedimentation must be considered during site engineering. Developments need utilities. How utilities will be brought to a site is often left up to the site engineer. The sizing of sewers and water mains is part of the engineering process. Storm sewers may be needed, as might fire hydrants. Routing the locations of utilities is another task to be dealt with. Engineers earn their money when it comes to large developments.

The handling of storm water can be a significant issue when developing land. There can be many rules affecting the treatment of storm water. In some cases, storm water will be piped to a storm sewer. Some cities allow storm water and sanitary sewage to share a common sewer, but many jurisdictions prohibit this practice. It's very common for a city to require two sewers, one for sanitary sewage and one for storm water. If there is no storm sewer available, what will happen with runoff water? Can you pipe it into a retention or detention pond? Perhaps, but there could be several regulations affecting how this might be done. Can a pipe be run on a gravity grade to a spot away from a building and then discharge onto open ground? In some places, yes, but other jurisdictions may frown on this. Can underground dry wells (holes filled with gravel and covered with earth) be used to collect storm water? Probably, but you will have to check local code requirements.

When storm water is discharged into surface areas, there is concern for pollution of the local water table. Someone, you or your engineer, must determine the depth of the water table. County extension offices can usually provide data on the depth of the water table in various locations. Once the depth of the water table is known, you will need to know how much soil is required between the bottom of the discharge point and the water table. Local code requirements vary, so check with your local agencies to determine the depth requirements.

Soil types differ in their perk rates. You need to know this and the rates in order to make a decision about potential pollution. The bottom elevation of a catch basin, pond, or dry well is known as the *invert*. This is the point where measurement begins between the storm water and the water table. In other words, if you have a detention pond that is 8 feet deep and a water table 12 feet deep, the distance between the storm water and the water table would be 4 feet. It's important that there be enough vertical distance between the water table and the surface water for the soil to cleanse the storm water before it enters the water table.

If your development work will include construction, your engineers will have to work with construction codes. Developers who are into conversion work, where buildings are bought, converted, and then sold or leased, also run into code issues. Meeting code requirements is a standard procedure for many of the experts involved with land development. Most local codes are well documented to eliminate confusion. Charts and tables are often provided in code books to aid planners (Figs. 11.1 and 11.2).

## Grading Designs

Grading designs for a development affect the control of storm water. Obviously, the lay of the land has a lot to do with the way that water runs. When you and your engineer are working on a grading plan, you should also be working on a storm-water plan. It makes sense to work on both concepts at the same time, since they are so tightly connected. The first step is the grading.

The less you have to alter existing land conditions, the better off you are. You will be saving time and money if you can work with the natural lay of the land. Developers who work with large parcels or who do extreme-density projects usually have to cut and fill their projects. Smaller developments, where building lots are larger and the density of housing is less, can sometimes avoid most of the cutting and filling.

You and your engineers have to look very closely at what your grading needs will be. If the work will be extensive, you can count on spending some serious money for work that most people will simply take for granted. If you invested tens of thousands of dollars in recreational amenities, such as a swimming pool and tennis courts, potential buyers would see value. Putting the same amount of money in dirt may be much more important, but buyers will not normally have much appreciation for your investment. It can be hard to recover your costs associated with earthwork.

When you have to cut and fill a site, you are exposing yourself to potential problems that would not exist if the ground alterations could be avoided. For example, when you cut away natural soil you create a

Minimum plumbing fixtures, Table 922.2 of the code.

| Building or occupancy[2] | Occupant content[2] | Water closets[3] | Lavatories[4] | Bathtubs, showers, and miscellaneous fixtures |
|---|---|---|---|---|
| Dwelling or apt. house | Not applicable | 1 for each dwelling or dwelling unit | 1 for each dwelling or dwelling unit | Washing machine connection per unit.[5] Bathtub or shower—one per dwelling or dwelling unit. Kitchen sink—One per dwelling or dwelling unit |
| Schools: preschool, day care, or nursery | Average daily attendance | Each 15 children or fraction thereof — 1 Fixture | Each 15 children or fraction thereof — 1 Fixture | |
| Schools: Elementary & secondary | Average daily attendance | (see Water closets table below) | (see Lavatories table below) | One drinking fountain for each 3 classrooms, but not less than one each floor. |
| Office[6] and public buildings | 100 sq ft per person | (see Water closets table below) | (see Lavatories table below) | (see Drinking Fountains table below) |

**Schools: Elementary & secondary — Water closets[3]**

| Persons (total) | Male | Female |
|---|---|---|
| 1–50 | 2 | 2 |
| 51–100 | 3 | 3 |
| 101–150 | 4 | 4 |
| 151–200 | 5 | 5 |
| For each additional 50 persons over 200, add | 1 | 1 |

**Schools: Elementary & secondary — Lavatories[4]**

| Persons (total) | Male | Female |
|---|---|---|
| 1–120 | 1 | 1 |
| 121–240 | 2 | 2 |
| For each additional 120 persons over 240, add | 1 | 1 |

**Office and public buildings — Water closets[3]**

| Persons (total) | Male | Female |
|---|---|---|
| 1–15 | 1 | 1 |
| 16–35 | 1 | 2 |
| 36–55 | 2 | 2 |
| 56–100 | 2 | 3 |
| 101–150 | 3 | 4 |
| For each additional 100 persons over 150, add | 1 | 1.5[7] |

**Office and public buildings — Lavatories[4]**

| Persons (total) | Male | Female |
|---|---|---|
| 1–15 | 1 | 1 |
| 16–35 | 1 | 2 |
| 36–60 | 2 | 2 |
| 61–125 | 2 | 3 |
| For each additional 120 persons over 125, add | 1 | 1.5[7] |

**Office and public buildings — Drinking Fountains**

| Persons | Fixtures |
|---|---|
| 1–100 | 1 |
| 101–250 | 2 |
| 251–500 | 3 |

Not less than one fixture each floor subject to access.

## FIGURE 11.1

Minimum plumbing fixtures, Table 922.2 of the code. (*Reproduced from the 1991 edition of The Standard Plumbing Code® with permission of the copyright holder, Southern Building Code Congress, International, Inc. All rights reserved.*)

125

| Building or occupancy[2] | Occupant content[2] | Water closets[3] | | | Lavatories[4] | | | Bathtubs, showers, and miscellaneous fixtures |
|---|---|---|---|---|---|---|---|---|
| | | Persons (total) | Male | Female | Persons (total) | Male | Female | Drinking Fountains |
| Common toilet facilities or areas of commercial buildings of multiple tentants[8,9] | Use the sq ft per person ratio applicable to the single type occupancy(s) occupying the greatest aggregate floor area (Consider separately each floor area of a divided floor) | 1–50 | 2 | 2 | 1–15 | 1 | 1 | Persons — Fixtures |
| | | 51–100 | 3 | 4 | 16–35 | 1 | 2 | 1–100 — 1 |
| | | 101–150 | 4 | 5 | 36–60 | 2 | 2 | 101–250 — 2 |
| | | For each additional 100 persons over 150, add | 1 | 1.5[7] | 61–125 | 2 | 3 | 251–500 — 3 |
| | | | | | For each additional 120 persons over 125, add | 1 | 1.5[7] | 501–1000 — 4 |
| | | | | | | | | Not less than one fixture each floor subject to access. |
| Retail stores[6] | 200 sq ft per person | 1–35 | 1 | 1 | 1–15 | 1 | 1 | Drinking Fountains |
| | | 36–55 | 1 | 2 | 16–35 | 1 | 2 | Persons — Fixtures |
| | | 56–80 | 2 | 3 | 36–60 | 1 | 3 | 1–100 — 1 |
| | | 81–100 | 2 | 4 | 61–125 | 2 | 4 | 101–250 — 2 |
| | | 101–150 | 2 | 5 | For each additional 200 persons over 125, add | 1 | 1.75[7] | 251–500 — 3 |
| | | For each additional 200 persons over 150, add | 1 | 1.75[7] | | | | 501–1000 — 4 |
| | | | | | | | | Not less than one fixture each floor subject to access. |
| Restaurants,[6] clubs, and lounges | 40 sq ft per person | 1–50 | 2 | 2 | 1–150 | 1 | 1 | Comply with Board of Health Requirements. |
| | | 51–100 | 3 | 3 | 151–200 | 2 | 2 | |
| | | 101–300 | 4 | 4 | 201–400 | 3 | 3 | |
| | | For each additional 300 persons over 300, add | 1 | 2 | For each additional 200 persons over 400, add | 1 | 1 | |

| Building or occupancy[2] | Occupant content[2] | Water closets[3] | | | Lavatories[4] | | | Bathtubs, showers, and miscellaneous fixtures |
|---|---|---|---|---|---|---|---|---|
| | | Persons (total) | Male | Female | Persons (total) | Male | Female | |
| Do it yourself laundries[6] | 50 sq ft per person | 1–50<br>51–100 | 1<br>1 | 1<br>2 | 1–100 | 1 | 1 | One drinking fountain and one service sink. |
| Beauty shops and barber shops[6] | 50 sq ft per person | 1–35<br>36–75 | 1<br>2 | 1<br>2 | 1–75 | 1 | 1 | One drinking fountain and one service or other utility sink. |
| Heavy manufacturing,[10] warehouses,[11] foundries, and similar establishments[12,14] | Occupant content per shift, substantiated by owner. Also see 922.3.2 | 1–10<br>11–25<br>26–50<br>51–75<br>76–100<br>For each additional 60 persons over 100, add | 1<br>2<br>3<br>4<br>5<br><br>1 | 1<br>1<br>1<br>1<br>1<br><br>0.1[7] | 1–15<br>16–35<br>36–60<br>61–90<br>91–125<br>For each additional 100 persons over 125, add | Male[14]<br>1<br>2<br>3<br>4<br>5<br>1 | Female[14]<br>1<br>1<br>1<br>1<br>1<br>0.1[7] | One drinking fountain for each 75 persons. One shower for each 15 persons exposed to excessive heat or to skin contamination with poisonous, infectious, or irritating material. |
| Light mfg.,[10] Light warehousing,[11] and workshops, etc.[12,13] | Occupant content per shift, substantiated by owner. Also see 922.3.2 | 1–25<br>26–75<br>76–100<br>For each additional 60 persons over 100, add | 1<br>2<br>3<br>1 | 1<br>2<br>3<br>1 | 1–35<br>36–100<br>101–200<br>For each additional 100 persons over 200, add | Male[14]<br>1<br>2<br>3<br>1 | Female[14]<br>1<br>2<br>3<br>1 | One drinking fountain for each 75 persons. One shower for each 15 persons exposed to excessive heat or to skin contamination with poisonous, infectious, or irritating material. |

| Building or occupancy[2] | Occupant content[2] | Water closets[3] | | | Lavatories[4] | | | Bathtubs, showers, and miscellaneous fixtures |
|---|---|---|---|---|---|---|---|---|
| | | Persons (total) | Male[16] | Female[16] | Persons (total) | Male[16] | Female[16] | |
| Dormitories[15] | 50 sq ft per person (calculated on sleeping area only) | 1–10 | 1 | 1 | 1–12 | 1 | 1 | Washing machines may be used in lieu of laundry tubs.[15] One shower for each 8 persons. In women's dorms add tubs in the ratio 1 for each 30 females. Over 150 persons add 1 shower for each 20 persons. |
| | | 11–30 | 1 | 2 | 13–30 | 2 | 2 | |
| | | 31–100 | 3 | 4 | For each additional 30 persons over 30, add | 1 | 1 | |
| | | For each additional 50 persons over 100, add | 1 | 1 | | | | |
| | | Persons (total) | Male | Female | Persons (total) | Male | Female | Drinking Fountains |
| Theaters, auditoriums, churches, waiting rooms at transportation terminals, and stations | 70 sq ft per person (calculated from assembly area). Other areas considered public buildings. | 1–50 | 2 | 2 | 1–200 | 1 | 1 | Persons — Fixtures |
| | | 51–100 | 3 | 3 | 201–400 | 2 | 2 | 1–100 — 1 |
| | | 101–200 | 4 | 4 | 401–750 | 3 | 3 | 101–350 — 2 |
| | | 201–400 | 5 | 5 | For each additional 350 persons over 750, add | 1 | 1 | Over 350 add one fixture for each 400. |
| | | For each additional 250 persons over 400, add | 1 | 1 | | | | |

[1] The figures shown are based upon one fixture being the minimum required for the number of persons indicated or any fraction thereof.

[2] The occupant content and the number of required facilities for occupancies other than listed shall be determined by the Plumbing Official. Plumbing facilities in the occupancies or tenancies of similar use may be determined by the Plumbing Official from this table.

[3] Urinals shall be required in male restrooms of elementary or secondary schools, restaurants, clubs, lounges, waiting rooms of transportation terminals, auditoriums, theaters, and churches at a rate equal to ⅓ of the required water closets in Table 922.2. Required urinals can be substituted for up to ⅓ of the required water closets. The installation of urinals shall be optional in the female restrooms of previously stated occupancies and shall be optional in both male and female restrooms of all other occupancies. Optional urinals may be substituted for up to ⅓ of the required water closets in the male and female restrooms.

[4] Twenty-four linear inches of wash sink or 18 inches of a circular basin, when provided with water outlets for such space, shall be considered equivalent to 1 lavatory.

[5] When central washing facilities are provided in lieu of washing machine connections in each living unit, central facilities shall be located for the building served at the ratio of not less than one washing machine for each 12 living units, but in no case less than two machines for each building of 15 living units or less. See 914.5.

[6] A single facility consisting of one water closet and one lavatory may be used by both males and females in the following occupancies subject to the building area limitations:

| Occupancy | Maximum Building Area (sq ft) |
| --- | --- |
| Office | 1200 |
| Retail Store (excluding service stations) | 1500 |
| Restaurant | 500 |
| Laundries (Self Service) | 1400 |
| Beauty and Barber Shops | 900 |

## FIGURE 11.1

(Continued) Minimum plumbing fixtures, Table 922.2 of the code. (Reproduced from the 1991 edition of The Standard Plumbing Code® with permission of the copyright holder, Southern Building Code Congress, International, Inc. All rights reserved.)

| Fixture type | Fixture-unit value as load factors | Minimum size of trap (in) |
|---|---|---|
| Bathroom group consisting of water closet, lavatory, and bathtub or shower | 6 | |
| Bathtub[1] (with or without overhead shower) or whirlpool attachments | 2 | 1½ |
| Bidet | 2 | Nominal 1½ |
| Combination sink and tray | 3 | 1½ |
| Combination sink and tray with food disposal unit | 4 | Separate traps 1½ |
| Dental unit or cuspidor | 1 | 1¼ |
| Dental lavatory | 1 | 1¼ |
| Drinking fountain | ½ | 1 |
| Dishwashing machine[2] domestic. | 2 | 1½ |
| Floor drains[5] | 1 | 2 |
| Kitchen sink, domestic | 2 | 1½ |
| Kitchen sink, domestic with food waste grinder and/or dishwasher | 3 | 1½ |
| Lavatory[4] | 1 | Small P.O. 1¼ |
| Lavatory[4] | 2 | Large P.O. 1½ |
| Lavatory, barber, beauty parlor | 2 | 1½ |
| Lavatory, surgeon's | 2 | 1½ |
| Laundry tray (1 or 2 compartments) | 2 | 1½ |
| Shower stall, domestic | 2 | 2 |
| Showers (group) per head[2] | 3 | |
| Sinks | | |
| Surgeon's | 3 | 1½ |
| Flushing rim (with valve) | 8 | 3 |
| Service (trap standard) | 3 | 3 |
| Service (P trap) | 2 | 2 |
| Pot, scullery, etc.[2] | 4 | 1½ |
| Urinal, pedestal, siphon jet, blowout | 8 | Note 6 |
| Urinal, wall lip | 4 | Note 6 |
| Urinal, washout | 4 | Note 6 |
| Washing machines (commercial)[3] | | |
| Washing machine (residential) | 3 | 2 |
| Wash sink[2] (circular or multiple) each set of faucets | 2 | Nominal 1½ |
| Water closet, flushometer tank, public or private | 3 | Note 6 |
| Water closet, private installation | 4 | Note 6 |
| Water closet, public installation | 6 | Note 6 |

[1] A showerhead over a bathtub or whirlpool bathtub attachments does not increase the fixture value.

[2] See 1304.2 and 1304.3 for methods of computing unit value of fixtures not listed in Table 1304.1 or for rating of devices with intermittent flows.

[3] See Table 1304.2.

[4] Lavatories with 1¼ or 1½-inch trap have the same load value; larger P.O. plugs have greater flow rate.

[5] Size of floor drain shall be determined by the area of the floor to be drained. The drainage fixture unit value need not be greater than 1 unless the drain receives indirect discharge from plumbing fixtures, air conditioner, or refrigeration equipment.

[6] Trap size shall be consistent with fixture type as defined in industry standards.

**FIGURE 11.2**

Fixture units per fixture or group, Table 1304.1 of the code. (*Reproduced from the 1991 edition of The Standard Plumbing Code® with permission of the copyright holder, Southern Building Code Congress, International, Inc. All rights reserved.*)

potential for erosion and sediment movement. Not only will this likely require an additional investment in containment control, the process can slow your project down. Hauling in fill dirt is a very expensive proposition, and filled land often settles over time, which can create depressions that give the development drainage problems.

Sometimes the dirt cut from one section of a project can be used as fill for another piece of the project. While this method is not as nice as not having to cut at all, it is better than having to buy fill dirt and having it trucked into the site. Overall grading is a factor that should be weighed when assessing a piece of land for viability as a development project. Try to avoid land that will require extensive earthwork. If you can't avoid the need for cutting and filling, have your engineer design a plan that will minimize the work.

Before a grading plan can be completed, some benchmarks must be established. Engineers and surveyors can work together to establish desirable grades. For example, what will the finished grade level for housing be? How high above the finished grade level will the finished floor level of homes be? What will be required for parking areas and walkways? How will your roads be affected by various grades? As your engineer answers these questions you can begin to look for a spot elevation. This is a chosen elevation that will be used as a benchmark to meet your goals for all of the other desired elevations. More than one spot elevation will be used to establish a network of measurements with which your engineer can work.

The engineering process for setting grades can be very complicated. However, the engineering reports are not difficult for most developers to understand. Let me give you a quick example. Assume that your surveyors have delivered an elevation survey to you and your engineer. The engineer has taken all spot elevations and plotted a house location on the survey. If you review the drawing, you can see almost exactly how the land around the home will affect drainage issues. Obviously, you want the land to slope away from the structure. But the slope must be within the required guidelines of local code restrictions for intended use. In this case, the intended use is a lawn. Your engineer will include notes on code requirements, recommended slope values, and actual slope values. You can see quickly how your plans fit the formula.

When you combine an elevation survey with spot elevations, you can determine many factors needed for construction. Surveyors can shoot elevations and mark them for all of your development construction. For example, you can see on a grade stake just where the top of a road curb will be. The completed use of spot elevations may affect sewer depths, water service locations, finished floor grades, finished grade elevations, the depth of retention and detention ponds, required depths for sump pumps in basements, and so forth.

Doing a site grading study for a single house is fairly simply and easy to understand. But, if you are doing the same work for a project that will contain 200 homes, the process becomes much more intricate. All of the homes must be considered, as must all of the open space, roads, parking areas, and other elements of the development. Designing a plan that will accommodate all of the housing units and infrastructure takes experience, talent, and a lot of attention to detail. This is when it feels very good to have competent engineers doing the math for you.

There are four types of calculations that may normally be used by a site engineer who is computing the needs of cutting and filling a site. If the site is small and will require little excavation, the prism method may be used. With this procedure, the engineer will multiply the area of excavations by the average height of the corners. In doing so, the engineer arrives at a figure to relate to the approximate volume of cutting or filling. Most developers should leave all final calculations to their experts.

The contour method is one where the areas between existing and proposed contours are added together. Then the total is multiplied by the distance between the contours. The amount of cutting or filling is determined by the solution of the formula. While you may not be able to compute the needs for filling or cutting yourself, you should be able to understand the engineering report without much trouble.

Engineers may use the cross-sectional method to determine the needs for filling and cutting. They do this by drawing lines through a site plan to create sections. The sections are usually about 50 feet apart in scale. A planimeter, which is a tool that measures the areas of planes, is used to determine the planes. Each section is figured individually and then added together to arrive at the total requirements for cutting and filling.

Another method that might be used is the average-end method. A cross section of an area reveals top and bottom areas as parallel planes.

The two planes are added together and then divided by a formula of two multiplied by one. When done properly, the formula reveals the amount of cutting or filling that will be needed.

You don't have to worry about taking math classes at night to be a developer. It is not up to you to do your own engineering. But, you should strive to understand as much of what you are seeing as you can. The fastest way to gain the knowledge is to question your engineer. If you get into asking a lot of questions, you may have to pay the engineers for their time in tutoring you. But, simple questions should be answered quickly and probably without added cost. Learn what you can, where you can.

# Storm Water Drainage

ealing with storm water drainage is important when you develop a piece of land. As you alter the land, you create new needs for handling runoff water. The size and nature of a development have a direct impact on how sophisticated a storm water plan must be. In the case of a single house, the creation of a drainage system is usually easy. Most builders surround their foundations with slotted drain pipe that is bedded in and covered by a layer of crushed stone, which is further covered with dirt. The drain water might run to a sump location for pumping, but it will generally be piped to a suitable discharge location with a gravity installation.

Gutters installed on houses and piped to underground drains are very effective at keeping rainwater from eroding the soil around a foundation. The subsurface drains for gutters may tie into the foundation drains that are carrying storm water to its discharge pump. If a sump pump is installed in a house, the discharge hose from the sump pump may also intersect with the underground drainage piping at some point. The discharge location for the drainage pipe may be a dry well or a storm sewer. Check local code requirements to see what options are available to you in this regard. Basically, the handling of storm water for a house that sits on a well-drained lot is easy and not very expensive. However, most projects require somewhat more effort, thought, and money to protect from excessive storm water.

While a single residential project can be protected from storm water with a simple, inexpensive system, a major development can require extensive work. The engineering process for major projects can be quite expensive. There are multiple factors that must be considered during the design process of a storm water management design. Here are the four primary concerns to be considered during the planning phase of managing storm water:

- Quality of groundwater
- Peak flow changes
- Total runoff water
- Quality of lakes and rivers

Building a development can create many changes in the natural dispersion of storm water. Think about it. If you take a natural area and install paved parking areas, homes, sidewalks, and other impervious barriers you are bound to create more runoff water. There simply isn't as much earth available to absorb the water.

When engineers are developing a plan to deal with storm water, they must consider the effect that their plans will have on all other types of water. This means drinking water, groundwater, lakes, streams, ponds, and sediment and erosion control. It's not enough to contain or remove storm water. The process must include a plan to protect other types of water.

Every parcel of land has its own natural flow routes for storm water. Some of these routes may be destroyed during the development process. If you can maintain the routes during and after developing, you might reduce your overall development cost. For example, if there is a natural wet-weather stream that runs quietly behind your major development area you might be able to use the natural lay of the land to funnel water to a retention or detention pond. You might run into environmental problems, though, so have your environmental experts confirm that your drainage plan is acceptable to all governing authorities.

With the right designs, storm water can be recycled. Building numerous ponds to catch storm water and then using the water to irrigate the land or a golf course is a great idea. Most developers prefer using multiple ponds over using a single pond. The proper use of land-scaping helps prevent erosion and can slow the rate of flow for the runoff. There are many techniques that can be used to make storm water systems both attractive and effective. Your engineers will have to decide between a closed system and an open system. Most people agree that open systems are more desirable. So, let's discuss the differences between the two systems and see what you think.

## Closed Drainage Systems

Closed drainage systems are generally considered less desirable than open systems. Cost and maintenance are two factors that come into play when choosing a system type. The installation of a closed system usually requires extensive piping. Closed systems are designed to be run underground and out of sight. The components of a closed system can include pipes, catch basins, inlets, and both retention and detention areas. Some developers like closed systems since they are not visible. Keeping the drainage system out of sight is preferable at times.

If you opt for a closed drainage system, you have many factors to consider. Most developers start by planning the routes of drainage piping. You, or your engineers, must look at the area to be drained. Then, a decision will have to be made for routing and sizing pipes. Planning the details of a storm water system is way beyond the capabilities of most developers. Some master plumbers possess the ability to create a system, but the design work is normally done by engineers.

Sizing pipes for a drainage system can be a complex task. The formulas used are normally set forth in the local plumbing code. Total expected rainfall must be calculated, as well as maximum runoff potential (Figs. 12.1 and 12.2). Piping must be sized to accommodate maximum water flow. In the case of site drainage, inverts are needed to direct surface runoff into the underground piping. Inverts are merely devices that collect surface water and deliver it into a drainage system. Grates are used to cover the openings of inverts. Most local jurisdictions require the use of sediment traps in conjunction with inverts. Sometimes filters are used in place of traps. State and local code requirements dictate the precise requirements for sediment control. Developers must have a good idea of what will be required for drainage before a reasonable cost estimate for the infrastructure of a project can be completed.

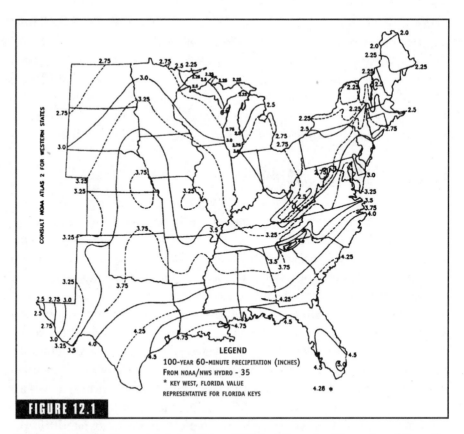

**FIGURE 12.1**

**Rainfall rates for primary roof drains, Figure 1506.4 of the code.** (*Reproduced from the 1991 edition of* The Standard Plumbing Code® *with permission of the copyright holder, Southern Building Code Congress, International, Inc. All rights reserved.*)

Most major drainage systems installed below ground require catch basins. These basins are expensive and should be kept to a minimum. Proper design can reduce the number of catch basins needed for a closed system. The basins are meant to retain sediment as storm water passes through a drainage system. Catch basins may be called for under inlets of a system, at changes of direction in a piping system, and close to streets.

Most catch basins are made of formed concrete. The concept behind a catch basin is similar to that of a septic tank. A pipe delivers water to the basin and allows the water to flow into the holding tank. Heavy sediment sinks to the bottom of the enclosure. An outlet pipe is installed at some distance above the bottom of the tank, but below the inlet pipe. As sediment drops to the bottom of the catch basin, water is

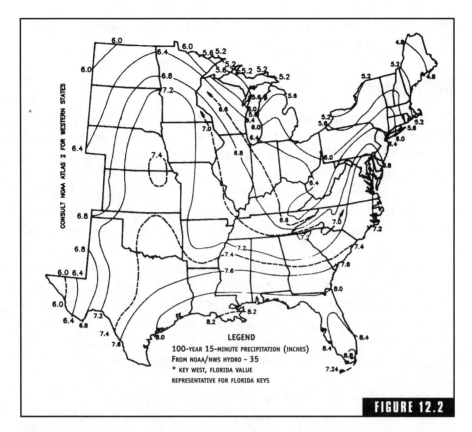

**Rainfall rates for secondary roof drains, Figure 1507.3 of the code. (***Reproduced from the 1991 edition of* **The Standard Plumbing Code**® *with permission of the copyright holder, Southern Building Code Congress, International, Inc. All rights reserved.***)**

allowed to flow into the outlet pipe and on through the drainage system.

Piping diagrams for storm water should be drawn to minimize turns in the piping. As with any type of plumbing, bends in the piping can cause stoppages in the flow of water if debris enters the system. It is best to route piping to avoid having it placed under buildings and other elements that would make gaining access to the pipe unreasonable. Since closed systems are installed below grade, they can be expensive to repair. Don't add to this expense by making access to the pipe difficult to obtain.

Cost can be a prohibitive factor for closed systems. Open systems are generally less expensive to construct. However, when the water flow is too great for an open system, a closed system must be used. In cases where an open system is considered to be an eyesore, a closed system is the answer.

# Open Systems

Open systems for the control of storm water are common. Open swales carry water to retention or detention areas. These systems work well for some projects. If the maximum amount of runoff is not excessive, an open system is a cost-effective option. The overall design of a development can have a lot to do with the viability of an open drainage system. Most developers strive to make their open drainage systems as attractive as possible. This can mean added expense, but the end result is often worth the cost.

It would be easy to run a swale in a straight line to a retention pond. Getting from point A to point B with a straight line is both the most direct route and the least expensive path. But it probably is not the best path. It is generally better to create multiple ponds, rather than one large pond. Also, winding swale paths tend to look more natural and they provide more opportunity for vegetation and attractive appearance.

When designed properly, detention and retention ponds can become an enhancement to a development. Retention ponds can be stocked with fish to give residents a source of recreation. In some cases, retention ponds can be used as ice skating areas in winter. Size and depth of ponds vary with the needs of drainage for a project. Having deep ponds in residential areas can pose a hazard. Potential buyers may shy away from the development because of fear of drowning.

When ponds are created, the edges of the pond area should slope gently to the center of the pond. Steep drop-offs increase the risk of drowning. Ponds that deepen with gentle slopes are, by nature, less threatening. Landscaping in and around the pond is also important. When a detention pond is used there will be times when the pond is not holding substantial water. Without the proper landscaping, the bottom of the pond will be an ugly eyesore of sediment and mud. Planting the bottom of the pond with vegetation that will thrive in and out of water makes a low-water condition more attractive. In addition, the vegetation acts as a filter when water enters a pond.

Given a choice between open and closed systems, open systems will normally be less expensive and easier to maintain. In addition to lower costs, open systems can provide relaxing recreational opportunities. There are times when a combination system is required for proper site drainage. Each site is different. You and your engineers must spend enough time during the design process to create the best solution for drainage that is available to you.

The deciding point on the type of system to use is often determined by the amount of runoff water expected. High volumes of runoff call for a closed system. Residential developments normally have more land left in a natural state than a commercial site. Logically, it's more common for runoff to be higher with commercial sites. This indicates a likelihood that closed systems will be used with commercial projects while open systems may be used with residential systems.

Let's assume that you are working on a residential development. The project is large and will contain a variety of amenities. Many of the housing areas will have limited runoff and can be served by an open drainage system. Some parts of the development will have substantial pavement and concrete. These areas will produce rapid, high-volume runoff. This type of project will need a combination system. You will use a closed system for the paved areas and an open system for the natural areas. Of course, your engineers will make final determinations on what your project will require.

## Looking at the Land

Looking at the land that you plan to develop can tell you much about drainage needs. A visual inspection can reveal patterns where water is presently running. Of course, your development alterations will change current trends in the runoff water. Amazingly, some developers fail to think of this. The land that you are looking at in its raw form is not the project that you will be draining. You and your experts must consider what the project needs will be once development is complete.

Your engineers can come up with a good preliminary plan for drainage early in your planning stages. The engineers will have to know the master plan, street locations, types of buildings and their placement, and other factors that affect drainage. Topo maps are used to trace natural water flow. Calculations are made on the basis of existing conditions and proposed changes. It is during this stage of planning that engineers may be able to make adjustments to lower the cost of drainage for storm water. Minor changes in construction plans could save you considerable money in the infrastructure of your development.

## Sectional Designs

Sectional designs are not uncommon for developments with mixed landscaping. Obviously, a project that has varying topography and different levels of development will need different types of drainage control. You might break your development down into sections and then design a drainage system for each section. Part of the design may be a closed system, while the rest of it is an open design. You might use one large retention pond to control drainage in one part of the development while a series of smaller detention ponds might be used in another section.

The amount of development in an area certainly affects drainage. A lot of concrete or pavement creates different needs than a wooded section of land would. Various soil types also affect the need for runoff drainage. You will need soil studies to determine how much runoff water a section of a development can handle under given conditions. Whenever soil types differ, you must alter your plans for drainage control.

Engineers must factor in many considerations when developing a drainage plan. As a developer, you should rely on your experts to provide you with a suitable storm water system. Be aware of the basics so that you can talk with your engineers and understand most of what they lay out in front of you. But, don't attempt to design your own drainage system when dealing with a sizable project. Your job may not require extensive drainage. Maybe you will need nothing more than a driveway culvert and some subsoil drains for gutters. If this is the case, consider yourself lucky. However, if you are doing a major project, the engineering and installation of a storm drainage system will be an expense that you can't afford to overlook.

# Deciphering the Dirt

Deciphering the dirt of a project is a job that is best left to soil scientists and engineers. But it never hurts to have a good idea of what the experts will be talking about. On some sites, the primary concern for soils is that they will perk well enough to allow the installation of a septic system. Large sites can be much more involved. In many cases, the soils of a site control much of the development potential—not to mention the cost of a project. Many factors influence the viability of a project, and the soil conditions are certainly a major consideration.

Most builders and developers are not overly concerned with scientific data pertaining to soils. If the ground will support foundations, drain properly, and support a successful development, that is generally all that builders and developers are interested in. How much do you want to know about soils? Do you really care that the official name for a soil scientist is agronomist? Probably not. Even if you don't care to know the difference between soil types and characteristics, you should invest some time in understanding the basic terms that you will be dealing with as a developer.

What is soil? Do you know what soil is made up of? Well, there are three components to soil. The first element of soil is the particles that most people think of as dirt. But mixed in with the particles is water and gases. Soil that is fully saturated has all of the voids between the particles filled with water. If the soil dries out completely, the voids are filled only with gasses. Under normal conditions, water and gases fill the voids between the particles. Engineers must assess the phases of soil to arrive at their engineering data. The relationships of gases, water, and particles must be established in a weight-to-volume factor. Once engineers have the basic evaluation of the soil, they can establish the soil properties for such elements as shear strength, shrinking, swelling, and consolidation.

Texture for soil is often talked about. Many people refer to soil by its texture. How many times have you heard people talk about sandy soil or clayey soil? The texture of soil is determined by the relative amounts of the individual particles making up soil. Different tools are used to identify particle sizes. Sieves are used to sort particles by size. Hydrometers are used to measure the amount of soil in suspension. The process is much more complicated than most builders or developers are willing to get involved in. But, hey, that's why we have engineers. Without getting into scientific formulas and procedures outside of the realm of duties normally associated with being a land developer, let's just look at how the soils on a project will affect your business.

## Types of Soils

There are many types of soils to be encountered. Many soils are transported in one way or another. The physical aspects of soil types can be judged, to some extent, by the means of transportation. We're not talking about trucking dirt into a site. No, the transportation referred to here has to do with natural movement.

Alluvial and lacustrine soils are created by sedimentation. Alluvial soils are left by running water. Lacustrine soil is the result of deposits in lakes. Since alluvial deposits are transported by running water, a natural filtering process takes place. Large particles tend to sink to the bottom of a stream while smaller particles are moved with the water. The separation process is natural and effective. Both alluvial and lacustrine soils tend to make poor foundation materials. Because of the makeup of alluvial and lacustrine soils, they are generally medium to fine sands, silt, or clay. The drainage factor for this type of soil is poor. Building a foundation on alluvial or lacustrine soil is risky, since the soils are usually soft, loose, and highly compressible.

Glacial soils are called *moraines.* The soils are pushed, eroded, or carried along with glacier movement. Particle sizes range from a clay consistency to large rocks. Characteristics of glacial soils can vary greatly. However, glacial deposits generally offer a good base for foundation construction.

Eolian soils are transported by wind. As you might imagine, this means that the soil must be small and light. Sand is the most common type of eolian soil. If you have ever been to a desert or a large beach, you have probably seen sand dunes, which are representative of eolian soils. Sand is not a great foundation soil to work with.

Colluvial soils are transported by gravity. In most cases, this type of soil is the result of hillsides deteriorating. Rock chips compose most of the colluvial soil. Since the soil has moved once, it is likely to move again. This makes colluvial soil undesirable as a foundation material. Organic soil is no better. This is soil that is made up of decaying plant life. Peat is what organic soil is best known as. Because of the compressible nature of peat, it is unsuitable for foundation construction.

## Bearing Capacity

The bearing capacity of soil is a primary concern when planning a development deal. You must know what the soil's ability is to support structure loads created during your development. This means buildings, roads, and other improvements. A first concern is the strength of existing soil, but you will also want to know how excavated soil that might be reused on your project will hold up. When embankments will be created, you have to know how stable the soil used to build the embankment will be. If you find that some of the soil is substandard in strength, your engineers might be able to recommend a way of improving its bearing capacity by adding chemicals or materials to the soil. In any event, you must establish that the soil will be suitable for your development plans.

Bearing capacity is increased when soil is compacted. When soil is compacted, the void ratio is decreased, which increases the soil's strength. Compaction does many things. Soil that is compacted will be stronger and will not be as likely to settle over time. In the case of foundations, settling soil can result in cracks. So compacted soil that will not be prone to settling is better than soil that is not compressed. Soil used on embankments will be more stable if it is compacted.

In most construction work, compacting soil is simply a matter of pressing dirt together with either a tamper or a roller. In the most simple of terms, this is true. However, the compaction of soil increases the soil density by rearranging soil particles. Engineers may talk about the fracture of grains of soil and the bonds between them. You might hear the experts talk about bending the soil. Terms like cohesive resistance may be used. What does it all mean? It means compacting the dirt with a tamper or a roller. Sometimes water is added to the soil to improve the compaction rate. As far as most developers are concerned, knowing that compacted soil is stronger and more stable than loose soil is enough to move on with.

Soil requires a moisture content to be compacted to its maximum density. When fill dirt is hauled in it is usually compacted to accept weight loads. Arriving at maximum density is desirable. The moisture content required for maximum strength varies from soil type to soil type. For example, sandy soil does well with a moisture content of about 8 percent. Clay, on the other hand, compacts best with a moisture content of about 20 percent. Project engineers will evaluate fill areas and call for certain compaction specifications as needed to meet the requirements of your development.

As most builders know, soil compacts best when the soil depth is kept shallow. For example, a plumber would not backfill a sewer ditch with 3 feet of dirt and then run a tamper over it. The ditch would be filled with layers of dirt and each layer would be tamped before the next layer of dirt was introduced into the ditch. Compaction in stages is the best way to arrive at maximum strength.

Soil that is being added to an area and compacted should be added a little at a time. Most soils should be added in layers that are not more than 8 inches thick. Each layer is compacted before the next layer is added. In some cases, water is applied to the layers of fill to increase the compaction rate. The layers are often called *lifts*. Some types of fill, such as gravel and sand, might be added in lifts that run up to a foot in depth. Compacting soil in layers takes time. It might seem tempting to fill an area with dirt as fast as possible and move on with other parts of the development. This would be a costly mistake. Soil that is not compacted properly is likely to cause any number of problems for a developer. Don't cut corners on soil compaction. Factor in the time and cost required to do the job properly and stick to a proved plan for suitable compaction.

# Compaction Equipment Options

Compaction equipment options exist for developers. What is the best type of compaction equipment to use on your project? Your site contractor will be the one who is most likely to decide on the type of equipment to be used. However, your engineers may specify the type of equipment that must be used to create a satisfactory compaction. As a developer, you should have a general idea of what type of equipment is used for various jobs. Rollers are the most common type of equipment used for large-scale soil compaction. But, there are different types of rollers. Should your project be prepared with a smooth roller, a sheepsfoot roller, or a vibratory roller? You may decide to leave decisions pertaining to equipment up to your engineers and contractors, but let's take just a few moments to look at the roles of different types of rollers.

### Sheepsfoot Rollers

Sheepsfoot rollers use drum wheels that have a large number of bumps or protrusions on them. The protrusions direct a lot of pressure in small areas for tight compaction. Water can be used to fill the roller drum for additional weight. Clay is compacted very well with a sheepsfoot roller. The bumps on the roller wheel can usually deliver pressures up to 1000 pounds per square inch (psi).

### Smooth Rollers

Smooth drum rollers are used most often for finish work. Since the roller drum is smooth, it maintains full contact with soil at all times. Any type of soil, except rocky soil, can be compacted with a smooth roller. Since the roller drum maintains full contact, it does not create a tremendous amount of pressure per square inch. Compare a sheepsfoot roller at 1000 psi compaction to a smooth roller at about 55 psi.

### Rubber Rollers

Rollers with rubber tires might not seem like much of a compaction tool, but they are. Pneumatic tires are spaced close together with a rubber roller. Weight is added to the equipment to obtain compaction pressures up to about 150 psi. You can get up to 80 percent coverage with a rubber-tired roller. However, this type of roller should not be used for initial compaction of some clay soils.

### Vibrating Rollers

Vibrating rollers are often used in road work. Like other rollers, vibrating rollers compress soil with the weight of the roller, but as an added bonus, the pounding of the vibrating roller packs soil even more tightly. Both granular soil and rock fill can be compacted with a vibrating roller. But the roller must be set up properly for the type of material being compacted. For example, rock fill would call for the roller to set for a heavy weight with a low-frequency vibration. Sand, on the other hand, would call for the roller to produce light to medium weight and high-frequency vibrations.

### Power Tampers

Power tampers are used where compaction areas are small and difficult to gain access to. The tamper is usually gas-powered and operated by one person who walks behind the equipment. When trenches are backfilled, power tampers are most likely to be used. Since the tampers are small and fairly easy to handle, they can be put in a small trench and operated by a single person. Any type of inorganic soil can be compacted with a power tamper.

## Stability

The stability of soil is directly related to its shear strength. What is shear strength? It is a rating of soil that is determined by calculating the resistance to sliding between soil particles. Physical characteristics of soil determine the shear strength potential. For example, the confining pressure, surface roughness of particles, and soil density all affect the shear strength of a soil. Voids between soil particles are known as *pore spaces*. Water can flow through pore spaces and affect shear strength.

The stability of slopes must be considered carefully. Embankments fail for various reasons. The strength of any fill material on a slope can affect slope stability. Existing soil strength must also be considered in terms of slope failure. Drainage on a slope is another factor to consider when evaluating the possible failure of an embankment. Engineers can devise methods for stabilizing most types of soil. Building an embankment is not as simple as just piling up dirt. Erosion and general failure must be assessed.

## Taken for Granted

The consistency of land is often taken for granted by builders and developers. People walk over a piece of land and don't often give much thought to the soil under their feet. Once development is started, the soil issues can become much more intense. A lot of money can be lost if the reading of the soil for a project is not done correctly. Developers cannot afford to skim over soil issues. Someone has to dig deeply into all aspects of soil characteristics. Search out qualified experts and let them do their jobs. Don't attempt to become your own expert in soils analysis, but learn enough about soils so that you can understand most of what your experts present to you.

# Land Loss and Costs for Roads

Developers soon find that roads can account for a lot of lost land. And roads can be extremely expensive to build, even in the most rural settings. If you get into building paved streets to state standards, the cost can be staggering. As you are probably starting to see, there are a lot of elements that make developing land a tricky business. There are so many ways to make costly mistakes that the odds seem to be against you every step of the way. Sure, there are risks and dangers. It's easy to lose a bundle of money when you embark on a development deal. Having deep pockets helps, but profit is profit. If you are looking to make money, and most developers are, the net profit is your goal. Having a lot of money to throw into your mistakes can keep you out of the bankruptcy court, but it may not help you to turn a profit. To make money, you have to be smart, in tune with market conditions, and be willing to pay plenty of attention to detail.

Large developments require extensive road work. Major money will be on the line. Most people would be expecting to spend a lot of money to build paved streets with curbs and storm sewers throughout an extensive development. But would you expect to spend tons of money to put a gravel road into a country development (Fig. 14.1)?

| USDA-RD<br>Form RD 440-11<br>(Rev. 11-96) | ESTIMATE OF FUNDS NEEDED<br>FOR<br>30-Day Period Commencing | FORM APPROVED<br>OMB NO. 0575-0015 |
| --- | --- | --- |

Name of Borrower _____

| Items | Amount of Funds |
| --- | --- |
| Development | $ |
| Contract or Job<br>No. _____ | |
| Contract or Job<br>No. _____ | |
| Contract or Job<br>No. _____ | |
| Land and Rights-of-Way | |
| Legal Services | |
| Engineering Fees | |
| Interest | |
| Equipment | |
| Contingencies | |
| Refinancing | |
| Initial O&M | |
| Other | |
| TOTAL | $ |

Prepared by _____
*Name of Borrower*

By _____
_____

Date _____

Approved by _____
*RD County Supervisor/District Director*

Date _____

**FIGURE 14.1**

**Estimate form for road work.**

Don't think that roads are going to be cheap, regardless of where or how they are built. Having a modest gravel road installed can cost a small fortune.

Let's assume that you are aware that road work will be expensive. Maybe you focus most of your energy in getting estimates for the construction and engineering costs. Are you forgetting something? You might be, many inexperienced developers do. Even if you calculate your road needs accurately, you could still come out of your development with a lot less money than you had hoped for. If the roads come in on budget how could they cost you more money than you expected? If you did not take into consideration the amount of raw land that has to be dedicated to roads, you could lose substantial planned income from having less land to develop into buildable sites.

Simple roads require a certain amount of land. There is no question about this. Complex street systems eat up a lot of land. Far too many developers fail to plan for the land lost to road construction. It's easy to see a 20-acre parcel of land as 20 acres of buildable resource. But how much of the 20 acres will be left after roads are installed? If you are planning to sell quarter-acre lots, you might be thinking that you will have 80 sites to sell. But, how many lots will you really have?

Land is lost in many ways. Some raw land is lost to drainage needs. More land can be given up for recreational areas and common space. You can count on roads consuming a portion of your development parcel. All of these land losses must be factored in when you are estimating your total sale units. Engineers, land planners, and surveyors can help you arrive at a viable number of building lots. Remember though, the amount of land that you see on a plot plan will not yield as many building lots as you may hope for. In other words, factor in your land loss before you speculate on your potential number of sale units.

## Simple Access

Simple access roads are usually not difficult to design. In many cases the roads are just straight, or nearly straight, cuts through a property. As simple as they sound, the roads can still be extremely expensive to build. Construction cost is related to several factors. Existing ground conditions are a prime consideration when it comes to cost. Some land is solid enough to support a low-density road without much site work.

Other pieces of land require extensive preparation to accept a road that will last. Drainage is another factor in road cost. Distance is, of course, an element of expense for a road. Topography is another factor that can have a lot of influence on the cost of a road. There is no shortage of considerations in figuring the cost of a road.

Some developments require extensive engineering reports. Other sites don't call for much more than a site visit by a good road contractor. Many builders are able to design their own access roads for small developments. It's wise to get engineering reports for all roads, but a lot of builders and developers skip the engineering phase when the roads being installed are simple and designed for low traffic flow.

I've been involved in a lot of road work over the last couple of decades. Most of my personal jobs have been fairly small. But, I've partnered up with other developers on large jobs. My experience has shown me that no job is as easy as it appears to be. A driveway for a single-family home can give a builder nightmares. But long access roads can come together without much sweat. Every job is different.

## Straight and to the Point

Keeping an access road straight and to the point is usually the least expensive way to provide ingress and egress to building lots. I've developed tracts of land that contained hundreds of acres and required only one, fairly straight, road. This type of road construction is about as economical as it gets. Plus, a straight run limits land loss. By installing a road through the middle of a property, you can offer each building lot frontage on the road. All that is required is a serviceable road that has provisions for turning around at the end of the road. If the road runs through a property and ties into other roads at each end, you don't even need the cul-de-sac for turning around. It doesn't get any easier than this.

## Branches

Some land requires road access that consists of branches built off of the primary access road. Building the branches adds to the cost of construction, but the additional expense may be worthwhile. Cutting a straight road through the middle of a property might cause you to lose development potential. You may be able to get more building lots out of a parcel if you install branch access roads.

Branch roads give a developer the opportunity to have more lots fronting on a road with less land. Yet, the branch roads require land. Is the land lost to the road construction a waste? It depends on the project. The shape of a land parcel comes into play with road design. Zoning requirements and desired lot sizes are also factors to consider when thinking of branch roads. Many subdivisions must incorporate the use of branch roads to reach the highest and best use. Your land planner and engineers will be your best sources of suggestions for road layouts.

## Natural Road Sites

Natural road sites exist on some land. If you have walked much acreage, you've seen natural paths that lend themselves to road construction. The paths may be the result of old logging roads that were used many years ago. Sometimes the road sites are simply a result of topography. Almost anyone can spot some of the natural road sites. What are you looking for? Solid, high ground is a good start when you are looking for a road location. If there are gaps between trees or only small brush growing in a potential path, it's a plus. Negative factors can be hills, streams, low spots, and soft ground. When natural road sites exist you should try to use them.

Building a road, even a simple one, is not a cheap proposition. However, there are some situations where the cost is minimal in comparison to other sites. To describe this best, let me give you some examples from my road experience to compare.

The first long road construction that I was involved with was a straight run through the middle of old farm land. A natural site existed where farmers had traveled the same path for years when working the fields and getting from one location to another. Since there had been farm traffic over the years, the path was well compacted. Farmers had probably filled in the path with field rocks each year. By the time I started developing the land, I had a given path that was solid, even during wet seasons. There were trees to clear or stumps to pull. By road construction standards, the job was a piece of cake.

When I brought equipment to the site it was not difficult or time-consuming to prepare the road base for gravel. My crews cut some drainage ditches and then started building up the road with gravel.

Since I had a solid base to work with, the job moved along quickly and inexpensively. In a matter of about a week, I had a road that any car could travel easily. Cutting and filling was not needed. Base compaction was not required. All the crews had to do was dig the side ditches and place the gravel with a proper crown and slope. A job like that can spoil a developer. Not all jobs are that easy.

Another job that I dealt with had similar characteristics, but it offered more trouble to me. This road was long and somewhat winding. The base was solid in most areas but did contain some sinkholes. A stream crossed under the road at one point and a small river ran along one side of the road. The river was close enough to the road at some points to present a potential for flooding during periods of heavy rain. Another factor in this road was exposed bedrock in some areas. The bedrock was good as a base, but it made keeping gravel on the road difficult, especially where the road went over inclines.

As the road was surfaced with gravel, there were areas that seemed to sink away. This called for larger stone to build a solid base. Culvert piping was installed for the stream to run under the road. Berms were built on the side of the road where the river might invade it during heavy rains. Fine sandlike gravel was used on the bedrock to fill in cracks along the rock and to provide a somewhat slip-resistant material for finished gravel to be applied to. The cost of this road was considerably more than the road installed on the farm land, but the job was still cheap in terms of most road construction.

A third project produced a road job that was something of a nightmare. I had to install about 1 mile of road through a field that was extremely soft. Along the way, I had to get the road across a stream that ran through a gully that was probably about 6 feet deep. Once I got across the gully, I had to take the road up a hill, around a bend, and through a pine forest. When road construction began, the equipment struggled with mud in the field. To say that the site was a mess would be an understatement. Special arrangements had to be made to protect the stream to environmental standards, both for the crossing and for erosion from the hill on the other side of the water.

As my crews worked the land we found that the mud was going to eat up too much rock. To reduce the amount of material needed, black weblike material was placed in the roadbed to reduce the sinking of stone. The rolled material that went down prior to the rock base was very expensive, but it was the only way to minimize the problems associated with the mud. I had not planned on the added costs that were incurred with the mud problem, so I lost some money on the deal. If I'd had experts review the site in advance I probably would have known what to expect, but it was a simple job that I didn't think warranted engineering, except for the stream crossing. I learned that whatever I had saved in engineering fees had probably been lost, and then some, with the added cost of construction.

Builders and developers often feel that their field experience is enough to make decisions on road construction. Sometimes field experience is enough, but if you want to minimize surprises that can be costly, you should factor engineering costs into all of your road work. I didn't always do this, and it cost me more money than I thought I was saving on some jobs.

## Complex Roads

Complex road systems must be engineered. If you are going to do a development where there will be miles of paved roads, you would be extremely foolish to start construction without engineering reports. Some developers feel that having road contractors come to a site and make suggestions is enough. I strongly suggest that you pay for engineering reports for any major road work. The difference in cost between building a gravel road through some farm land and installing a paved road system in a large subdivision is immense. Mistakes made with paved roads are considerably more expensive than the same mistakes made with a gravel road. Don't attempt any major road work without plans from experts.

Typical developers don't delve deeply into the road planning process for large projects. Yet, a good developer should be aware of the amount of land that must be used for roads, curbs, parking areas, and turnarounds. These needs are often taken for granted, but they shouldn't be. The amount of land required for road construction, parking, and related features can be substantial. Losing land is like losing money. It is the land that you will be selling, and you won't be selling roads and parking lots.

Good designers can come up with road plans that are cost-effective and efficient. It is not wise to cut corners on design issues that may repel land buyers when your development is complete. To expand on this, let's talk briefly about your options for turnarounds on dead-end streets and how decisions pertaining to the turnarounds could affect your development.

When you think of a turnaround area what do you envision? Most people from urban areas think of cul-de-sacs. The use of cul-de-sacs is widespread and accepted as something of an industry standard. But, there are other, less expensive, types of turnarounds that could be used. How much money should you try to save? Reducing development costs is a great way to increase profits. But, if the cuts you make reduce sales or bring lower sale prices, your price cuts will prove to be frustrating.

Let's assume that you want to use cul-de-sacs for your turnaround areas. It is your desire to use island circles, which is a type of cul-de-sac that is circular in shape and that has an island inside of the travel area so that landscaping can be planted. This is a classy type of turnaround, but it is expensive. You weigh the cost and decide to do without the island feature. The decision will save you some money and you will still have a circular cul-de-sac for your turnaround. A decision like this may be quite sensible. But, what are your other options and how would they play out on paper?

Small developments that have low traffic flow can get by with T-shaped turnarounds. A T-shaped turn is not as easy to turn around in as a cul-de-sac is. A driver must pull into the T turn, pull forward in one direction, back up to the other end of the T turn, and then reenter the street. This takes time and can be difficult for some drivers to deal with. The amount of land and pavement needed for a T turn is less than what would be required for a cul-de-sac, so money can be saved. But are you buying trouble for your development. Saving money on the turnarounds could cost you in lost sales or unhappy residents.

A Y-shaped turnaround is similar to a T turn, except that the angles are easier to negotiate in a Y turn. More land and pavement is needed for a Y turn than would be needed for a T turn. However, a Y turn requires less land and pavement than a cul-de-sac. So, what should you do? Most developers would be willing to spend more for cul-de-sacs to ensure acceptance of their developments by land buyers. However, if you were dealing with a small development of say six houses on a gravel road, a Y turn would probably be fine. Generally speaking, cul-de-sacs are best.

You can go too far in trying to save money on road construction. Trying to avoid engineering reports can be a bad mistake. Failing to make the roads user-friendly will prove to be a problem. Being unwilling to spend a little extra money to make roads more attractive can hurt you. Major design issues will be handled by your experts. Your role in roads may not amount to much of anything. But at the very least, keep in mind that all of the areas used for roads and related needs will deplete the amount of raw land that you will have left to sell.

# Water Requirements

The water requirements for a development must be calculated in order to arrive at a cost projection for a project. Figuring the water requirements for a sizable development is a job for experts. Even small developments can have diverse water needs that should be designed by experts. There is more to water needs than just the water used by homes in your development. Irrigation is a need that some investors might overlook. Having water available for fire hydrants may be a necessity. If there are community buildings in your development, water will be needed for them. Some developments contain homes where fire sprinklers are standard equipment. The fire protection systems can require more water pressure and quantity. In short, the need for water in a development involves much more than what some developers realize.

Some parcels of land don't have access to city water mains. In some cases, entire communities run with well water. Community well systems can be expensive and unpredictable. Most developers look for land where water is readily available. Buying land where well water will be needed can be risky. But well water is used in many places without problems. I've done a lot of small developments where the only water came from wells. Whether you are counting on municipal water or well water, you should not take anything for granted.

I've made some expensive mistakes in dealing with city water mains. One development I did had a city water service running in front of it. I knew the water main was there and assumed that all I'd have to do was pay the city tap fee and connect to the water main. I was wrong. The water main was there, but it was too small to serve my little development. I was required to upgrade the water main and repair the street cuts out of my development profits. Ouch!

I've done jobs where I thought that the city would extend water service to my property at the city's expense. Cities often do this, but I ran into a situation where the city required me to do my own street cuts and repairs. Repairing street cuts to meet demanding state and local requirements can be very expensive. It only took one experience to teach me to ask for complete details before assuming anything about city policies.

The cost of installing water systems can be staggering. Developers who work with large developments should rely on experts to plan water systems. Builders and developers who are doing microdevelopments may not need any engineering help, but they still have to cover their bases. Wells for individual building lots are one thing, but any connection to any public utility is another thing. Developers need to identify the water requirements of their projects early in the planning stage.

## Types of Water Demand

There are two types of water demand—consumptive and nonconsumptive. Water that is needed for municipal, agricultural, or industry use is considered consumptive. Nonconsumptive use involves recreational use, transportation, and hydropower. Developers are most often concerned about the water requirements for the following uses:

- Residential needs
- Institutional needs
- Recreational needs
- Irrigation needs
- Commercial needs

- Industrial needs

- Firefighting needs

- Decorative needs

There are charts and tables available to help designers determine the water needs for a development. Most plumbing codes provide such tables. The amounts of water required by local codes can be somewhat shocking. Most people are not aware of how much water may be needed for a single household. For example, you may find that the minimum required daily water rate for a residential development equates to 100 gallons of water per day, per person. If you were planning for a shopping center, you might have to figure on up to 300 gallons of water per each 1000 square feet of floor space. Designers normally handle the calculation of water requirements for developers, so you should not have to become too personally involved with the process.

When water systems are sized they must allow for the delivery of enough water to cover peak demands and fire flows and to handle increased future demands. Most of the time that system will work at far less than its ability. But, the system must be large enough to meet all demands when necessary. In addition to peak demand, water pressure has to be considered. Again, normal use and fire flow must be factored into the sizing. Since water mains are usually installed below ground and follow the topography of land, more pressure is needed to push water over hilly terrain. In order for a water main to have adequate pressure it may be necessary for individual buildings to be equipped with pressure-reducing valves. For example, a residence may be limited by plumbing code to a maximum working pressure of no more than 80 pounds per square inch (psi). If a water main is delivering pressure at a rate of 125 psi, a pressure-reducing valve will have to be installed in the home to lower the pressure to an acceptable level.

Local authorities normally set minimum requirements for water pressure needs. State agencies often handle this part of the design function. Fire flow requirements are usually established by individual municipalities. The requirements for minimum pressure in water mains must be reviewed in sizing a system for a new development. Again, this work should be done by your experts.

# Routing Water Mains

The routing of water mains can require considerable planning. Depending on where you will be developing land, you may find that routing requirements for your water system are somewhat carved in stone. Jurisdictions often set guidelines for the placement of water lines. For example, you can expect that a rule is in place to keep all water pipes at least 10 feet away from all sewer pipes. This rule protects the pipes in case one or the other, or both, develop leaks. When water mains are allowed closer than 10 feet to a sewer, the water main is likely to be required to be installed on an elevated shelf that is at least 18 inches above the sewer. Additional safeguards may be required to prevent contamination of the water system.

Actual placement of water mains can be restricted to certain locations. For example, a city may require that all water mains be placed a fixed distance from the centerline of streets or curbs. You may be required to install all water mains on only one side of a street to maintain conformity. I've heard of situations where cities were very strict about where water mains could be installed, so this is an issue that must be confirmed. The experts you have designing your project should take care of this for you.

Depending on what your designers come up with, you may have to create easements for the installation of your water system. If easements are going to be needed, you need to create them before you start selling lots. Developers try to keep easements on outparcels and common areas. Whenever possible, avoid running water mains through lots you plan to sell. If you do have to encroach on individual lots, keep the water mains as close to the property lines as possible.

Residential developments don't pose as many problems in the placement of water mains as commercial sites do. However, high-density residential developments can be as difficult to work with as commercial sites. What makes commercial projects and high-density projects more troublesome? Space is generally very limited with commercial projects. The same can be true for town house and condo projects. When there is limited land to work with, the placement of utilities can be very difficult.

When you consider the size of water mains, they can require substantial room. Small residential developments might be served by a water main with a diameter of as little as 4 inches. However, a 6-inch diameter is generally considered about the smallest size suitable for residential projects. Large projects may require water mains with diameters of 24 inches. Routing sewers and water mains can be a bit like running a maze. Designers can really have their work cut out for them if there is limited land to work with.

Developers must consider the quality of the land where they plan to install utilities. Having enough land is one thing, having enough land that is suitable for an installation can be quite another thing. For example, I could buy 60 acres of land here in Maine and be hard pressed to find a suitable path for water and sewer lines. How could this be with so much land? Ledge—bedrock—could make installing pipes below grade extremely difficult and expensive.

Sewers and water mains are normally buried. Minimum ground cover for a small sewer is usually 12 inches. Water mains should be installed below the local frostline, which could easily range from 20 to 48 inches, or more. Can you imagine what it would cost to create a path through bedrock for a water main that had to be buried 48 inches deep? I have run into bedrock when running water services to individual homes. In such cases, I got minimal bury depth and installed in-pipe heat tape to protect the pipe from freezing during cold temperatures. This is feasible for a single water service for a house, but it certainly wouldn't make sense for a development. If a water service and a sewer are installed in a common trench, the water pipe must be above the sewer and on an independent shelf within the trench (Fig. 15.1). This is to reduce the risk of contamination if the pipes were to leak.

Part of the design process for routing water mains involves valve locations and the placement of fire hydrants, connections, and so forth. Determining placement for fire hydrants is a job that must be done with careful attention to fire codes and local regulations.

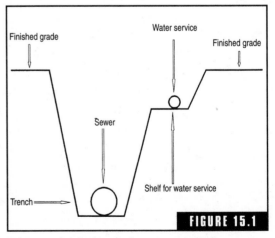

**Water service and sewer in common trench.**

# Fire Hydrants

Fire hydrants are not installed in all developments. Some areas simply don't have the resources for fire hydrants. But many developments are required to be equipped with hydrants for fire fighting. In these cases, designers must work within the confines of established rules. There are some basic guidelines that might be followed, but it is more likely that there will be specific regulations to observe. Since solid rules vary, let's talk about the basics.

It's pretty obvious that fire hydrants have to be readily accessible and placed in conspicuous locations that are close enough to buildings to make the hydrants worthwhile. A few developers resist having fire hydrants sprouting up all over a development. The view of these developers is that the hydrants detract from the aesthetic quality of a development. Well, if you share these feelings, get over it. You have to make fire fighting equipment readily available. Now your designers may be able to come up with some creative ways to reduce any potential negative impact on the appearance of your development.

It is common for fire hydrants to be installed within a few feet of the edge of a street or curb. Connections on the hydrants should face the street. Precise locations should take into consideration the ease or difficulty with which firefighters will be able to connect to the hydrants. You may find that hydrants must be installed a certain distance from buildings. There are two reasons for this. Hydrants must be close enough to buildings to make them effective, but the hydrants must be far enough from buildings that might be burning to make it safe for firefighters to connect to the hydrants.

The rules for hydrant placing can vary with the type of development that you are involved in. Typical residential developments might require different hydrant placement than a town house project would. Commercial developments are certainly likely to require different placement for hydrants. Some commercial buildings have manifold hookups on exterior walls so that fire hoses can be connected directly to the building. When this is the case, the manifold is usually kept within 100 feet of a fire hydrant. The spacing between fire hydrants varies. It is common for hydrant spacing to run between 300 to 1000 feet. Your designers, with the help of local regulations, will spot the locations for fire hydrants. Good designers will take into consideration the need for visual appeal and will keep obtrusive locations to a minimum.

# Tapping in

Tapping into existing water mains can be very tricky. Some existing water mains cannot be shut down, not even for short periods of time. When this is the case, the tap-in requires special equipment and skill. In simple terms, two halves of pipe are placed over the existing water main and strapped into place. The strapping process basically involves the use of flanges on the pipe halves being bolted together. A cutting tool that fits over a valve cuts into the water main through the open water valve. Once access is gained to the main, the cutter is removed and the valve is closed. When all goes as planned, the remainder of the work is dry and typical.

When isolation valves are available, an existing water main can be shut down long enough for a dry tap to be made. While the hookup is being connected, water to buildings downstream is turned off. This is the simplest way of tapping in, but it is not always practical. Wet taps are often required and they tend to be more expensive than dry taps. This is an issue that you should investigate while putting together your numbers for the cost of a development.

There may be an existing water main available for your project. Sometimes each building can have an individual tap into an existing water main. Other circumstances require one large tap-in that is developed into a complete distribution system within a development. Either way, there will be tap fees, and they can cost thousands of dollars. Let me tell you a quick story about a developer I once knew who learned about tap fees the hard way.

A developer in Virginia purchased a parcel of land that was cut into several house lots. I believe the development housed eight single-family homes. All of the land had frontage on a city street. A city water main and sewer were available in the street that ran in front of the property. The developer wasn't too concerned with details since his development was small. He researched enough to find out that there were water and sewer services available, but he stopped short of where his research should have gone. He forgot to ask about the tap fees!

The developer built the houses simultaneously. It was his intent to do all of the water and sewer connections at the same time. His plan was to save money on equipment movement fees and time by doing all of the hookups at once. It all made sense until the connection permits were applied for. Once the developer went to the city, he found that the tap fees for his desired connections were sizable. The houses being built were priced in the low $60,000s. With a 20 percent markup, the builder/developer was expecting a gross profit of about $12,000 per house. Well, he didn't get it. The tap fees were, as I recall, about $1800 each. Keep in mind that this was many years ago. It could have been worse, but it was bad enough. The moral to this story is to get all your cost data in place before you begin your development.

## Wells

Water wells are sometimes used to provide water for developments. This might involve a community water supply that is distributed through a water main system or individual wells for each building in a community. Individual wells are fairly simple. Community water services are not really complicated, but they can require several pumping stations and holding tanks, in addition to normal distribution piping. Cost is certainly a factor in determining which type of well system to use when municipal water mains are not available for tapping into.

Some home buyers are reluctant to buy houses where their domestic water comes from a well. This is something that you must consider when doing your marketing research. There are many areas where wells are common and meet with no resistance. However, if you are developing an area where most homes are served by municipal water mains, you may find it difficult to sell your building lots. Research this aspect carefully before you commit to a development.

When a community well system is used, it is likely to be made up of several wells and pumping stations. Large holding tanks are needed for community well systems. Ongoing maintenance of the system may also be a cost factor. I have seen developments of this type, but I've never undertaken one myself, and I wouldn't. Personally, I think that the process is too much to deal with, but that's only my personal preference. However, I have done many projects where individual wells were used.

Individual wells are usually either drilled wells or dug wells. Dug wells are common in the south and drilled wells are the norm in the north. Drilled wells are more dependable, but they are also more expensive. Most developers who install wells use whichever type of well is most common in the local area. I've installed both types of wells. A few of the dug wells, also known as shallow wells, came back to haunt me. They sometimes went dry during hot, dry summer months. A few of the plumbing systems served by the wells sucked sand into the water lines. I have never experienced any problems with drilled wells. So, my vote goes to drilled wells, but both are suitable subject to local conditions.

If you are dealing with individual wells, you avoid the cost of expensive distribution systems. However, the cost of the wells and related well equipment, such as pumps and pressure tanks, adds up quickly. Usually, if a public water main is available a developer must use it. It may be cheaper to use wells, but most jurisdictions will not allow the use of private water or sewer systems when public systems are available. Clearly, this issue is something that you must address fully before cementing your costs for construction. I strongly suggest that you have your experts look into the matter for you.

# Flood Zones, Wetlands, and Other Deal-Stoppers

F lood zones, wetlands, and other deal-stoppers can be a developer's worst nightmare. There are simply some elements of land that can't be worked around. Developers who buy land without adequate research can wind up in deep financial trouble. I guess I've been lucky. While I've come very close to being devastated by land problems, I've never taken a direct hit. Even so, I have lost money that I hadn't planned on spending because of land elements. Developers who deal with environmental issues have to be able to take a lot of heat and maintain their cool.

Most developers shy away from anything that might be close to an environmental issue, but there are some who have no fear. Then there are those who are willing to walk the line and hope that they don't get too close to the edge. Over the years, I have done my share of line walking and I've known some developers who have shown total disregard to environmental laws.

Personally, I have a great respect for environmental issues. There isn't enough money to make me destroy natural resources that should be protected. When I say that I've worked the edge, I simply mean that I've built in areas where I've taken heat and been proved to be in the right. The last house I built for myself is an example of such a situation and it's a good example of how even careful builders and developers can wind up in hot water, so let me tell you a little about it.

I bought 25 acres of land to build my personal home on. The 7 acres on which I chose to build fronted on a small river. The river was in view of the home location, but I couldn't see any flood risk or wetlands issues. However, to be safe, I asked the Department of Environmental Protection (DEP) to inspect the site. A representative from the DEP came out and assured me that there was no threat to the river or the wetlands from my proposed construction. My next step was to have the local building inspector come out for a site visit.

The local building inspector assured me that the land was fine to build on and that getting a building permit would not be a problem, subject to a soils test. I had a soils test done and it was fine. Everything seemed to be fine. Once I was convinced that the deal was safe, I removed all contingencies from my purchase contract and bought the land. A few weeks later, when I applied for my building permit, the permit application was denied. The reason I was given was that the lot was not a legal building lot. I was told that it was an illegal subdivision of a larger parcel. A few weeks ago I had been told that the lot was fine, and all of a sudden, I was in a world of trouble.

Without detailing all of the steps required, I went to the zoning board. The next step was the local board of appeals. My attorney and I had done exhaustive research to prove that the town was wrong in their opinion of the land status. Long story short: I won my appeal and got my building permit. Now I'd done everything reasonable to make sure that the parcel was an approved building lot and still ran into roadblocks. Because of my experience, knowledge, and persistence, I won. If I had been an average home buyer I might have given up.

After the fiasco of the building permit I thought that my troubles were over, and they were, for a while. When I financed the home, I got a construction loan that would convert to a permanent mortgage. The house was finished and the permanent mortgage went into effect. After several months I decided to refinance the loan for a better interest rate. When I did, another problem came up. The bank told me that the house was built in a flood zone. I was shocked and didn't believe it. A survey crew was sent out by the bank.

The bank's survey crew told me that the house was "probably" in the flood zone. I looked into getting flood insurance and found that since the town where my home was located didn't participate in the flood program that I could not get flood insurance. I was steamed. Then I found out that I couldn't sue the town since they were not insured and that a legal tort protected such towns. Things were going from bad to worse.

I was in jeopardy of not being able to get my new loan. Both the new bank and the old bank were on my case. I hired a surveyor who just happened to be on the town council to do a full survey of not only my land but of the entire river area. It was very expensive, but it proved that my house was not in danger of flooding. This resolved the issue for good. My expense was considerable and the mental anguish was extreme, but I won. All of this fighting should have been unnecessary. The land I bought was not a problem piece, but it turned into one.

As you can tell from my personal story, even experienced builders and developers can do all that is reasonable to do and still wind up in a mess. You might just imagine what could happen to a developer who was careless. Environmental issues are a big factor in land development, so let's get down to the nitty gritty.

## Working With Wetlands

Working with wetlands is a high-risk venture. Any land containing even a small section of wetlands is a potential time bomb for a developer. I've seen tiny frog ponds kill development deals. In fact, I can remember a piece of land where the mere presence of ferns and cattails scared off a major developer. It doesn't take much to put a piece of property under the scrutiny of environmental concerns.

Several laws pertaining to environmental issues are on the books. There is a law that prohibits unauthorized obstruction or alteration of any navigable water. The law keeps developers from filling in such waters as well as excavating material from the waters. This is a serious situation and most developers respect it. Remember when I told you earlier that I knew of developers who had no respect for laws? Well, this particular law was violated by a developer I used to know. The developer filled in wetland areas for development. He did the fill fast and knew that he would be caught.

I had lunch with him after the fact and we discussed his actions. At the time, he was in deep legal trouble. His attitude at the time was that it was his land and that he would do what he wanted to with it. He told me that he had filled the wetland quickly so that the authorities would have to make him remove the fill, rather than stop him from placing the fill. The last I heard, the developer was juggling court dates and fighting his fight. Personally, I don't agree with what he did, but he did it.

Another law on the books has to do with the risk of discharging pollutants into navigable waters. Then there is the law that deals with the transportation of dredged materials headed for disposal in an ocean. One of the laws that impacts land developers most is the Emergency Wetlands Resources Act of 1986. This law ensures the conservation of wetland resources. Any wetland area can fall under multiple laws.

Any developer wishing to fill in a wetland area must apply for a permit. The permit application will be reviewed by both the U.S. Army Corps of Engineers (Corps) and the Environmental Protection Agency (EPA). Getting approval for such a fill request is unlikely. To obtain approval, you must demonstrate that you have no practicable alternatives to your filling of the wetlands. Further, you must prove that your fill will not cause significant damage to the aquatic ecosystem. The EPA have veto power over the Corps in such matters.

What is a wetland? You could probably get many answers to this question, but the definition given by the governing bodies is the definition that matters most. According to the environmental authorities a wetland area is an area that is inundated or saturated by surface or groundwater at a frequency and duration sufficient to support, and that under normal circumstances does support, a prevalence of vegetation typically adapted for life in saturated soil conditions. Wetlands generally include swamps, marshes, bogs, and similar areas. What you have just read is the official definition of a wetland, but don't assume that the definition given is all that there is to the matter. The interpretation of the definition can be broad, so you must be cautious.

Wetlands may be regulated by state, federal, and local agencies. Passing muster with one agency doesn't exempt you from the others. If you have any reason to believe that your project might fall into a wetland classification, you need to involve experts to remove any doubts or risks that might jump up in your face. If you violate a wetland regulation you may be responsible for either civil or criminal action against you. Trying to beat or cheat the system simply isn't worth the price you may have to pay.

There are many rules that apply to the disturbance of wetlands. If you have plans for clearing land, dredging areas, or filling sections of your development you will certainly trigger wetland regulations if the land falls under the wetland protection. Other activities can also put you in harm's way, so just don't do anything in any area where you might be nailed for a wetland infraction.

# Flood Areas

Flood areas are bad for developers. The benchmark for flood areas is usually the 100-year flood boundary. This is an area of land that has been flooded within the last 100 years. Most communities participate in a flood program that allows homeowners to acquire flood insurance at reasonable rates. Even at the reasonable rates, flood insurance is an expense that is not required for properties that are not considered to be at risk of flooding. If you create a development where flood insurance is required, selling the lots could be difficult. On the outside chance that you get caught up in a deal where flood insurance is needed but not available, you are in deep trouble.

Local authorities normally have flood maps available for inspection. However, the maps may be old and difficult to read. This is the problem that I ran into with my personal home. The flood maps were old and were not drawn in great detail. It took a detailed survey, which I had to pay for, to change the mind of the powers that be. Have your engineers establish local flood areas and make sure that your building sites are not in them.

# Hazardous Waste

Hazardous waste is a component of modern land developing that old-time developers didn't have to worry so much about. Times have changed, and hazardous waste is a serious consideration in modern development practices. The EPA offers a list of materials that are considered to be hazardous. Materials not listed may also be considered to be hazardous if they exhibit any of the following characteristics:

- Corrosivity
- Toxicity

- Reactivity

- Ignitability

If you become involved with hazardous wastes you may have a lot of hoops to jump through. The most innocent piece of property can harbor hidden waste and high cleanup costs. If you violate regulations pertaining to hazardous wastes, you could have to foot the bill for all cleanup costs, which will not be cheap. In addition to the cleanup costs, you could be hit with fines of up to $25,000 for each violation.

There is no way that I know of to be absolutely sure that a parcel of land might not be hiding hazardous waste. Research of past use of the land is about the best defense that you have. It is possible to do expensive scans of the property, but if general research doesn't raise any red flags there is probably no need for high-tech, expensive scans.

## Other Environmental Concerns

Other environmental concerns for developers could range from destroying natural habitat for an endangered species to erosion. The list of potential risks can be a long one. This is why you need to bring in an environmental expert to clear your project before you go too far in starting the developing process. Specialists can be expensive, but they are a real bargain if you compare the risks and costs of what could happen without them.

So far we have talked about hard-line environmental issues. The subjects covered to this point are dealt with under some form of legal protection. But there are other issues that you could face as a developer that are not so clearly defined in legal documents. Sometimes a developer's worst enemy is the public, and you might find yourself in some situation where public disapproval is your biggest drawback to a development.

## Angry Citizens

Angry citizens can be extremely difficult to deal with. Your development plans can meet all requirements, be signed off on and still fall into a trap that is hard to emerge from. I've had this happen on a small scale and I've known other developers who have dealt with the problems on a much larger scale. People don't always embrace new developments. While there may be no legal reason or way for the public to stop your development, the people can certainly make the profitability of your project suffer. Let me give you a few quick examples from my past that will highlight this facet of developing.

I bought some leftover lots in a subdivision to build on. The subdivision was several years old and residents had become accustomed to using the vacant lots for their own purposes, such as mulch disposal. When I bought the lots there was some distress that the vacant lots were about to grow houses. One neighboring resident was especially nasty about my company building in the area. The resident was rude to my workers and would not cooperate with us in any way. When I had surveyors stake the house out so that footings could be dug, the survey stakes came up missing the next day. I paid the surveyors to stake out the house again, and again the stakes were gone when the backhoe operator arrived the next morning. Finally, I paid a third time to have the house staked off and had the surveyors drive iron stakes below the ground level. The next morning I was on the site with my metal detector and found the stakes for the house corners. This problem cost me a few days and a few hundred dollars more for extra surveys, but I finally got the footings in. All in all, compared to some horror stories, my experience wasn't too bad.

I have know of developers who encountered many problems with developments due to unhappy neighbors. The types of problems ranged from people pouring sugar into the fuel tanks of heavy equipment to windows being broken out of houses on a regular basis. If the people near your land don't support your development plans you could run into expensive vandalism. While I have no first-hand knowledge of anyone forming a blockade or a physical protest on a project I have heard of such events.

If your project is approved and legal you have remedies against people who stand in your way, but that might be of little help in the real world. Calling the police daily or filing lawsuits robs you of development time. You may find it prudent to interview residents in the adjacent areas of your development to see if there will be any mass disapproval.

Land development is a business that can be plagued with problems. It is probably impossible to avoid all potential problems. However, with enough knowledge, experience, and research you can dodge most of the bullets. There are plenty of traps waiting for the unsuspecting developer, so keep your guard up and cover all of the bases that you can. Some problems are sure to slip through your defenses, but you can head most of them off with proper preparation.

# Location, Location, Location

Real estate professionals have long had a saying about the most important element in determining the value of real estate: The key to high value is location, location, and location. There is a lot of truth in the adage. Many old-time investors can be heard saying that they try to own the worst properties in the best neighborhoods. Land developers can prosper by cashing in on the right locations at bargain prices. But don't be fooled into thinking that every low price equates to a bargain. Bad land at any price is not a good buy. Developers have to weigh many factors when deciding what type of land to acquire and where to buy it.

The type of development that you wish to create will determine, to a large extent, the type of land that you will need. Your type of development will also indicate the various types of locations that may be suitable for the project. Land that is ideal for a medical complex might not be worth considering for a shopping center or a residential subdivision. Prices for land vary greatly depending on location, zoning, and other factors. Sometimes the best land bargain may be an expensive piece of property. Do you really care how much the land costs if you make a terrific profit? You could get in as much, or more, trouble, by purchasing cheap land as you would by investing in prime property at a premium price. However, you must work the numbers for each deal to determine what you should do.

The first step in choosing your land location is determining what your land needs are. If you plan to build a series of do-it-yourself car washes, you will want a location that is visible and where there is enough vehicular traffic to warrant the construction. Developing land for a group of private storage buildings could require a different type of land and location. For one thing, the storage facility might be suitable for land that doesn't have access to water and sewer services and that will not perk for private waste disposal. Land without water and sewer facilities would not work for a car wash, but it could work for the storage facility.

If your interest is in creating office space, you will most likely want land in an urban setting. Rural land might support some office space, but being closer to the city would probably be smarter. Much of the decision-making process is a matter of common sense. Some of the thought process is based on creative use of land. Money is always a consideration. And developers must know their market; this is where demographic studies come into play.

Would you be better off to build a complex of high-end condos near a subdivision of single-family homes or in an area where other condos have been built? More information is needed to answer this type of question. You can base a decision on your personal opinion, but if you want to make money consistently, you have to perform plenty of research. Getting to know your customers before you present them with something to buy is a major step toward becoming successful.

## Matching up Your Needs

Matching up your needs with available land is not difficult. Once you know what your land needs are, matching them to land that is available is simple. We discussed this in earlier chapters. But what happens when you find three parcels that all fit your criteria? How will you decide which parcel is your best bet? Comparing each piece and reviewing all available data on each parcel is the best way to refine your buying decision. Let's look at a short example of what you might face in a three-way comparison.

Assume that you want to build a development of Victorian homes. You want each home to be situated on lots that have a minimum of a quarter-acre in area. According to your research, the homes should have a minimum of three bedrooms and at least two bathrooms. Your plan calls for some larger homes, too, that will have four bedrooms and two and a half baths. The development plan that you have in mind calls for the development to be created in the shape of a semicircle. The street will be horseshoe-shaped and will serve all of the homes. Your plans are drawn and you want enough land to build at least 12 homes. Considering lot sizes, the subdivision street, and other land needs, you have determined that you need at least 7 acres of land. You know that you might get by with a little less acreage and you wouldn't mind having a little more, but your plan indicates that 7 acres is likely to be the best size for your development.

After doing some research, you find three parcels of land that might work for your development. All three parcels have water and sewer hookups available. The size of each parcel is within your guidelines, but Parcel 1 has more rolling land than the other two parcels do, and this could increase development cost. Parcel 2 has very few trees, and this could reduce the value of the building lots. On the other hand, the lack of trees would reduce the cost of clearing the building lots. So far, Parcel 3 seems like the best choice.

The prices of all three parcels are similar, with Parcel 3 being the most expensive by about $5000. Parcel 1 is the cheapest piece. In terms of land for development, the price differences between the parcels is not really enough to throw much weight in either direction. You know that you will have to base your buying decision on other factors.

You will be building Victorian homes for families. Most home buyers will have or will be planning to have children. You can use demographic reports to profile your buyers (Figs. 17.1 and 17.2). This prompts you to look into the proximity of schools and playgrounds. You also check to see what types of medical facilities are nearby. Then you check out the day-care facilities. Parcel 3, your first choice, doesn't fare well when compared to the other two parcels with kids' issues being a measuring stick. Parcel 1 appears to have the most conveniences to offer parents. Parcel 3 would be great for retirement housing, but there is not much in the area to offer children and their parents. This causes you to rule out Parcel 3.

Now you are down to two parcels of similar price. One has rolling land and the other has very few trees. When you look more closely at

## U.S. Census Bureau

### Housing Vacancy Survey
### First Quarter 1999

Table 7.  Homeownership Rates by Age of Householder:
First Quarter 1999 and 1999

| Age of householder | First Quarter 1999 | First Quarter 1998 | Standard error on 1999 rate | Standard error on difference |
|---|---|---|---|---|
| United States.............. | 66.7 | 65.9 | 0.2 | 0.2 |
| Less than 25 years..... | 18.4 | 17.5 | 0.6 | 0.8 |
| 25 to 29 years......... | 36.6 | 36.4 | 0.6 | 0.9 |
| 30 to 34 years......... | 53.5 | 52.8 | 0.6 | 0.8 |
| 35 to 39 years......... | 64.1 | 62.4 | 0.5 | 0.7 |
| 40 to 44 years......... | 69.7 | 69.4 | 0.5 | 0.7 |
| 45 to 49 years......... | 74.4 | 74.1 | 0.5 | 0.7 |
| 50 to 54 years......... | 78.3 | 78.0 | 0.5 | 0.7 |
| 55 to 59 years......... | 80.9 | 79.0 | 0.6 | 0.8 |
| 60 to 64 years......... | 81.4 | 81.8 | 0.6 | 0.8 |
| 65 to 69 years......... | 83.2 | 81.8 | 0.6 | 0.8 |
| 70 to 74 years......... | 82.1 | 82.9 | 0.6 | 0.9 |
| 75 years and over...... | 76.6 | 75.6 | 0.5 | 0.7 |
| Less than 35 years... | 39.4 | 39.0 | 0.4 | 0.5 |
| 35 to 44 years....... | 67.0 | 65.9 | 0.4 | 0.5 |
| 45 to 54 years....... | 76.2 | 75.9 | 0.4 | 0.5 |
| 55 to 64 years....... | 81.1 | 80.3 | 0.4 | 0.6 |
| 65 years and over.... | 79.8 | 79.1 | 0.3 | 0.5 |

**FIGURE 17.1**

Housing vacancy survey.

the two parcels you notice something about Parcel 2 that you had not paid attention to before. With your horseshoe street you need enough road frontage to have your street connect to the main street in two places. As you scale out the road frontage and compare it to your needs you see that there is not enough road frontage with Parcel 2. This new information kills this deal and points you back to Parcel 1.

After more consideration, you decide to buy Parcel 1. The rolling land will make construction a bit more expensive, but the appearance of the homes will benefit from the different elevations. More importantly, the parcel fits all of your needs for success. As it turns out, Parcel 1 is the least expensive piece of land you were considering and it was also the best piece of land for your needs. Sometimes things work out this way.

You don't have to buy the most expensive land on the market to get good land. But you must be willing to pay enough to ensure that you are getting land that will give you good odds for success in your development plans. Demographics can be a big help in deciding what land locations are suitable for your development. The example used above showed an impact of demographics. Knowing that your home buyers either had or would have children helped you to pinpoint your land needs better.

## Demographics

Demographics is the statistical study of populations (Fig. 17.3). A demographic study can be fairly simple, maybe just the number of males versus the number of females in a town, or quite complex. Items that might be determined in a complex study might include the age of the population, income, family status, level of education, and so forth. Developers can use demographic data to determine what types of developments are most likely to be successful.

Let's say that you are planning to build a community of condominiums. How many bedrooms should the units have in them? Rule-of-thumb planning would indicate that three-bedroom units will attract the most interest. This may be true, but will your target market be able to afford three-bedroom units? You need to know what your buyers are likely to want and what they are probably able to afford. It might be determined that your complex of condos should offer one-bedroom units at lower prices to coincide with your buying public. Maybe you should offer loft units as an option. To know what to build, you have to know what people in the area will want and what they can afford to pay. This type of information comes from demographic studies.

Demographic studies may be developed by local or state agencies. To get refined, detailed studies you may have to hire a research firm to conduct a survey specific to the information that you are in search of. Looking around an area might be all that you have to do. By observing the cars, the age of people, and the other housing in an area, you can make assumptions. But we all know that assumptions can be dangerous. Developers who are working with large projects can afford to pay

# U.S. Census Bureau

## Survey of Market Absorption
## Fourth Quarter 1998

Table 5. Absorption Rates of Condominium and Cooperative Apartments:
       1992 to 1998
(Buildings with five units or more. Percents are computed using
unrounded data)

| Quarter of completion | Total condominium and cooperative apartments completed | Standard error* | Percent of all units in buildings with 5 or more units | Standard error* |
|---|---|---|---|---|
| **1998** | | | | |
| July-September\p | 9,800 | 2,600 | 13 | 3.4 |
| April-June | \r6,800 | 890 | 10 | 1.5 |
| January-March | \r7,300 | 1,540 | 13 | 2.5 |
| **1997** | | | | |
| October-December | 9,800 | 2,290 | 13 | 3.1 |
| July-September | 7,400 | 1,560 | 11 | 2.5 |
| April-June | 9,200 | 1,690 | 16 | 3.0 |
| January-March | 9,500 | 2,540 | 19 | 4.3 |
| **1996** | | | | |
| October-December | 14,200 | 4,020 | 23 | 6.4 |
| July-September | 10,600 | 1,540 | 15 | 2.1 |
| April-June | 6,400 | 850 | 10 | 1.7 |
| January-March | 5,600 | 840 | 11 | 1.8 |
| **1995** | | | | |
| October-December | 9,400 | 1,790 | 16 | 3.1 |
| July-September | 10,100 | 1,290 | 16 | 2.0 |
| April-June | 9,600 | 1,750 | 19 | 3.3 |
| January-March | 7,200 | 1,190 | 20 | 3.3 |
| **1994** | | | | |
| October-December | 8,200 | 1,460 | 17 | 3.4 |
| July-September | 8,300 | 1,110 | 18 | 3.2 |
| April-June | 9,200 | 1,970 | 25 | 5.4 |
| January-March | 8,800 | 1,450 | 36 | 4.6 |
| **1993** | | | | |
| October-December | 9,500 | 1,410 | 30 | 4.8 |
| July-September | 7,000 | 870 | 21 | 4.0 |
| April-June | 8,500 | 1,140 | 27 | 4.2 |
| January-March | 7,000 | 1,140 | 25 | 4.3 |
| **1992** | | | | |
| October-December | 7,900 | 1,170 | 19 | 3.0 |
| July-September | 8,200 | 1,280 | 19 | 3.1 |
| April-June | 7,200 | 2,120 | 19 | 5.5 |
| January-March | 7,800 | 950 | 24 | 3.1 |

**FIGURE 17.2**

Absorption rates of condominium and cooperative apartments from 1992 to 1998.

| Quarter of completion | Percent absorbed within- | | | |
| | 3 months | | 6 months | |
| | Percent | Standard error* | Percent | Standard error* |
|---|---|---|---|---|
| **1998** | | | | |
| July-September\p | 72 | 13.6 | (NA) | (NA) |
| April-June | \r82 | 3.4 | 92 | 1.7 |
| January-March | 81 | 4.6 | 91 | 1.9 |
| **1997** | | | | |
| October-December | 86 | 2.6 | 93 | 1.6 |
| July-September | 74 | 5.1 | 94 | 1.1 |
| April-June | 84 | 3.6 | 92 | 1.8 |
| January-March | 76 | 7.8 | 89 | 5.6 |
| **1996** | | | | |
| October-December | 90 | 2.8 | 95 | 1.7 |
| July-September | 71 | 3.4 | 83 | 2.4 |
| April-June | 80 | 4.6 | 91 | 1.3 |
| January-March | 76 | 2.3 | 88 | 1.4 |
| **1995** | | | | |
| October-December | 83 | 3.0 | 90 | 2.2 |
| July-September | 77 | 4.4 | 87 | 2.7 |
| April-June | 69 | 4.9 | 79 | 6.4 |
| January-March | 66 | 9.1 | 76 | 9.0 |
| **1994** | | | | |
| October-December | 73 | 4.5 | 86 | 2.8 |
| July-September | 72 | 2.7 | 83 | 5.7 |
| April-June | 79 | 2.9 | 88 | 2.4 |
| January-March | 82 | 3.2 | 89 | 2.2 |
| **1993** | | | | |
| October-December | 83 | 2.9 | 92 | 1.4 |
| July-September | 68 | 7.5 | 75 | 6.3 |
| April-June | 76 | 2.4 | 85 | 2.4 |
| January-March | 76 | 2.6 | 86 | 2.4 |
| **1992** | | | | |
| October-December | 71 | 1.8 | 83 | 1.6 |
| July-September | 71 | 2.8 | 85 | 1.9 |
| April-June | 69 | 5.5 | 82 | 3.5 |
| January-March | 64 | 2.4 | 74 | 2.0 |

| Quarter of completion | Percent absorbed within- | | | |
| | 9 months | | 12 months | |
| | Percent | Standard error* | Percent | Standard error* |
|---|---|---|---|---|
| **1998** | | | | |
| July-September\p | (NA) | (NA) | (NA) | (NA) |
| April-June | (NA) | (NA) | (NA) | (NA) |
| January-March | 95 | 1.3 | (NA) | (NA) |

**FIGURE 17.2**

Absorption rates of condominium and cooperative apartments from 1992 to 1998.
(*Continued*)

| | | | | |
|---|---|---|---|---|
| **1997** | | | | |
| October-December | 96 | 0.9 | 97 | 0.6 |
| July-September | 97 | 0.7 | 98 | 0.5 |
| April-June | 94 | 1.5 | 97 | 0.8 |
| January-March | 93 | 4.4 | 94 | 4.0 |
| **1996** | | | | |
| October-December | 96 | 1.3 | 99 | (Z) |
| July-September | 92 | 1.6 | 95 | 0.7 |
| April-June | 95 | 1.0 | 96 | 0.9 |
| January-March | 92 | 1.2 | 94 | 0.9 |
| **1995** | | | | |
| October-December | 93 | 1.7 | 94 | 1.6 |
| July-September | 92 | 2.3 | 96 | 0.9 |
| April-June | 87 | 4.9 | 90 | 4.7 |
| January-March | 82 | 9.7 | 86 | 10.0 |
| **1994** | | | | |
| October-December | 91 | 2.3 | 94 | 2.1 |
| July-September | 88 | 5.3 | 90 | 4.9 |
| April-June | 92 | 2.4 | 94 | 1.5 |
| January-March | 92 | 1.4 | 94 | 0.9 |
| **1993** | | | | |
| October-December | 95 | 0.9 | 97 | 0.7 |
| July-September | 81 | 6.8 | 85 | 7.0 |
| April-June | 89 | 2.0 | 93 | 0.9 |
| January-March | 93 | 1.3 | 95 | 1.0 |
| **1992** | | | | |
| October-December | 90 | 1.1 | 93 | 1.0 |
| July-September | 91 | 1.2 | 93 | 1.1 |
| April-June | 87 | 3.3 | 89 | 2.6 |
| January-March | 80 | 2.1 | 84 | 1.8 |

\* One standard error (68-percent confidence interval)
NA Not available.  p Preliminary.  r Revised.
Z Fewer than 50 units or less than one-half of one percent.

**FIGURE 17.2**

Absorption rates of condominium and cooperative apartments from 1992 to 1998. (*Continued*)

for detailed, personalized studies. Small developers may not have a budget for such a study.

If you are on a tight budget and can't afford a customized study, you still have options. Check with your local town or city offices to see if any census or demographic studies are available. Contact real estate agencies and see if they will share any demographic information with you. Real estate appraisers also may be able to provide you with demographic data. If you are working on a project that is noncompetitive with other developers in your area, you might get some demographic details from the other developers. While some of these sources may charge you something for the information, the cost will probably be much lower than it would be if you commissioned your own study.

In order for demographic studies to be of value they must address the issues that you are interested in. For example, if you are planning to create a golf course community, you will be investing a lot of money in the golf course. The recreational opportunity should add considerable value to the development, but will people in the area be interested in living around a golf course? Will they be able to pay the higher cost for such housing? You need to know the answers to these questions before you build a golf course. A demographic study can give you the answers.

Let's say that you are thinking of developing land for the construction of professional office space. Will the area support the new offices? Researching this type of question can be easier than figuring out if a golf course is a viable amenity to a housing project. Get on the phone and call rental agencies. See if they have regular requests for professional office space. Ask if there is more demand for space than there is space available. Don't rely completely on the results of your phone calls, but keep notes on your findings. You can try other types of research to complement your phone calls. For example, maybe you should run a few ads in the local newspaper offering free information on a coming development of professional office space. If you get very few responses you should be nervous about your plans. But if you are flooded with requests for brochures you should feel pretty good about your plans.

Straight demographic reports are easy to interpret. Most small developers use many types of studies to determine how well their developments might work out. Your engineers should be able to provide you with substantial demographic data. I've hired people to sit down for hours at a time and make phone calls to interview people about what they would like in a new development. Cold calling people can be a waste of time, but sometimes the information received is worth the time and expense. Most developers experiment with different means of gathering information until they hit on procedures that work best for their individual needs.

## U.S. Census Bureau

### Housing Vacancies and Homeownership
### Historical Tables

Table 11A.  Median asking Rent for the U.S. and Regions:  1988 to Present

Median Rent (dollars)

| | U.S. Total | Northeast | Midwest | South | West |
|---|---|---|---|---|---|
| **1988** | | | | | |
| 1st Qtr | 330 | 416 | 300 | 303 | 390 |
| 2nd Qtr | 344 | 406 | 304 | 317 | 431 |
| 3rd Qtr | 347 | 420 | 304 | 308 | 429 |
| 4th Qtr | 350 | 424 | 297 | 316 | 476 |
| Annual | 343 | 417 | 301 | 311 | 428 |
| **1989** | | | | | |
| 1st Qtr | 345 | 437 | 300 | 314 | 419 |
| 2nd Qtr | 358 | 447 | 331 | 312 | 456 |
| 3rd Qtr | 355 | 445 | 325 | 315 | 468 |
| 4th Qtr | 370 | 483 | 334 | 317 | 474 |
| Annual | 358 | 459 | 320 | 316 | 456 |
| **1989/r** | | | | | |
| 1st Qtr | 331 | 440 | 297 | 299 | 410 |
| 2nd Qtr | 344 | 442 | 297 | 298 | 458 |
| 3rd Qtr | 345 | 457 | 298 | 308 | 465 |
| 4th Qtr | 358 | 477 | 324 | 309 | 450 |
| Annual | 346 | 453 | 304 | 304 | 444 |
| **1990** | | | | | |
| 1st Qtr | 368 | 475 | 336 | 309 | 511 |
| 2nd Qtr | 363 | 456 | 305 | 312 | 497 |
| 3rd Qtr | 374 | 518 | 316 | 329 | 455 |
| 4th Qtr | 380 | 499 | 320 | 325 | 525 |
| Annual | 371 | 487 | 319 | 318 | 500 |
| **1991** | | | | | |
| 1st Qtr | 385 | 522 | 337 | 325 | 509 |
| 2nd Qtr | 395 | 476 | 356 | 353 | 508 |
| 3rd Qtr | 402 | 487 | 314 | 354 | 516 |
| 4th Qtr | 414 | 504 | 346 | 357 | 556 |
| Annual | 398 | 498 | 339 | 347 | 523 |
| **1992** | | | | | |
| 1st Qtr | 401 | 469 | 338 | 344 | 505 |
| 2nd Qtr | 404 | 489 | 349 | 347 | 518 |
| 3rd Qtr | 409 | 479 | 348 | 359 | 528 |
| 4th Qtr | 430 | 482 | 352 | 366 | 571 |

**FIGURE 17.3**

A statistical study.

| | | | | | |
|---|---|---|---|---|---|
| Annual | 411 | 476 | 347 | 354 | 533 |
| **1993** | | | | | |
| 1st Qtr | 422 | 473 | 365 | 367 | 529 |
| 2nd Qtr | 436 | 502 | 361 | 387 | 539 |
| 3rd Qtr | 427 | 480 | 351 | 362 | 563 |
| 4th Qtr | 444 | 482 | 363 | 377 | 559 |
| Annual | 431 | 483 | 360 | 372 | 548 |
| **1993/r** | | | | | |
| 1st Qtr | 420 | 473 | 367 | 363 | 526 |
| 2nd Qtr | 435 | 502 | 361 | 385 | 536 |
| 3rd Qtr | 426 | 480 | 351 | 361 | 562 |
| 4th Qtr | 444 | 482 | 363 | 375 | 562 |
| Annual | 430 | 483 | 360 | 370 | 547 |
| **1994** | | | | | |
| 1st Qtr | 431 | 481 | 362 | 377 | 544 |
| 2nd Qtr | 430 | 478 | 363 | 379 | 531 |
| 3rd Qtr | 425 | 445 | 369 | 363 | 529 |
| 4th Qtr | 427 | 462 | 372 | 380 | 551 |
| Annual | 429 | 467 | 367 | 375 | 536 |
| **1995** | | | | | |
| 1st Qtr | 433 | 510 | 364 | 385 | 539 |
| 2nd Qtr | 419 | 436 | 351 | 386 | 540 |
| 3rd Qtr | 437 | 486 | 387 | 390 | 537 |
| 4th Qtr | 445 | 441 | 390 | 413 | 550 |
| Annual | 438 | 473 | 371 | 393 | 541 |
| **1996** | | | | | |
| 1st Qtr | 428 | 434 | 387 | 402 | 524 |
| 2nd Qtr | 435 | 454 | 365 | 409 | 535 |
| 3rd Qtr | 449 | 476 | 371 | 422 | 536 |
| 4th Qtr | 458 | 470 | 383 | 441 | 547 |
| Annual | 444 | 457 | 377 | 417 | 535 |
| **1997** | | | | | |
| 1st Qtr | 436 | 488 | 381 | 396 | 535 |
| 2nd Qtr | 431 | 450 | 380 | 401 | 539 |
| 3rd Qtr | 448 | 496 | 375 | 408 | 522 |
| 4th Qtr | 455 | 516 | 395 | 411 | 543 |
| **1998** | | | | | |
| 1st Qtr | 457 | 495 | 414 | 410 | 554 |
| 2nd Qtr | 452 | 494 | 409 | 405 | 551 |
| 3rd Qtr | 463 | 525 | 389 | 426 | 547 |
| 4th Qtr | 466 | 521 | 417 | 435 | 559 |
| **1999** | | | | | |
| 1st Qtr | 444 | 509 | 397 | 406 | 563 |

Table 11B.  Median Asking Sales Price for the U.S. and Regions: 1988 to Present

**FIGURE 17.3**

A statistical study. (*Continued*)

Median Sales Price (dollars)

| | U.S. Total | Northeast | Midwest | South | West |
|---|---|---|---|---|---|
| **1988** | | | | | |
| 1st Qtr | 57,000 | 136,700 | 38,000 | 52,200 | 79,200 |
| 2nd Qtr | 63,500 | 124,000 | 44,500 | 56,300 | 91,100 |
| 3rd Qtr | 60,300 | 114,000 | 38,400 | 58,500 | 74,400 |
| 4th Qtr | 59,100 | 125,000 | 32,100 | 57,200 | 73,900 |
| Annual | 59,200 | 124,500 | 38,100 | 56,400 | 81,300 |
| **1989** | | | | | |
| 1st Qtr | 61,600 | 108,100 | 40,100 | 59,300 | 70,700 |
| 2nd Qtr | 64,300 | 108,900 | 42,600 | 62,600 | 73,200 |
| 3rd Qtr | 57,600 | 119,700 | 41,200 | 53,500 | 71,600 |
| 4th Qtr | 57,400 | 115,800 | 34,400 | 59,200 | 85,900 |
| Annual | 59,500 | 108,100 | 36,800 | 57,900 | 72,700 |
| **1989/r** | | | | | |
| 1st Qtr | 55,700 | 95,600 | 37,800 | 55,200 | 59,500 |
| 2nd Qtr | 56,000 | 93,900 | 32,200 | 53,200 | 67,100 |
| 3rd Qtr | 53,300 | 116,800 | 32,600 | 49,800 | 63,600 |
| 4th Qtr | 51,900 | 113,600 | 32,300 | 52,100 | 68,200 |
| Annual | 54,200 | 102,400 | 33,100 | 52,300 | 64,600 |
| **1990** | | | | | |
| 1st Qtr | 48,900 | 97,700 | 33,500 | 41,900 | 100,100 |
| 2nd Qtr | 65,900 | 112,300 | 39,300 | 49,500 | 131,800 |
| 3rd Qtr | 69,000 | 125,900 | 42,900 | 56,600 | 120,700 |
| 4th Qtr | 64,600 | 103,600 | 41,900 | 52,500 | 127,500 |
| Annual | 62,700 | 109,900 | 39,200 | 50,400 | 120,500 |
| **1991** | | | | | |
| 1st Qtr | 68,700 | 99,300 | 48,500 | 54,100 | 125,700 |
| 2nd Qtr | 65,000 | 115,700 | 46,300 | 51,300 | 105,600 |
| 3rd Qtr | 58,600 | 73,600 | 47,000 | 46,100 | 99,800 |
| 4th Qtr | 63,700 | 109,900 | 51,400 | 50,600 | 137,400 |
| Annual | 63,700 | 101,600 | 48,300 | 49,700 | 120,900 |
| **1992** | | | | | |
| 1st Qtr | 68,700 | 102,000 | 47,300 | 52,000 | 133,500 |
| 2nd Qtr | 72,500 | 97,400 | 33,900 | 59,700 | 153,700 |
| 3rd Qtr | 75,200 | 99,300 | 43,500 | 57,200 | 123,100 |
| 4th Qtr | 76,800 | 91,500 | 41,200 | 63,200 | 133,300 |
| Annual | 73,300 | 96,800 | 41,500 | 57,700 | 134,900 |
| **1993** | | | | | |
| 1st Qtr | 72,600 | 101,600 | 49,800 | 60,500 | 135,700 |
| 2nd Qtr | 70,300 | 99,500 | 42,700 | 61,800 | 119,000 |
| 3rd Qtr | 67,300 | 91,200 | 46,800 | 54,400 | 122,300 |
| 4th Qtr | 69,400 | 107,900 | 48,500 | 57,700 | 124,200 |
| Annual | 69,900 | 99,700 | 46,900 | 58,600 | 125,800 |
| **1993/r** | | | | | |
| 1st Qtr | 71,500 | 102,700 | 50,500 | 63,500 | 135,300 |

**FIGURE 17.3**

A statistical study. (*Continued*)

| | | | | | |
|---|---|---|---|---|---|
| 2nd Qtr | 70,200 | 99,600 | 42,700 | 62,000 | 118,000 |
| 3rd Qtr | 67,200 | 91,400 | 46,800 | 54,400 | 121,200 |
| 4th Qtr | 69,200 | 107,700 | 48,100 | 57,600 | 124,000 |
| Annual | 69,600 | 99,900 | 46,900 | 59,800 | 124,900 |
| **1994** | | | | | |
| 1st Qtr | 77,300 | 113,900 | 49,800 | 67,300 | 104,600 |
| 2nd Qtr | 69,300 | 110,000 | 49,800 | 61,600 | 107,200 |
| 3rd Qtr | 70,700 | 98,400 | 47,600 | 63,400 | 114,600 |
| 4th Qtr | 72,800 | 108,600 | 61,200 | 61,900 | 98,200 |
| Annual | 72,200 | 107,100 | 51,000 | 63,200 | 105,100 |
| **1995** | | | | | |
| 1st Qtr | 77,800 | 100,000 | 55,400 | 65,200 | 143,200 |
| 2nd Qtr | 79,900 | 90,100 | 57,800 | 70,200 | 138,100 |
| 3rd Qtr | 77,200 | 107,000 | 65,500 | 64,700 | 100,000 |
| 4th Qtr | 75,200 | 114,100 | 65,700 | 62,200 | 119,100 |
| Annual | 77,500 | 102,600 | 61,400 | 65,400 | 128,300 |
| **1996** | | | | | |
| 1st Qtr | 80,600 | 93,300 | 69,600 | 67,500 | 128,600 |
| 2nd Qtr | 79,300 | 112,800 | 67,700 | 68,400 | 108,900 |
| 3rd Qtr | 82,800 | 98,200 | 62,000 | 72,300 | 123,200 |
| 4th Qtr | 81,500 | 92,400 | 63,600 | 71,500 | 123,100 |
| Annual | 81,200 | 95,700 | 66,800 | 70,300 | 121,900 |
| **1997** | | | | | |
| 1st Qtr | 87,900 | 117,200 | 86,400 | 73,900 | 110,300 |
| 2nd Qtr | 88,600 | 101,700 | 72,000 | 81,500 | 116,200 |
| 3rd Qtr | 87,300 | 93,500 | 83,900 | 74.700 | 127,700 |
| 4th Qtr | 86,300 | 83,300 | 77,600 | 77,500 | 123,300 |
| **1998** | | | | | |
| 1st Qtr | 84,400 | 82,600 | 78,000 | 78,900 | 127,800 |
| 2nd Qtr | 85,600 | 96,100 | 73,500 | 78,500 | 121,300 |
| 3rd Qtr | 91,600 | 85,400 | 89,200 | 84,100 | 129,600 |
| 4th Qtr | 89,700 | 99,200 | 75,700 | 82,300 | 140,500 |
| **1999** | | | | | |
| 1st Qtr | 95,700 | 117,900 | 73,300 | 92,100 | 127,100 |

Source: Current Population Survey/Housing Vacancy Survey, Series H-111, Bureau of the Census, Washington DC 20233.

rRevised.

**FIGURE 17.3**

A statistical study. (*Continued*)

# Traffic Studies

Traffic studies are another form of research that can be important for some developers. For example, if you are planning to build a minimall it would be wise to know how much traffic passes your proposed site on a regular basis. Getting a traffic study done will not tell you everything you want to know, but it will give you an idea of the number of potential customers in a given area. Any type of retail development should benefit from having a traffic study done. You may be able to find some traffic reports through local agencies, but hiring an independent firm to conduct a study for you will most likely reveal the best data for you to work with.

Traffic studies can be done in different ways. The easiest way is to have a traffic counter installed. This is simply a piece of equipment that counts each vehicle that passes. The downside to this type of study is that you have no idea what types of vehicles are moving through the proposed area. Having a person on hand to watch traffic while the traffic counter records overall activity will give you a better description of the type of traffic that you will be dealing with. For example, if there is construction in the area and there are dozens upon dozens of dump trucks running back and forth, it could skew your numbers if no one was watching the traffic. A human spotter could note the high activity of repeat construction traffic.

Cutting corners on research is a bad move for land developers in most cases. Your research is your best tool in making wise development decisions. While the cost of professional studies will often run into thousands of dollars, the studies usually pay for themselves many times over.

## Proximity Research

Proximity research is an excellent way of matching a piece of property with your proposed buyers. Assuming that you have a general profile of your prospective buyers and what their needs and desires are, you can do your own proximity research. Assume that you are going to develop a tract of land for a miniature golf course. What will patrons of the golf course be interested in? Many of the customers will probably be playing golf with their children. Would having a pizza restaurant and a burger joint close by be an advantage? Sure it would. How about an ice cream shop? Yep. Making sure that food and drink are available is a good idea, unless your development is going to offer such services. Then you might prefer a place where such facilities were not so close by.

If you are developing a piece of inner-city land you might want to make sure that there is good public transportation close by. Many city dwellers rely on public transportation as the only means of mobility. If you are creating an office building in a city, parking could be a major concern. If you don't have enough land to facilitate the parking, how will you handle the overflow? Can you make a deal with a nearby parking garage? These are the types of things that you look carefully at as you pick and choose your properties.

Your marketing team, if you have one, should define your potential buyers. If you are wearing the marketing hat, you have to fulfill that function. Someone has to pinpoint the type of buyers that you are going to sell the development to. Once the target market is known, you can close in on what their needs and desires are likely to be. Once you figure out the trigger buttons that will influence someone to buy into your development, you go out and make sure that the needed elements are present. For example, if your marketing team says that you must have a grocery store within 1.5 miles of your project, find out if there is such a store. You can pay others to do proximity research or you can do it yourself. Once you know what you are looking for, there is no reason why you shouldn't be able to handle this phase of your planning personally.

## Failed Projects

Most developed areas have some projects that have failed. Some of the projects will have failed before they were ever completed. Others will have been built and then sputtered. You should look into all of the projects that have failed in the area where you are thinking of developing land. Looking at the past 5 years should be sufficient. Find out what failed and why it failed. You can learn a lot from the past, and no developer wants to see history repeat itself when it comes to a development going belly up. For all you know, the land that you are considering may be in a flood or earthquake zone (Fig. 17-4)

How will you get leads on projects that failed? Some of them will be obvious. They will be the ones that have been sitting vacant and deteriorating for the last year or so. Other projects are more difficult to spot. A consultation with an appraiser who works the area is one fast way of finding out what you want to know. Talking to real estate brokers is another way to look into failed projects. You could go back through old newspapers and public records, but this would take a lot of time, and talking to appraisers, brokers, and other developers will probably tell you what you need to know.

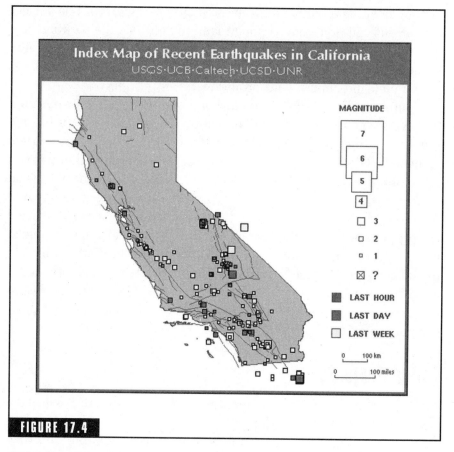

**FIGURE 17.4**

Earthquake map.

# Growth Status

The growth status of an area is always important and it can have a lot of influence on property values. There are three basic stages within which real estate is rated. There are areas that are in growth patterns. Some areas are stable. Other areas are declining. Another type of area that is not talked about as often is an area that is being revitalized. As you might imagine, you should stay out of declining areas.

Many inexperienced investors buy into stable areas. This can be okay, but it is not likely to produce fast profits and it could result in a loss. An area that is stable today could be declining in a year. Growth areas that are established are usually the best buys. Revitalization regions can also be very good, so long as the funding for the projects doesn't run out and sales are as expected.

Making money in real estate can be risky. Buying into new and unknown projects can be especially risky. But it is usually the unknown projects that produce the most profit in the least amount of time. Investors often buy investment properties, such as town houses, before they have been built. In the business, this is called buying in the dirt. With the right project, an investor can buy from blueprints and sell soon after construction is completed for a tidy profit. This, of course, assumes that the project is well received.

Developers prosper more quickly with investors who are willing to buy in the dirt. Getting contracts for homes that are not yet built makes it possible for developers to borrow against the contracts. Just as investors buy in the dirt in hopes of quick profits, developers sometimes buy on the fly in the same quest. Buying into the unknown is even more risky for developers than it is for investors who are speculating on housing sales. Developers take the first risks, and the biggest risks. You should strive to lower your risk by making sure that the land that you buy to develop is in the best location possible. Put in the time and the money required to reduce your risks.

# Plans and Specifications

Plans and specifications are a critical element of any development. The plans and specs start with the land and extend into construction. Land planners and engineers usually are the first on the team for creating plans and specifications for a development. Architects usually aren't far behind. Of course, not all developments are large enough to warrant the expense of so many professional planners. A small developer may buy stock house plans and have little more than a survey crew involved in general planning. The developer may create most specifications personally.

The degree of complexity for drawings can vary greatly. It could take several months to get a general development plan drawn. Even then there would probably be many alterations from time to time that would add to the total time for a completed plan. But, most jurisdictions require complete plans and specifications before code approval will be issued. Simple plans can work for small developments. A surveyor and some stock house plans might be all that you will need to get a project off the ground. On the other hand, if you are going after a major development, plan on months and months of planning.

# Many Layers

There can be many layers to a development plan. When complete plans and specifications are created for a development, they may contain a number of components. Scaled drawings are certainly one component of the process. Cross-sectional drawings are also a part of complete plans. Today's designers frequently rely on computer-aided drafting (CAD) programs to create computerized drawings. CAD programs open up a fast, new world for designers. Work that could take a team of architects months to accomplish manually can be done by a single designer in less time when a CAD system is used. Getting 3-D drawings is easy with CAD programs.

In addition to drawings, written specifications are needed for development projects. The specs can cover everything from fill materials to landscaping materials. Having detailed specifications is both important and impressive. Lenders like to see specifications that leave nothing to the imagination. To get a better idea of what to expect from professional plans and specs, let's take a professional package apart, layer by layer.

## Overview

The overview plan will show a wealth of information. Roads will be shown on an overview plan. Details of the roads will include centerlines, driving surfaces, shoulders, curb lines, and property lines. In addition to the roads for a development, an overview will plot the course of utilities. A detailed plan will show the location of power poles and underground utilities. Storm drainage routes should be listed on the overall plan. Locations for water and sewer pipes should also be drawn on the plan. Basically, all utilities and objects that may affect them, such as trees, should be shown on a plan view.

## Side Views

Side views are normally shown as a part of a development plan. These views could pertain to roads or the slope of land. Designers often refer to the side views as *profiles* or *profile plans*. Reference points must be established on the cross-sectional views. In the case of roads, the reference point is often the centerline of the road. The use of cross-sectional drawings is common in all types of land designs and architectural drawings.

Linear projects normally use cross sections that are drawn on 90° angles. When used with geometric plans, cross sections show only dimensions and slopes. Structural cross sections, however, show the types and depths of materials to be used in construction. There are many reasons for having cross sections drawn.

Developers use cross-sectional drawings to calculate the demand of earthwork. The grading of land can be shown well with cross-sectional drawings. Renderings of cross sections can show developers how a section of land will look with different types of grading. With the use of computers, it can be fast and easy to see many different looks in a matter of minutes. The use of 3-D drawings makes it possible for designers and developers to lay out drainage patterns, slopes, and just about everything else in a development project before the first shovelful of dirt is moved.

## Detailed Pages

Detailed pages in a design plan often provide blowups of small details. Since plans are drawn to scale, small objects can be difficult to see and identify. But, when a detail cut is provided, the small object is drawn much larger. A typical scale for precision drawings is one where each quarter of an inch on the plan equals 1 foot. In other words, a line that represents a fence and that is 1 inch long would be equal to 4 feet of fencing.

Detail sections on master plans can be drawn as a plan, a profile, a cross section, or any other type of diagram that will be helpful. For example, a small picnic area on a master plan might be little more than a dot on a large piece of paper. To show how the picnic area should look, a detail would be included. Detail pages are used in all sorts of plans. Builders may see detail sheets that show how kitchen cabinets look or how a particular door might look.

## Cover Sheets

Cover sheets are a part of most plan packages. These sheets offer general information. Cover sheets are usually meant to provide a quick reference to a complete plan package. For example, a cover sheet could include such information as the name of a project, a basic description of the job, a table of contents for what is included in the full package, and so on.

In addition to cover sheets, an index sheet may be included in packages for larger projects. An index sheet for a large production plan is similar to the index of this book. Having an index makes it easy to locate specific elements of a plan. Detailed plans for large projects can involve what seems likes tons of paper. Having an index so that you can turn quickly to a particular place in the plan is very advantageous.

# Types of Plans

How many types of plans will you have to deal with as a developer? It depends largely on the type of projects that you are working with. A very simple development might be drawn on a single sheet of drafting paper. Or, you could have stacks of reports containing hundreds of pieces of paper in each report. If you have no other plan, you will have a master plan. In a small development, the master plan might only be a page or two long. Complex developments could have master plans created for individual components of a development. For example, you might have a master plan for sewer and water supplies and another master plan for roads. Then there could be a master plan for construction. Another master plan for storm drainage could be a part of your plan package.

Your overall master plan is the plan that will most likely be submitted for code approval. In some cases, code officials may require you to provide master plans for individual elements of a development. Since there are different code officials and different segments of regulations, each phase of the development may have to be approved by individual branches of the code enforcement system. Once all of the individual units are approved, the master plan may have to be approved on its own merit. You can think of the individual master plans as stepping stones toward gaining final approval of the master plan.

## A First Step

A first step toward the development process is a plan for altering present conditions. This plan is sometimes called a *demolition plan*. The name implies tearing something down, like a building, but it applies to other forms of demolition, such as excavation work. Think of a wooded parcel of land. Which trees will be saved and which ones will be removed? The removal of trees counts as demolition and should be shown on a demolition plan. Underground utilities are another concern when new development is scheduled. It is not in your best interest to demolish underground pipes, conduits, or cables.

Topo maps are normally used as a part of a demolition plan. Any existence of underground utilities must be marked clearly on a development plan. The person who creates your demo plan has a lot of responsibility. Having a contractor dig up a gas main could be disastrous. The depth of a demo map ranges in detail, but every demo map should be as complete as possible.

A common consideration in a demo plan is the effect that earthwork will have on adjacent properties and structures. For example, if digging will take place near a sidewalk, fence, or other structure, the structure should be shown on the plan, along with a safe distance for equipment to maintain between construction and the object. Detailed instructions might be provided on angles of excavation to protect adjoining structures, such as parking areas on neighboring land.

## A Grade Plan

A grade plan should be drawn to indicate what the finished grading of a project will look like. Some developers refer to grading plans as elevation plans. In addition to showing swales, slopes, and finished grades, a grading plan may show trench depths and compaction requirements. Rough grading plans should also be included on a grade plan. A typical grade plan will consist of many lines and measurements that will be used to arrive at the desired result when developers are working the earth.

## Utility Plans

Utility plans show the proposed or existing locations of all utilities on or planned to be on the site. Most modern utilities are run below ground in developments. It's important that the routing of utilities will not interfere with other development necessities. A detailed utility plan will show the proposed locations of all utility components, such as valves, junction boxes, relay boxes, transformers, and so forth. Detailed sections of a utility plan may produce a view of proposed trenches and how they are to be backfilled, and may even include cross-sectional cuts of the trench design and its proposed contents.

### Traffic

Traffic is a major concern with large developments. It's common for a separate traffic plan to be drawn for a development. Not all projects require a traffic plan. When a traffic plan is drawn, it may include such details as the location of traffic lights, guard rails, road edges, road shoulders, driving surfaces, hike/bike lanes, traffic patterns, road entrances to the main roadways, and so forth. It's normal for traffic plans to be reviewed by an appropriate agency to confirm that safety is sufficient in the design. Civil engineers usually create traffic plans and it's not unusual to find engineers who specialize in the design of traffic plans.

### Construction Plan

A construction plan will often be drawn to show proposed boundaries for building lots. These plans can show the placement of proposed construction. A developer's construction plan is not the same as a builder's plans and specifications. The developer's plan shows an overview of all construction for a development. In fact, the plan is often referred to as a *development plan*. The plan usually details all setback requirements that must be observed by builders.

All sorts of information can show up on a construction plan. Developers who have very strict covenants and restrictions may indicate on a construction plan any number of design requirements for a house built on a particular lot. For example, one lot may be labeled for the construction of a colonial-style home with brown siding and a black roof. Construction plans from developers don't usually get this specific, but they can. Builders can refer to construction plans to aid in their decision of which lots to buy and build on.

## Building Plans and Specifications

Building plans and specifications may be a required part of an overall development plan. Developers often call building plans *improvement plans*. A developer may not be able to gain approval for a development project if the master plan doesn't include an improvement plan. Some developers create their own improvement plans while others work closely with builders to establish a building plan. Someone has to provide blueprints of structures to be built and complete specifications for all elements of the construction process.

Blueprints for building plans normally show front, rear, and side elevations of the structures to be built. Floor plans are also shown. Framing plans are included as a part of a standard set of blueprints. Depending on the type of project, there can be diagrams that show the routing of plumbing, heating, and electrical systems, as well as any other systems, such as fire protection systems. There will normally be detail plans showing roofing, sheathing, siding, and other elements of construction. Exterior plans will show parking areas, driveways, sidewalks, decks, porches, and similar items. Drainage plans for the structure should also be shown in the set of blueprints. A grading plan for the finished grade and landscaping around a building should also be a part of a builder's plan.

Specifications for construction should be very detailed. A plan should not call merely for wood siding. Instead, the plan might define cedar siding as being the material of choice. The type of roofing material to be used should be itemized within the specifications. It takes time to nail down all of the particulars of a construction project, but intricate specifications result in better projects that run more smoothly.

## Changes

Changes often occur once a project is under construction. Unforeseen problems pop up that require on-site changes. When these changes are needed, they should be reflected on an amended plan. For example, you might be having a sewer installed and run into bedrock that is not sensible to penetrate. If you turn the sewer to go around the rock, the change in direction should be reflected on the plans filed for your project. Failure to record such changes can create big problems later on if someone has to locate the sewer.

Some changes can be made at the developer's discretion. However, there are times when change must be approved by code officers or engineers. If you run into a problem on site, you should check with your experts to see if any major consideration should be given to the change before it is authorized. Even small alterations can have a ripple effect. Since most developers are not experts in all aspects of the projects that they create, depending on expert advice is the best bet.

# Cutting Costs

Cutting the costs of development is something that nearly every developer is interested in. There is nothing wrong with adding to your profit, so long as your means of doing so don't have a negative effect on your development. Good planners can often find ways to accomplish a goal in a less-expensive manner. It may be up to you to make a judgment call on whether a cost-cutting decision is worthwhile. Getting too picky on prices can be bad. There are times when trying to save a little money can cost you a lot of money. Let me give you an example of a cost-cutting method that could be used but normally shouldn't be.

Assume that you are developing a major development of town houses. The housing units have two full bathrooms in them. Many of the homes have full basements that may be finished into living space by homeowners at some later date. Since the proposed housing will have only two toilets in each unit, you are able to install sewers that have a 3-inch diameter. Since 3-inch pipe costs less than 4-inch pipe and since code will allow you to install the smaller sewer lines to the houses, it makes sense to run the smaller pipe. Or does it?

A 4-inch sewer can handle a large number of plumbing fixture units. This is also true of a 3-inch pipe. But, most local plumbing codes will not allow a 3-inch sewer to serve more than two toilets. A 4-inch sewer can take the discharge from far more toilets than what you would find in a house. Your project will meet code requirements with 3-inch building sewers. But what happens if a homeowner decides later to add a toilet in a finished basement? The unfortunate homeowner will have to pay to have the building sewer replaced with a larger pipe or will have to run a separate building sewer to the main sewer. Either option is expensive for the homeowner. This problem would be avoided if you install 4-inch building sewers during construction. Does saving a few dollars per house justify the inconvenience that you may be creating for future homeowners?

Let's say that you save $40 per house by using a 3-inch sewer. This adds up when you consider that you might be building 300 homes.

There are thousands of dollars to be saved by using the smaller pipe, and you will not be violating any building codes. But, what happens if several home buyers find out that they can't add another toilet and they make a lot of noise about it. You could get a reputation for being a cheapskate builder or developer. All of a sudden, the money you saved doesn't seem so great.

The example I've just given you is only one situation where you might have to make a personal judgment call. There can be many times during the planning of a development where you might be given opportunities to reduce development costs. Sometimes the savings can be made without risk of future problems. Something as simple as using a different type of foundation shrub might save you a lot of money and probably wouldn't offend anyone. You have to weigh the consequences of your actions. If you have doubts, talk to other builders and developers. Ask real estate brokers for their opinions. Make your decisions carefully and base them on research.

Once you have your plans completed, you can put them out to bids with contractors. This is a critical part of your profit-making procedure. Knowing how to work with contractors and subcontractors can make a huge difference in how much money you make or lose. So, let's go to the next chapter and explore the next step in your career as a land developer.

# Getting Development Bids

Getting development bids is a part of the development process that can result in more profit than you had hoped for. Experienced developers usually have a pretty good idea of what to expect in terms of contractor costs. There are always gaps to be filled in, but developers with several projects to their credit have a good feel for what costs are likely to run. New developers don't usually have this advantage. But in the end, the experienced investors don't always have the best angle. Sometimes rookie developers make the best deal when bargaining for services.

Some developers feel that putting a job out to bids is exciting, and it can be. When you start shopping for prices you have a chance to increase your profits. If you started into a deal with a certain amount of money budgeted for site work and you shave a few thousand off of your estimate, it's money in your pocket. There are developers who see the bidding process as one of the most important parts of land developing.

Independent contractors are frequently used during land development. It is rare to find a developer who has in-house people and equipment for site work. Bids range from prices for surveying work to prices for landscaping. Each phase of the development process offers an opportunity for extra income. But the money doesn't come without some work on the part of the developer. And the tables can be turned to where the bid process results in lost income. If you guesstimate a price for work and the job turns out to cost more, you are on the losing end. It could be said that getting bids is the gambling part of the project. Are you a good poker player? If you are, you just might make your mark on the spreadsheets.

Putting a job out to bids is not as simple as some people believe it is (Fig. 19.1). There are people who think that developers make a few phone calls and get all the prices that they need for a development project. This simply is not the case. Bidding a job out can be a lot of work, and it is certainly important work. There generally is no shortage of potential contractors to work with, but the quality of some contractors may be suspect. Developers must get more than prices (Fig. 19.2). They must get references and a sense of security about the contractors that they plan to work with.

Large developers often hire someone to solicit bids for them. It is usually their project manager. Smaller developers generally do the bidding work themselves. I've paid people to collect bids for me, but I've always maintained an active hand in reviewing the bids. And I can't recall a time when I authorized any work from anyone I had not met personally. Call it a quirk, if you like, but I believe it's important to meet the people who will be working with my company.

We talked much earlier about lining up your experts and giving them examples of the types of services that you would require. Getting bids from some experts is difficult. A lawyer might give you a ballpark figure for certain aspects of a job, such as running a title search, but most attorneys are going to bill their time out as they go. Engineers and others are also likely to work on a billable-time basis. Some experts, like surveyors, may give you some fixed prices to hang your hat on. It never hurts to ask for committed prices from your team of experts (Fig. 19.3), but don't be surprised if you can't get them. Estimates may be the best that you are able to get. Some contractors will try to get your work on a time-and-material basis. Personally, I would avoid time-and-material deals with contractors. It is in your best interest to have firm prices that you can depend on whenever you can get them. Contractors should be willing to give you firm quotes.

# Estimates Are Not Quotes

Estimates are not quotes. Generally speaking, estimates can prove to be worthless, since vendors are not normally required to honor them. Quotes, on the other hand, are firm prices that should be made part of a contract before work is started. Don't confuse estimates with quotes.

---

Your Company Name
Your Company Address
Your Company Phone and Fax Numbers

### LETTER SOLICITING BIDS FROM SUBCONTRACTORS

Date: _____

Subcontractor address: _____

_____

_____

Dear: _____

I am soliciting bids for the work listed below, and I would like to offer you the opportunity to participate in the bidding. If you are interested in giving quoted prices for the labor / material for this job,
please let me hear from you. The job will start _____. Financing has been arranged and the
job will be started on schedule. Your quote, if you choose to enter one, must be received no later
than _____.

The proposed work is as follows: _____

_____

_____

_____

Thank you for your time and consideration in this request.

Sincerely,

Your Name
Title

**FIGURE 19.1**

---

Form letter for soliciting bids from contractors.

Entering into a job with nothing more than estimates is risky business. Very few seasoned developers or contractors will do any business based on mere estimates. Quotes (Fig. 19.4) are almost always required. There are exceptions, of course, but quotes are the way to go.

---

Your Company Name

Your Company Address

Your Company Phone and Fax Numbers

**BID REQUEST**

Contractor's name: _____

Contractor's address: _____

Contractor's city/state/zip: _____

Contractor's phone number: _____

Job location: _____

Plans and specifications dated: _____

Bid requested from: _____

Type of work: _____

Description of material to be quoted: _____

_____

_____

All quotes to be based on attached plans and specifications. No substitutions allowed without written consent of customer.

Please provide quoted prices for the following: _____

_____

_____

_____

_____

All bids must be submitted by: _____

**FIGURE 19.2**

---

Bid request form.

Some special circumstances might warrant a time-and-material basis, but working without firm, committed prices is dangerous.

I've worked with contractors for some 23 years. During this time I've been a subcontractor, a general contractor, and a developer. If there is one rule that I have learned to live by during these years, it is to

---

**Your Company Name**
**Your Company Address**
**Your Company Phone and Fax Numbers**

**WORK ESTIMATE**

Date: _____

Customer name: _____

Customer address: _____

Customer phone number(s):_____

**DESCRIPTION OF WORK**

Your Company Name will supply all labor and material for the following work:

_____

_____

_____

_____

**PAYMENT FOR WORK**

Estimated price: _____ ($ _____)

Payable as follows: _____

_____

If you have any questions, please don't hesitate to call. Upon acceptance, a formal contract will be issued.

Respectfully submitted,

Your Name
Title

**FIGURE 19.3**

Work estimate.

always work with written contracts (Fig. 19.5) that clearly state firm prices. It is better for subcontractors and contractors to have an undisputed agreement between each other. Most of the problems that I've encountered over the years have come from confusion on issues that were not addressed in writing.

---

Your Company Name
Your Company Address
Your Company Phone and Fax Numbers

### QUOTE

This agreement, made this _____ day of _____, 19__, shall set forth the whole agreement, in its entirety, by and between Your Company Name, herein called Contractor, and _____, herein called Owners.

Job name: _____

Job location: _____

The Contractor and Owners agree to the following: Contractor shall perform all work as described below and provide all material to complete the work described below. Contractor shall supply all labor and material to complete the work according to the attached plans and specifications. The work shall include the following: _____

_____

_____

_____

_____

### SCHEDULE

The work described above shall begin within _____ days of notice from Owners, with an estimated start date of _____. The Contractor shall complete the above work in a professional and expedient manner within _____ days from the start date.

### PAYMENT SCHEDULE

Payment shall be made as follows: _____

_____

_____

This agreement, entered into on _____, shall constitute the whole agreement between Contractor and Owners.


_____          _____
Contractor                      Date          Owner                         Date


                                              _____
                                              Owner                         Date

**FIGURE 19.4**

Quote.

USDA-FmHA
Form FmHA 1924-6
(Rev. 8-93)

*Position* **6**

**CONSTRUCTION CONTRACT**

**FORM APPROVED**
**OMB NO. 0575-0042**

State _____

County _____

This Contract, made this _____ day of _____ , 1 9 — ,

by _____ of _____

(hereinafter called the "Owner"), and _____ of

_____ (hereinafter called the "Contractor").

WITNESSETH that the parties hereto agree as follows:

(A) The Contractor will furnish materials and perform the work for:

for the consideration of _____ dollars ($ _____ ),
in accordance with the "General Conditions" shown in this contract and the specifications and the drawings as follows:

(B)  The Contractor will start work by _____ , 1 9 _ _ , and will complete

the work by _____ , 19 ___ (See paragraph III of General Conditions).

(C)  The Owner will make payments as follows: (Check [ ] *proper payment clause and effectively xxxxxxxx out all of
the clauses not applicable.*)

☐ 1. ONE LUMP SUM will be made for the whole contract, upon acceptance by the owner and the Farmers Home Administration, of all work required hereunder and compliance by the contractor with all the terms and conditions of this contract.

☐ 2. PARTIAL PAYMENTS NOT TO EXCEED 60 PERCENT of the value of the work in place (less the aggregate of previous payments) will be made at intervals of_____. The value of work in place shall be as estimated by the contractor and approved by the Farmers Home Administration. Prior to receiving any partial payment, the contractor must furnish the owner with a statement showing the total amount owed to date for materials and labor procured under this contract and, if required by the owner or the Farmers Home Administration, must also submit evidence showing that previous partial payments were properly applied and that the current payment will be properly applied. Upon completion of the whole contract and acceptance of the work as required hereunder, by the owner and the Farmers Home Administration, and compliance by the contractor with all terms and conditions of this contract, the amount due the contractor will be paid.

☐ 3. PARTIAL PAYMENTS IN THE AMOUNT OF 90 PERCENT of the value of the work in place and of the value of the materials suitably stored at the site (less the aggregate of previous payments) will be made at intervals of_____ _____ . The value of the work and materials in place or on site shall be as estimated by the contractor and approved by the owner and the Farmers Home. Administration. Upon acceptance by the owner and the Farmers Home Administration of all work required hereunder, and compliance by the contractor with all terms and conditions of this contract, the amount due the contractor will be paid. The contractor shall, before the owner signs the contract, deliver to the owner a surety bond in the amount of the contract.

(D) The items described below (the Notice of Requirement for Affirmative Action to Ensure Equal Employment Opportunity required by Executive Order 11246, the Equal Opportunity Clause published at 41 CFR 60-1.4 (a) and (b), and the Standard Federal Equal Employment Opportunity Construction Contract Specifications required by Executive Order 11 246) apply, during the performance of this contract, if the contract exceeds $10,000 (This also includes subsequent loans and grants, or contract change orders made during the construction period of the original contract, which will cause the total to exceed $10,000.) to the following: (1) AN contractors or subcontractors who hold any Federal or federally assisted construction contract, (2) All grants, contracts and loans (direct, insured, or guaranteed) let by the FmHA, and (3) All construction work performed by construction contractors and subcontractors for Federal nonconstruction contractors and subcontractors if the construction work is necessary in whole or in part to the performance of a nonconstruction contract or subcontract. The items are applicable to all of a contractor's or subcontractor's employees who are en aged in "on site" construction including those construction employees who work on a non-Federal or non-federally assisted construction site. The items, however, will not pre-empt state and local government regulations of the construction industry, and will not relieve contractors and subcontractors of the obligations they may have under other affirmative action or equal opportunity programs.

**FIGURE 19.5**

**A construction contract.**

2

<u>NOTICE OF REQUIREMENT FOR AFFIRMATIVE ACTION TO ENSURE EQUAL EMPLOYMENT OPPORTUNITY</u> (Executive Order 11 246)

Date ————————————————City———————————————————————— DOL Region .................................

Goals and Timetables for WOMEN (Exhibit D, FmHA Instruction 1901-E)

| Timetable | Trade | Goal (o/o) |
|---|---|---|
| From 4-1-78 until 3-31-79 | All trades | 3.1 |
| From 4-1-79 until 3-31-80 | All trades | 5.1 |
| From 4-1-80 until 3-31-81 | All trades | 6.9 |

Goals and Timetables for ALL MINORITIES (Exhibit D, FmHA Instruction 1901-E)

### EQUAL OPPORTUNITY CLAUSE (41 CFR 60–1.4 (a) and (b))

(1) The contractor will not discriminate against any employee or applicant for employment because of race, color, religion, sex or national origin. The contractor will take affirmative action to ensure that applicants are employed, and that employees are treated during employment, without regard to their race, color, religion, sex or national origin. Such action shall include, but not be limited, to the following: employment, upgrading, demotion or transfer; recruitment or recruitment advertising; layoff or termination; rates of pay or other forms of compensation; and selection for training, including apprenticeship. The contractor agrees to post in conspicuous places, available to employees and applicants for employment, notices to be provided by the Farmers Home Administration setting forth the provisions of this nondiscrimination clause.

(2) The contractor will, in all solicitations or advertisements for employees placed by or on behalf of the contractor, state that all qualified applicants will receive consideration for employment without regard to race, color, religion, sex or national origin.

(3) The contractor will send to each labor union or representative of workers with which contractor has a collective bargaining agreement or other contract or understanding, a notice, to be provided by the Farmers Home Administration, advising the said labor union or workers' representative of the contractor's commitments under this agreement as required pursuant to Section 301 of Executive Order 11246 of September 24, 1965, and shall post copies of the notice in conspicuous places available to employees and applicants for employment.

(4) The contractor will comply with all provisions of such Executive Order and of all relevant rules, regulations, and orders of the Secretary of Labor and of any prior authority which remain in effect.

(5) The contractor will furnish all information and reports required by such Executive Order, rules, regulations, and orders, or pursuant thereto, and will permit access to books, records, and accounts by the Farmers Home Administration and the Secretary of Labor for purposes of investigation to ascertain compliance with such rules, regulations, and orders.

(6) In the event of the contractor's noncompliance with the nondiscrimination clauses of this contract or with any of the said rules, regulations, or orders, this contract may be cancelled, terminated or suspended in whole or in part and the contractor may be declared ineligible for further contracts in accordance with procedures authorized in such Executive Order and such other sanctions may be imposed and remedies invoked as provided in the Executive Order or by any such rules, regulations, or order, or as otherwise provided by law.

(7) The contractor will include the provisions of paragraphs (1) through (7) in every subcontract or purchase order, unless exempted by such rules, regulations, or orders, so that such provisions will be binding upon each such subcontractor or vendor. The contractor will take such action as the Farmers Home Administration may direct as a means of enforcing such provisions, including sanctions for noncompliance: Provided, <u>however,</u> that in the event the contractor becomes involved in, or is threatened with, litigation with a subcontractor or vendor as a result of such direction by the Farmers Home Administration, the contractor may request the United States to enter into such litigation to protect the interest of the United States.

FmHA **1924-6**

**FIGURE 19.5**

A construction contract. (*Continued*)

## STANDARD FEDERAL EQUAL EMPLOYMENT OPPORTUNITY CONSTRUCTION CONTRACT SPECIFICATIONS (EX. O. 11246)

3

1. As used in these specifications:

a. "Covered area" means the geographical area described in the solicitation from which this contract resulted;

b. "Director" means Director, Office of Federal Contract Compliance Programs, United States Department of Labor, or any person to whom the Director delegates authority;

c. "Employer identification number" means the Federal Social Security number used on the Employer's Quarterly Federal Tax Return, U.S. Treasury Department Form 941.

d. "Minority" includes:

(i) Black (all persons having origins in any of the Black African racial groups not of Hispanic origin);

(ii) Hispanic (all persons of Mexican, Puerto Rican, Cuban, Central or South American or other Spanish Culture or origin, regardless of race);

(iii) Asian and Pacific Islander (all persons having origins in any of the original peoples of the Far East, Southeast Asia, the Indian Subcontinent, or the Pacific Islands); and

(iv) American Indian or Alaskan Native (all persons having origins in any of the original peoples of North America and maintaining identifiable tribal affiliations through membership and participation or community identification).

2. Whenever the Contractor, or any Subcontractor at any tier, subcontracts a portion of the work involving any construction trade, it shall physically include in each subcontract in excess of $10,000 the provisions of these specifications and the Notice which contains the applicable goals for minority and female participation and which is set forth in the solicitations from which this contract resulted.

3. If the Contractor is participating (pursuant to 41 CFR 60-4.5) in a Hometown Plan approved by the U.S. Department of Labor in the covered area either individually or through an association, its affirmative action obligations on all work in the Plan area (including goals and timetables) shall be in accordance with that Plan for those trades which have unions participating in the Plan. Contractors must be able to demonstrate their participation in and compliance with the provisions of any such Hometown Plan. Each Contractor or Subcontractor participating in an approved Plan is individually required to comply with its obligations under the EEO clause, and to make a good faith effort to achieve each goal under the Plan in each trade in which it has employees. The overall good faith performance by other Contractors or Subcontractors toward a goal in an approved Plan does not excuse any covered Contractor's or Subcontractor's failure to take good faith efforts to achieve the Plan goals and timetables.

4. The Contractor shall implement the specific affirmative action standards provided in paragraphs 7a through p of these specifications. The goals set forth in the solicitation from which this contract resulted are expressed as percentages of the total hours of employment and training of minority and female utilization the Contractor should reasonably be able to achieve in each construction trade in which it has employees in the covered area. The Contractor is expected to make substantially uniform progress toward its goals in each craft during the period specified.

5. Neither the provisions of any collective bargaining agreement, nor the failure by a union with whom the Contractor has a collective bargaining agreement, to refer either minorities or women shall excuse the Contractor's obligations under these specifications, Executive Order 11246, or the regulations promulgated pursuant thereto.

6. In order for the nonworking training hours of apprentices and trainees to be counted in meeting the goals, such apprentices and trainees must be employed by the Contractor during the training period, and the Contractor must have made a commitment to employ the apprentices and trainees at the completion of their training, subject to the availability of employment opportunities. Trainees must be trained pursuant to training programs approved by the U.S. Department of Labor.

7. The Contractor shall take specific affirmative actions to ensure equal employment opportunity. The evaluation of the Contractors compliance with these specifications shall be based upon its effort to achieve maximum results from its actions. The Contractor shall document these efforts fully, and shall implement affirmative action steps at least as extensive as the following:

a. Ensure and maintain a working environment free of harassment, intimidation, and coercion at all sites, and in all facilities at which the Contractor's employees are assigned to work. The Contractor, where possible, will assign two or more women to each construction projects. The Contractor shall specifically ensure that all foremen, superintendents, and other on-site supervisory personnel are aware of and carry out the Contractor's obligation to maintain such a working environment, with specific attention to minority or female individuals working at such sites or in such facilities.

b. Establish and maintain a current list of minority and female recruitment sources, provide written notification to minority and female recruitment sources and to community organizations when the Contractor or its unions have employment opportunities available, and maintain a record of the organizations' responses.

c. Maintain a current file of the names, addresses and telephone numbers of each minority and female off-the-street applicant and minority or female referral from a union, a recruitment source or community organization and of what action was taken with respect to each such individual. If such individual was sent to the union hiring hall for referral and was not referred back to the Contractor by the union or, if referred, not employed by the Contractor, this shall be documented in the file with the reason therefor, along with whatever additional actions the Contractor may have taken.

d. Provide immediate written notification to the Director when the unions or unions with which the Contractor has a collective bargaining agreement has not referred to the Contractor a minority person or woman sent by the Contractor, or when the Contractor has other information that the union referral process has impeded the Contractor's efforts to meet its obligations.

e. Develop on-the-job training opportunities and/or participate in training programs for the area which expressly include minorities and women, including upgrading programs and apprenticeship and trainee programs relevant to the Contractor's employment needs, especially those programs funded or approved by the Department of Labor. The Contractor shall provide notice of these programs to the sources complied under 7b above.

f. Disseminate the Contractor's EEO policy by providing notice of the policy to unions and training programs and requesting their cooperation in assisting the Contractor in meeting its EEO obligations; by including it in any policy manual and collective bargaining agreement; by publicizing it in the company newspaper, annual report, etc.; by specific review of the policy with all management personnel and with all minority and female employees at least once a year; and by posting the company EEO policy on bulletin boards accessible to all employees at each location where construction work is performed.

g. Review, at least annually, the company's EEO policy and affirmative action obligations under these specifications with all employees having any responsibility for hiring, assignment, layoff, termination or other employment decisions including specific review of these items with onsite supervisory personnel such as Superintendents, General Foremen, etc., prior to the initiation of construction work at any job site. A written record shall be made and maintained identifying the time and place of these meetings, persons attending, subject matter discussed, and disposition of the subject matter.

h. Disseminate the Contractor's EEO policy externally by including it in any advertising in the news media, specifically including minority and female news media, and providing written notification to and discussing the Contractor's EEO policy with other Contractors and Subcontractors with whom the Contractor does or anticipates doing business.

i. Direct its recruitment efforts, both oral and written, to minority, female and community organizations, to schools with minority and female students and to minority and female recruitment and training organizations serving the Contractor's recruitment area and employment needs. Not later than one month prior to the date for the acceptance of applications for apprenticeship or other training by any recruitment source, the Contractor shall send written notification to organizations such as the above, describing the openings, screening procedures, and tests to be used in the selection process.

j. Encourage present minority and female employees to recruit other minority persons and women and, where reasonable, provide after school, summer and vacation employment to minority and female youth both on the site and in other areas of a Contractor's workforce.

k. Validate all tests and other selection requirements where there is an obligation to do so under 41 CFR Part 60-3.

l. Conduct, at least annually, an inventory and evaluation at least of all minority and female personnel for promotional opportunities and encourage these employees to seek or to prepare for, through appropriate training, etc., such opportunities.

m. Ensure that seniority practices, job classifications, work assignments and other personnel practices, do not have a discriminatory effect by continually monitoring all personnel and employment related activities to ensure that the EEO policy and the Contractor's obligations under these specifications are being carried out.

n. Ensure that all facilities and company activities are nonsegregated except that separate or single-user toilet and necessary changing facilities shall be provided to assure privacy between the sexes.

FmHA 1924-6

**FIGURE 19.5**

**A construction contract. (Continued)**

Estimates can be helpful during planning, but they are so undependable that I would rather not use them at all. There are no teeth in an estimate. I could tell you that I will provide my services for an estimate of $20,000 and wind up billing you for $30,000. If the estimate is based on an hourly rate and is not limited to a cutoff level, I could run up a terrific tab for you to foot.

Some contractors use low estimates to lure developers into trouble. It's sad to say, but true, that some contractors will stoop to almost any level to get a hook into a developer or general contractor. Creative use of estimates is usually the way that undesirable contractors get on the inside of a job. If you, as a developer, insist on quotes, you can avoid the scams associated with estimates.

4

o. Document and maintain a record of all solicitations of offers for subcontracts from minority and female construction contractors and suppliers, including circulation of solicitations to minority and female contractor associations and other business associations.

p. Conduct a review, at least annually, of all supervisors' adherence to and performance under the Contractor's EEO policies and affirmative action obligations.

8. Contractors are encouraged to participate in voluntary associations which assist in fulfilling one or more of their affirmative action obligations (7a through p). The effort of a contractor association, joint contractor-union, contractor-community, or other similar group of which the contractor is a member and participant, may be asserted as fulfilling any one "or more of its obligations under 7a through p of these Specifications provided that the contractor actively participates in the group, makes every effort to assure that the group has a positive impact on the employment of minorities and women in the industry, ensures that the concrete benefits of the program are reflected in the Contractor's minority and female workforce participation, makes a good faith effort to meet its individual goals and timetables, and can provide access to documentation which demonstrates the effectiveness of actions taken on behalf of the Contractor. The obligation to comply, however, is the Contractor's and failure of such a group to fulfill an obligation shall not be a defense for the Contractor's noncompliance.

9. A single goal for minorities and a separate single goal for women have been established. The Contractor, however, is required to provide equal employment opportunity and to take affirmative action for all minority groups, both male and female, and all women, both minority and non-minority. Consequently, the Contractor may be in violation of the Executive Order if a particular group is employed in a substantially disparate manner (for example, even though the Contractor has achieved its goals for women generally, the Contractor may be in violation of the Executive Order if a specific minority group of women is underutilized).

10. The Contractor shall not use the goals and timetables or affirmative action standards to discriminate against any person because of race, color, religion, sex, or national origin.

11. The Contractor shall not enter into any Subcontract with any person or firm debarred from Government contracts pursuant to Executive Order 11246.

12. The Contractor shall carry out such sanctions and penalties for violation of these specifications and of the Equal Opportunity Clause, including suspension, termination and cancellation of existing subcontracts as may be imposed or ordered pursuant to Executive Order 11246, as amended, and its implementing regulations, by the Office of Federal Contract Compliance Programs. Any Contractor who fails to carry out such sanctions and penalties shall be in violation of these specifications and Executive Order 11246, as amended.

13. The Contractor, in fulfilling its obligations under these specifications, shall implement specific affirmative action steps, at least as extensive as those standards prescribed in paragraph 7 of these specifications, so as to achieve maximum results from its efforts to ensure equal employment opportunist y. If the Contractor fails to comply with the requirements of the Executive Order, the implementing regulations, or these specifications, the Director shall proceed in accordance with 41 CFR 60-4.8.

14. The Contractor shall designate a responsible official to monitor all employment related activity to ensure that the company EEO policy is being carried out, to submit reports relating to the provisions hereof as may be required by the Government and to keep records. Records shall at least include for each employee the name, address, telephone numbers, construction trade, union affiliation if any, employee identification number when assigned, social security number, race, sex, status (e.g., mechanic, apprentice, trainee, helper, or laborer), dates of changes in status, hours worked per week in the indicated trade, rate of pay, and locations at which the work was performed. Records shall be maintained in an easily understandable and retrievable form; however, to the degree that existing records satisfy this requirement, contractors shall not be required to maintain separate records.

15. Nothing herein provided shall be construed as a limitation upon the application of other laws which establish different standards of compliance or upon the application of requirements for the hiring of local or other area residents (e.g., those under the Public Works Employment Act of 1977 and the Community Development Block Grant Program).

(E)    The contractor will determine if this contract is subject to a Hometown Plan. Check this block ❏ if contract is subject to a Hometown Plan. Effectively xxxxx out this provision if it is not. This contract is subject to the

_____ Plan. The applicable conditions are attached hereto and made a part hereof.

**FIGURE 19.5**

**A construction contract. (Continued)**

It would be too harsh, probably, to say that you should never use estimates. Almost every developer and contractor uses estimates from time to time. But, you must be aware that depending on estimates is dangerous. If you are using the estimates as a starting point for pushing numbers around, that's fine. But don't count on estimates to see you through a project.

---

IN WITNESS WHEREOF, the parties hereto have executed this contract as of the date first above written.

_____
*(Contractor)*

_____
*(Owner)*

## GENERAL CONDITIONS

I.     CHANGES IN WORK.–The Owner may at any time, with the approval of the official designated by the Farmers Home Administration (hereinafter called the Representative), make changes in the drawings and specifications, within the general scope thereof. If such changes cause an increase or decrease in the amount due under this contract or in the time required for its performance, an equitable adjustment will be made, and this contract will be modified accordingly by a "Contract Change Order". No charge for any extra work or material will be allowed unless the same has been ordered on such contract change order by the Owner with the approval of the Representative, and the price therefor stated in the order.

II.    INSPECTION OF WORK.–All materials and workmanship will be subject to inspection, examination, and test, by the Representative, who will have the right to reject defective material and workmanship or require its correction.

III.   COMPLETION OF WORK.–If the Contractor refuses or fails to complete the work within the time specified in paragraph B of this contract, or any extension thereof, the Owner may, with the approval of the Representative, terminate the Contractor's right to proceed. In such event the Owner may take over the work and prosecute the same to completion by contract or otherwise and the Contractor will be liable for any excess cost occasioned the Owner thereby; and the Owner may take possession of and utilize in completing the work such materials and equipment as may be on the site of the work and necessary therefor. If the Owner does not terminate the right of the Contract to proceed, the Contractor will continue the work, in which event, actual damages for delay will be impossible to determine, and, in lieu thereof, the Contractor may be required to pay to the

Owner the sum of $ _____ as liquidated damages for each calendar day of delay, and the Contractor will be liable for the amount thereof *Provided, however,* That the right of the Contractor to proceed will not be terminated because of delays in the completion of the completion of the work due to unforeseeable causes beyond the Contractor's control and without Contractor's fault or negligence.

IV.   RELEASES. –Prior to final payment, the Contractor will submit evidence that all payrolls, material bills, and other indebtedness connected with the work have been paid as required by the Owner or the Representative.

V.    OBLIGATION TO DISCHARGE LIENS. –Acceptance by the Owner and the Representative of the completed work performed by the Contractor and payment therefor by the Owner will not relieve the Contractor of obligation to the Owner (which obligation is hereby acknowledged) to discharge any and all liens for the benefit of subcontractors, laborers, material-person, or any other persons performing labor upon the work or furnishing material or machinery for the work covered by this contract, which have attached to or may subsequently attach to the property, or interest of the Owner.

VI. NOTICES AND APPROVAL IN WRITING.–Any notice, consent, or other act to be given or done hereunder will be valid only if in writing.

VII. ADDITIONAL REQUIREMENTS.–The contractor, in the performance of this contract, will comply with all applicable Equal Opportunity requirements. The provisions of FmHA Instruction 1901 -F concerning the protection of historical and archaeological properties and the provisions of FmHA Instruction 1940-G concerning environmental requirements apply. The contractor understands that should any archaeological resources be discovered during the construction process, the contractor will notify the owner and cease further construction activity that could affect the resource until the owner has consulted with FmHA and the contractor is informed of any steps to be taken or told to proceed with construction.

VIII. CLEANING UP.–The contractor shall keep the premises free from accumulation of waste material and rubbish and at the completion of the work shall remove from the premises all rubbish, implements and surplus materials and leave the building broom-clean.

IX. BUILDERS WARRANTY. –Upon completion of the work the contractor will; (Check [ ] proper warranty clause and effectively xxxxxxxx out the inapplicable clause.)

❑ execute Form FmHA 1924-19, "Builders Warranty".

❑ provide an FmHA-approved 10-year home warranty policy in accordance with Section 1924.9 and Exhibit L of FmHA Instruction 1924-A.

● U.S. Government Printing Office: 1993 - 555-047/80517                                    FmHA  1924-6

### FIGURE 19.5

**A construction contract.** *(Continued)*

Quotes are the only way to make solid cost projections on a project. Unfortunately, most quotes have time limits on them that may expire before you can take advantage of the quotes. Locking in quotes for several months can be very difficult. Even if contractors are willing to lock in their labor rates for months into the future, it will be nearly impossible for them to guarantee the cost of materials (Fig. 19.6) for a long period of time. This is a problem that all contractors and developers face.

---

Your Company Name
Your Company Address
Your Company Phone and Fax Numbers

### LETTER SOLICITING MATERIAL QUOTES

Date:

Dear:

I am soliciting bids for the work listed below, and I would like to offer you the opportunity to participate in the bidding. If you are interested in giving quoted prices on material(s) for this job, please let me hear from you at the above address.

The job will be started in _____ days/weeks. Financing has been arranged and the job will be started on schedule. Your quote, if you choose to enter one, must be received no later than

_____.

The proposed work is as follows:_____

_____

_____

Plans and specifications for the work are available upon request.

Thank you for your time and consideration in this request.

Sincerely,


Your Name

Title

**FIGURE 19.6**

Form letter for soliciting material quotes.

Development projects generally take many, many months to complete. Even home builders who can complete a house in 60 to 90 days have trouble locking in the prices for materials. Large builders sometimes have enough clout to get material suppliers to lock in prices. I've been fortunate to develop relationships with my suppliers to have them lock in material prices for the full term of construction. Builders who build only a few houses a year don't normally have this luxury.

When material prices can't be locked in long enough to hold a price until you need it, a quote is not much better than an estimate. If you are planning a large development, suppliers for your contractors and subcontractors may be willing to gamble on a price lock-in. You should at least try to get locked in on all prices. Most developers get the best bids that they can get and then factor in an additional amount of money to cover potential increases in material costs. This is a good move, but getting a firm lock that will stick with you is better.

When you begin seeking bids from contractors you should make it clear that you want quotes, not estimates. The bidding process is tough if you do it right. Don't get into it thinking that your job is easy, simple, or routine. Even if you have worked with contractors before, you have to treat every new project with respect. Now, let's get down to the art of taking bids.

## Locating Contractors

Locating contractors to bid your work can be more difficult than you might think. Sure, you can run through the advertisements in your local phone directory, but this approach is a total crap shoot. If you don't already know some reputable contractors, you should start your bidding price by getting some referrals (Fig. 19.7). If you are new to land development, you may not have many contacts in the industry. Don't worry, there are ways to shorten the learning curve.

Assuming that you have chosen your experts, you can ask them to recommend some local talent for your development needs. Many developers belong to various clubs. If you are a member of local clubs you might be able to do some networking that will produce leads for contractors. Builders can also be a good source of leads for subcontractors. If worst comes to worst, you can drive around and find contractors on jobs.

Touring sites in your general work area is a good way to preview contractors before you invite them to bid your work. Many developers ask contractors for references, but the best reference you can get is ongoing work that is being done by the contractors that you are interviewing. It's possible to fake references, but it's very hard to disguise work in progress. If you sit and watch a site that is being developed for a while, you can get a good idea of how the contractors on the job work.

---

**SUBCONTRACTOR QUESTIONNAIRE**

Company name: _____

Physical company address: _____

Company mailing address: _____

Company phone number: _____ After–hours phone number: _____

Company president/owner: _____

President/owner address: _____

President/owner phone number: _____ How long has company been in business: ____

Name of insurance company: _____

Insurance company phone number: _____

Does company have liability insurance? _____

Amount of liability insurance coverage: _____

Does company have worker's comp. insurance? _____

Type of work company is licensed to do: _____

List business or other license numbers: _____

Where are licenses held? _____

If applicable, are all workers licensed? _____

Are there any lawsuits pending against the company? _____

Has the company ever been sued? _____

Does the company use subcontractors? _____

Is the company bonded? _____

With whom is the company bonded? _____

Has the company had complaints filed against it? _____

Are there any judgments against the company? _____

**FIGURE 19.7**

Subcontractor questionnaire.

I have often had my field superintendents keep their eyes open for new sites under development. When my superintendents see a project going up they pay attention to who is doing the work. In fact, written reports from their day logs are saved for when we may need more contractors on our jobs.

Regardless of how you get leads on contractors there comes a time when you have to talk with several contractors to get bids on your job. Most developers like to see bids from at least three different contractors. I prefer to get five bids, unless I'm working with contractors whom I've worked with in the past.

## Soliciting Bids

Soliciting bids is a job that can be done in different ways. Some developers send bid packages out to all contractors who work within the area of expertise needed. It's common, especially for big jobs, to be listed in bid sheets that are distributed by companies who maintain subscribers for bid notifications. Most small developers pick up a telephone and call companies to see if they wish to bid work. Before you start asking for bids, you must have all of your paperwork in order. By paperwork I mean your plans and specifications for the work that contractors will be bidding on. Once you have your plans and specs ready, make contact with your potential contractors.

You may be surprised at how many contractors will have no interest in bidding your job. This seems crazy. Contractors are in business to work, yet some of them don't want to bid jobs. Why? There are many reasons. Extremely good contractors may be too busy to take on new customers. Some contractors don't have the skills to bid a job accurately, so they rely on jobs that they can work on an hourly basis. Except for times of major building booms, you can usually get plenty of contractors to offer bids, but it may take more work than you think to find the contractors.

All developers have their own way of soliciting bids. You can do it any way you like, but there are some trade secrets to it that can make your life easier. For example, let's say that you have five contractors bidding your site work. The prices come in after a week or two and you review them. Some more time passes as you sort through the bids. You decide on a particular contractor and contact the contractor's firm.

After meetings with the contractor and ongoing negotiations, which take considerable time, you find out that the contractor doesn't carry liability insurance and is not bondable. Boom! Your good lead and good bid bites the dust. How much time and money have you lost?

Losing time is bad; losing money is worse. And they usually go hand in hand. How could you have avoided the problem with the contractor. It's simple. You could have required proof of insurance and bonding ability (Figs. 19.8 and 19.9) before releasing a bid package to the contractor. Having contractors pass your basic tests before releasing bid packages is not only smart, it saves a lot of time. Why go through the motions with contractors whom you will not be willing or able to use regardless of their bids?

Most builders and developers have certain minimum requirements that the subcontractors must meet in order to work for them. Insurance coverage should certainly be one of them. Make a list of what you will require as minimum standards from any contractors who you would clear for working with you. If you are not sure of what you should require, consult your attorney. Get the list drawn up as a handout for your independent contractors. Include the list of requirements with your bid packages and make sure that all prospective bidders know that you are firm and nonnegotiable on the issues.

There may be other boilerplate information that you want to include in your bid packages. For example, you might make a detailed point of how you will not allow bidders to substitute materials for those that are specified. Material substitution (Fig. 19.10) is a common ploy used by some contractors who want to make their bids look attractive. You can't afford to accept this type of activity. Make it very clear that all specifications must be adhered to exactly. In the event that a substitution can't be avoided, insist that the bidding contractors provide a detailed report on the material substitution being offered. This will give you and your experts a chance to check out the substituted material for quality and value.

## Comparing Bids

Comparing bids is not as simple as just skimming the bottom line. Even small, simple jobs call for close scrutiny of the bid. If you are the one who is responsible for awarding bids, you must read each bid carefully. You can bet that there will be differences between the various bids, and I don't mean just the price. Contractors bidding a job usually make some alterations to the provided bid package. In theory, reviewing the bids should be as simple as looking at prices, but it seldom works out that way.

**Payment Bond**

**U.S. Department of Housing and Urban Development**
Office of Housing
Federal Housing Commissioner

**(This Bond is issued simultaneously with Performance Bond in favor of Owner conditioned on the full and faithful performance of the contract)**

Project Number:

Know All Men By These Presents, **that we,** ____________________

of ____________________

as Principal, (hereinafter called the Principal) and ____________________,

a ____________________ as Surety, (hereinafter called the Surety) are held and firmly bound

unto ____________________ as Obligee, (hereinafter called the "Owner"), for the use and

benefit of claimants as hereinafter defined, in the sum of ____________________ Dollars ($          ),
lawful money of the United States of America, for the payment of which Principal and Surety bind themselves, their heirs, executors, administrators, successors and assigns, jointly and severally, firmly by these presents.

**Whereas,** Principal has entered into a Construction Contract dated ____________ with Owner for the construction of a Housing Project designated as ____________________ a copy of which Construction Contract is by reference made a part hereof; and is hereinafter referred to as the Contract.

**Now, therefore, the conditions of this obligation** is such that, if Principal shall promptly make payment to all claimants as hereinafter defined, for all labor and material used or reasonably required for use in the performance of the Contract, then this obligation shall be void; otherwise it shall remain in full force and effect, subject, however, to the following conditions:

1. A Claimant is defined as one having a direct contract with the Principal or with a subcontractor of the Principal for labor, material, or both, used or reasonably required for use in the performance of the contract, labor and material being construed to include that part of water, gas, power, light, heat, oil, gasoline, telephone service or rental of equipment directly applicable to the Contract.

2. The above name Principal and Surety hereby jointly and severally agree with the Owner that every claimant as herein defined, who has not been paid in full before the expiration of a period of ninety (90) days after the date on which the last of such claimant's work or labor was done or performed, or materials were furnished by such claimant, may sue on this bond for the use of such claimant, prosecute the suit to final judgment for such sum or sums as may be justly due claimant, and have execution thereon. The Owner shall not be liable for the payment of any costs or expenses of any such suit.

3. No suit or action shall be commenced hereunder by any claimant:

a) Unless claimant, other than one having direct contract with the Principal, shall have given written notice to any two of the following: The Principal, the Owner, or the Surety above named, within ninety (90) days after such claimant did or performed the last of the work or labor, or furnished the last of the materials for which said claim is made, stating with substantial accuracy the amount claimed and the name of the party to whom the materials were furnished, or for whom the work or labor was done or performed. Such notice shall be served by mailing the same by registered mail or certified mail, postage prepaid, in an envelope addressed to the Principal, Owner or Surety, at any place where an office is regularly maintained for the transaction of business, or served in any manner in which legal process may be served in the state in which the aforesaid project is located, save that such service need not be made by a public officer.

b) After the expiration of one (1) year following the date on which Principal ceased work on said Contract, it being understood, however, that if any limitation embodied in this bond is prohibited by any law controlling the construction hereof, such limitation shall be deemed to be amended so as to be equal to the minimum period of limitation permitted by such law.

c) Other than in a state court of competent jurisdiction in and for the county or other political subdivision of the state in which the project, or any part thereof, is situated, or in the United States District Court for the district in which the project, or any part thereof, is situated, and not elsewhere.

4. The amount of this bond shall be reduced by and to the extent of any payment or payments made in good faith hereunder, inclusive of the payment by Surety of mechanics' liens which may be filed of record against said improvement, whether or not claim for the amount of such lien be presented under and against this bond.

Signed and Sealed this ____________ day of ____________, 19______.

Witness as to Principal: ____________________ (Seal)
(Principal)

____________________ By: ____________________

____________________
(Surety)

By: ____________________

form HUD-50052-A (11/89)

FIGURE 19.8

**A payment bond.**

If you have prepared a detailed bid package that leaves nothing to the imagination, you might get clean, easy-to-compare bids. Otherwise, you will have to sift through the bids and compare them closely. Some developers use bid packages where a contractor agrees to having priced all of the work contained in the package, fills in a blank with a price for all labor and material, and then signs the bid sheet. This is an ideal situation, but it is rare. It is much more common for contractors to offer you a letter as a bid or perhaps a quote on some type of form from their company. Receiving bids of this type is more risky for you. These are the bids that you have to go over with a magnifying glass.

I've received some very creative bids in my time. It's amazing how many contractors and suppliers fail to include certain details in their bids. To keep your prices dependable, you have to make sure that the bids are equal in all respects. You know, it's the old apples-to-apples thing. If you have three bids that are not identical in their description, they are nearly worthless. Prices for lemons, apples, and oranges can't be compared equally. You have to get bids that can be compared properly. Contractors don't always want you to have such contracts (Fig. 19.11), so insist on it. If they want the work badly enough, they will play by your rules.

Some subcontractors have to be convinced to bid jobs in a way that is acceptable to you. There are contractors who bid jobs only their way. Forget these people. If you can't get them to bid a job to your specifications, just imagine how difficult they will be to work with during the course of your project. You're boss, and you have the right to request bids to your standards. Don't settle for less.

$ _____

_____
(Surety)

**PAYMENT BOND**

No. _____

On Behalf of

_____

To

_____

_____

_____

Date _____, 19 _____

Expires _____, 19 _____

form HUD-50052-A (11/89)
ref. Handbook 4571.1

**FIGURE 19.8**

A payment bond. (*Continued*)

# Refining Bids

Refining bids may be necessary. Assume that you have encountered bids where types of materials had to be substituted. It's unlikely that all of your contractors substituted with the same alternative materials.

| BID BOND | DATE BOND EXECUTED *(Must not be later than bid opening date)* | OMB NO.: **9000-0045** Expires: 09/30/98 |
|---|---|---|

*(See instruction on reverse)*

Public reporting burden for this collection of information is estimated to average 25 minutes per response, including the time for reviewing instructions, searching existing data sources, gathering and maintaining the data needed, and completing and reviewing the collection of information. Send comments regarding this burden estimate or any other aspect of this collection of information, including suggestions for reducing this burden, to the FAR Secretariat (MVR), Federal Acquisition Policy Division, GSA, Washington, DC 20405.

PRINCIPAL *(Legal name and business address)*

TYPE OF ORGANIZATION *("X" one)*

☐ INDIVIDUAL  ☐ PARTNERSHIP
☐ JOINT VENTURE  ☐ CORPORATION
STATE OF INCORPORATION

SURETY(IES) *(Name(s) and business address(es)*

| PENAL SUM OF BOND | | | | BID IDENTIFICATION | |
|---|---|---|---|---|---|
| PERCENT OF BID PRICE | AMOUNT NOT TO EXCEED | | | BID DATE | INVITATION NO. |
| | MILLION(S) | THOUSAND(S) | HUNDRED(S) | CENTS | |
| | | | | | FOR *(Construction, Supplies, or Services)* | |

OBLIGATION:

We, the Principal and Surety(ies) are firmly bound to the United States of America (hereinafter called the Government) in the above penal sum. For payment of the penal sum, we bind ourselves, our heirs, executors, administrators, and successors, jointly and severally. However, where the Sureties are corporations acting as co-sureties, we, the Sureties, bind ourselves in such sum "jointly and severally" as well as "severally" only for the purpose of allowing a joint action or actions against any or all of us. For all other purposes, each Surety binds itself, jointly and severally with the Principal, for the payment of the sum shown opposite the name of the Surety. If no limit of liability is indicated, the limit of liability is the full amount of the penal sum.

CONDITIONS:

The Principal has submitted the bid identified above.

THEREFORE:

The above obligation is void if the Principal - (a) upon acceptance by the Government of the bid identified above, within the period specified therein for acceptance (sixty (60) days if no period is specified), executes the further contractual documents and gives the bond(s) required by the terms of the bid as accepted within the time specified (ten (10) days if no period is specified) after receipt of the forms by the principal; or (b) in the event of failure to execute such further contractual documents and give such bonds, pays the Government for any cost of procuring the work which exceeds the amount of the bid.

Each Surety executing this instrument agrees that its obligation is not impaired by any extension(s) of the time for acceptance of the bid that the Principal may grant to the Government. Notice to the surety(ies) of extension(s) are waived. However, waiver of the notice applies only to extensions aggregating not more than sixty (60) calendar days in addition to the period originally allowed for acceptance of the bid.

WITNESS:

The Principal and Surety(ies) executed this bid bond and affixed their seals on the above date.

**PRINCIPAL**

| SIGNATURE(S) | 1. | 2. | 3. | |
|---|---|---|---|---|
| | *(Seal)* | *(Seal)* | *(Seal)* | Corporate Seal |
| NAME(S) & TITLE(S) *(Typed)* | 1. | 2. | 3. | |

**INDIVIDUAL SURETY(IES)**

| SIGNATURE(S) | 1. | 2. | |
|---|---|---|---|
| | | *(Seal)* | *(Seal)* |
| NAME(S) *(Typed)* | 1. | 2. | |

**CORPORATE SURETY(IES)**

| SURETY A | NAME & ADDRESS | | STATE OF INC. | LIABILITY LIMIT $ | |
|---|---|---|---|---|---|
| | SIGNATURE(S) | 1. | | 2. | Corporate Seal |
| | NAME(S) & TITLE(S) *(Typed)* | 1. | | 2. | |

AUTHORIZED FOR LOCAL REPRODUCTION
Previous edition is usable

STANDARD FORM 24 (REV. )
Prescribed by GSA - FAR (48 CFR) 53.228(a)

**FIGURE 19.9**

A bid bond.

You may have to refine the bids to make them equal. This could be as simple as calling the contractors and having all of them agree to bid with identical substitutions. You may decide to take this step by mail or with e-mail. Face-to-face meetings might be the best way to distill comparable bids. The way in which you do it is not nearly as important as getting it done.

| CORPORATE SURETY(IES) *(Continued)* | | | | |
|---|---|---|---|---|
| **SURETY B** | | STATE OF INC. | LIABILITY LIMIT $ | |
| NAME & ADDRESS | | | | |
| SIGNATURE(S) | 1. | 2. | | Corporate Seal |
| NAME(S) & TITLE(S) *(Typed)* | 1. | 2. | | |
| **SURETY C** NAME & ADDRESS | | STATE OF INC. | LIABILITY LIMIT $ | |
| SIGNATURE(S) | 1. | 2. | | Corporate Seal |
| NAME(S) & TITLE(S) *(Typed)* | 1. | 2. | | |
| **SURETY D** NAME & ADDRESS | | STATE OF INC. | LIABILITY LIMIT $ | |
| SIGNATURE(S) | 1. | 2. | | Corporate Seal |
| NAME(S) & TITLE(S) *(Typed)* | 1. | 2. | | |
| **SURETY E** NAME & ADDRESS | | STATE OF INC. | LIABILITY LIMIT $ | |
| SIGNATURE(S) | 1. | 2. | | Corporate Seal |
| NAME(S) & TITLE(S) *(Typed)* | 1. | 2. | | |
| **SURETY F** NAME & ADDRESS | | STATE OF INC. | LIABILITY LIMIT $ | |
| SIGNATURE(S) | 1. | 2. | | Corporate Seal |
| NAME(S) & TITLE(S) *(Typed)* | 1. | 2. | | |
| **SURETY G** NAME & ADDRESS | | STATE OF INC. | LIABILITY LIMIT $ | |
| SIGNATURE(S) | 1. | 2. | | Corporate Seal |
| NAME(S) & TITLE(S) *(Typed)* | 1. | 2. | | |

### INSTRUCTIONS

1. This form is authorized for use when a bid guaranty is required. Any deviation from this form will require the written approval of the Administrator of General Services.

2. Insert the full legal name and business address of the Principal in the space designated "Principal" on the face of the form. An authorized person shall sign the bond. Any person signing in a representative capacity (e.g., an attorney-in-fact) must furnish evidence of authority if that representative is not a member of the firm, partnership, or joint venture, or an officer of the corporation involved.

3. The bond may express penal sum as a percentage of the bid price. In these cases, the bond may state a maximum dollar limitation (e.g., 20% of the bid price but the amount not to exceed _____ dollars).

4. (a) Corporations executing the bond as sureties must appear on the Department of the Treasury's list of approved sureties and must act within the limitation listed therein. Where more than one corporate surety is involved, their names and addresses shall appear in the spaces (Surety A, Surety B, etc.) headed "CORPORATE SURETY(IES)." In the space designed "SURETY(IES)" on the face of the form, insert only the letter identification of the sureties.

(b) Where individual sureties are involved, a completed Affidavit of Individual Surety (Standard Form 28), for each individual surety, shall accompany the bond. The Government may require the surety to furnish additional substantiating information concerning its financial capability.

5. Corporations executing the bond shall affix their corporate seals. Individuals shall execute the bond opposite the word "Corporate Seal"; and shall affix an adhesive seal if executed in Maine, New Hampshire, or any other jurisdiction requiring adhesive seals.

6. Type the name and title of each person signing this bond in the space provided.

7. In its application to negotiated contracts, the terms "bid" and "bidder" shall include "proposal" and "offeror."

**FIGURE 19.9**

STANDARD FORM 24 (REV. ) BACK

**A bid bond.** *(Continued)*

There may be other reasons for refining bids. You might find that you wish to make changes to your plans and specifications after a bid package goes out. Developers hope that this will not happen, but it sometimes does. The development business is full of surprises and changes. Just when you think that you have a firm plan it may become evident that something was missed or must be changed. If this hap-

---

Your Company Name
Your Company Address
Your Company Phone and Fax Numbers

**REQUEST FOR SUBSTITUTIONS**

Customer name: _____

Customer address: _____

Customer city/state/zip: _____

Customer phone number: _____

Job location: _____

Plans and specifications dated: _____

Bid requested from: _____

Type of work: _____

The following items are being substituted for the items specified in the attached plans and

specifications: _____

_____

_____

_____

_____

_____

Please indicate your acceptance of these substitutions by signing below.

_____    _____    _____    _____
Contractor                              Date     Customer                                Date

                                                 _____    _____
                                                 Customer                                Date

**FIGURE 19.10**

Request for substitutions form.

Your Company Name
Your Company Address
Your Company Phone and Fax Numbers

## PROPOSAL

Date: _____

Customer's name: _____

Address: _____

Phone number: _____

Job location: _____

### DESCRIPTION OF WORK

Your Company Name will supply, and/or coordinate, all labor and material for the above-referenced job as follows: _____

_____

_____

_____

_____

_____

_____

### PAYMENT SCHEDULE

Price: _____ dollars ($_____)

Payments to be made as follows: _____

_____

_____

All payments shall be made in full, upon presentation of each completed invoice. If payment is not made according to the terms above, Your Company Name will have the following rights and remedies. Your Company Name may charge a monthly service charge of _____ (_____%) percent, _____ (_____%) percent per year, from the first day default is made. Your Company Name may lien the property where the work has been done. Your Company Name may use all legal methods in the collection of monies owed to it. Your Company Name may seek compensation, at the rate of $_____ per hour, for attempts made to collect unpaid monies.

(Page 1 of 2. Please initial _____.)

**FIGURE 19.11**

Sample proposal.

Your Company Name may seek payment for legal fees and other costs of collection, to the full extent the law allows.

If the job is not ready for the service or materials requested, as scheduled, and the delay is not due to Your Company Name's actions, Your Company Name may charge the customer for lost time. This charge will be at a rate of $_____ per hour, per man, including travel time.

If you have any questions or don't understand this proposal, seek professional advice. Upon acceptance, this proposal becomes a binding contract between both parties.

Respectfully submitted,


Your Name
Title

### ACCEPTANCE

We, the undersigned, do hereby agree to, and accept, all the terms and conditions of this proposal. We fully understand the terms and conditions, and hereby consent to enter into this contract.

Your Company Name                          Customer

By:_____          _____

Title:_____         Date:_____

Date:_____

Proposal expires in 30 days, if not accepted by all parties.

**FIGURE 19.11**

Sample proposal. (*Continued*)

pens, you should get in touch with your contractors and refine any bids that you have requested or received. A written change order (Fig. 19.12) should be issued so that there can be no dispute as to what the changes are.

**FIGURE 19.12**

A change order.

Putting up with the paperwork of a development project is more than some developers wish to deal with. The volume of paperwork can be extreme, but it is necessary. If you don't have the patience or organizational skills to maintain good paper trails and files, hire someone to do it for you. Don't attempt to eliminate the paperwork. Sooner or later, developers without documentation generally wind up in trouble.

# Sales Projections

Sales projections are an essential part of successful land developing. No experienced developer will launch into a development deal without accurate sales projections. Some developers create their own sales projections while others hire consultants to do the projections for them. Many deals never get off the ground when sales projections will not support them. It's good business to make sure that there is adequate demand for what you plan to develop. And you have to make sure that your potential stable of buyers can afford to pay the price of admission. Having buyers lined up around a street corner is of little value if they don't have enough money or credit to buy what you are trying to sell.

The development of sales projections is a process that can follow proved paths. Yet much of the process is supposition. You can't be sure of what will happen until you attempt to make it happen. One problem with land developing is the time that it can take to turn out a salable product. What starts off as an excellent idea can turn sour quickly. You could be caught in a quagmire of financial problems. It has happened to me and many other experienced developers, so it could happen to you.

One of my worst problems during developing and building happened in the very early 1980s. I had started developing a project outside of northern Virginia. The development site was a mountain within a reasonable commuting distance to the cities. People liked living in the country and I'd done a lot of research. The results of my research showed that people would be anxious to buy vacation-type homes on the mountain. Many of the homes would be full-time residences, but some of them would be weekend places. In either case, the project was very viable at the time that I started it. Unfortunately, there was a turn of events that I didn't expect, and it could have cost me my entire business.

When I started the development, banks were offering mortgage money at about 12 percent interest. As a smart developer, I projected how the project would do if interest rates went up. The economy was not exactly stable during the time of the mountain development. But I had no idea of just how unstable the market would become.

The first home I built on the mountain was an A frame with a chalet look on the front elevation. My crews and I worked hard on that house, and we put it up quickly. I had gambled and built a house with some unusual features. For example, the downstairs bathroom had a sunken garden tub in it and a corner toilet. The exposed beams and ceiling fans were not too far off center, but the textured walls were a bit of a walk on the wild side. I had worked with the design of the house to make it memorable. It was my intent to live in it and to use it as a model home for the rest of the development.

Other homes had been built on the mountain before I moved into the project. The houses were mostly rustic and had sold well. All sales projections were favorable. What I had not anticipated was the runaway interest rates. Before we could complete the house, interest rates started climbing steadily. I had entered into the deal at an interest rate of 12 percent. By the time I completed the house and obtained my permanent mortgage the interest rate was 18 percent. This, of course, made a huge difference in the amount of my monthly payments.

The elevated interest rates kept climbing. General contractors were falling like flies to the high cost of financing. Builders were losing their businesses right and left. In addition to my developing and building business, I also owned a plumbing and remodeling business. The effect of the high interest rates was hitting contractors from all trades. To say that times were bad would be an understatement. I made a decision to cease all future development until the economy settled. But I was still stuck with a house that I could not afford to keep. The sales market didn't offer much hope of getting out of the house.

I talked with real estate brokers who told me that I'd have a great deal of trouble selling the house because of its unique features. Well, I didn't want to list the property with people who had a negative feeling about selling it, so I sold it myself. Out of the first three people to see the house, two of them made an offer to purchase the property. Amazingly, I sold the house right away and made a small profit. More importantly for me, I got out of a bad situation without losing my shirt doing it.

The keys to my escape were being the builder, the developer, and the salesperson. By being very active in all aspects of the business, I made a small profit where I might otherwise have been in a foreclosure suit. My research left me in a lurch when the interest rates ran skyward, but the same research proved to be instrumental in the sale. Why? Because both buyers wanted the house for its construction features and location, both of which were a result of my research. You can't overstate the importance of research and sales projections when it comes to winning in the development game.

## Getting Sales Projections

There are various methods available to you for obtaining sales projections. The easiest way to get sales information is to hire a consulting firm to perform the sales research for you. If you give the consultants criteria to work with, they can produce substantial reports for you to work with. The downside to hiring consultants is the cost and the lack of personal involvement. Many developers prefer to be involved in their own research. Some consulting firms will allow you to participate in the planning of sales projections, but many will not. If you want to be involved in the research, you should ask any consultants you are considering if you will be allowed to take part in the process.

Reports generated from consultants have the advantage of being objective. Your consultants should be offering pure facts without bias. This is something that is difficult for developers to do. If you believe in your project, you may skew the research without even realizing that you are cutting some corners. If you want to be especially thorough, you could hire a consulting firm and do your own sales projections to compare to the results of the consulting firm.

Historic data is one of the best ways to prove what has happened with previous development efforts. You can see what projects failed and which projects were successful. It's possible to tell how many days real estate was on the market before it sold. You can see what asking prices were and what the prices were for closed sales. A wealth of information is available from real estate brokers, real estate appraisers, and multiple-listing services. Most developers depend on this type of research for their sales projections.

Individual research can be conducted to prove that a project should be viable. For example, you could have a canvassing firm call people who fit the demographic profile for your project in an effort to get detailed information on what the people would be interested in buying. This process is sketchy at best. Many of the people called will not answer the questions asked, and some may not answer the questions honestly.

Talking with builders can also be a good way to project sales. Looking at ongoing developments can also help you to project potential sales. When it comes down to it, the most dependable means of sales projections is usually the comparable-sales method using historic data. But developers and builders often have gut feelings that are well worth following. Personally, I've been pretty successful in using historical data as my foundation and my gut feelings for the window dressing.

## Local Trends

Local trends can stimulate developers to follow a growing pattern of activity. But the trends may die out before a developer can complete a project. Many housing projects take years to develop and sell out. A lot can happen with trends over the course of years. I've seen developers fall into the trends trap. My experience in watching other developers has seen earth-sheltered houses fail, dome houses bite the dust, and passive solar homes go down in flames. All three types of housing were trendy for a while, but the trends didn't last when the developers were trying to cash in on them. I watched as development after development got off to a good start and then fizzled out. While this was happening, I was developing subdivisions of contemporary homes and colonial homes, which all proved successful. My house designs were not radical or trendy, but they stood the test of time.

You may not be involved with the construction of homes. Maybe your market is home builders and you are providing only building lots. Even straight land development projects can fall into the trendy traps. If you get too cute, you could lose money. Cutting lots into strange shapes, creating high-definition landmarks, eliminating expected amenities, or adding too many amenities could ruin your profit potential. Developers who stick to the basics usually have the longest survival history as successful developers. If you want to do something new and innovative, test-market it before you commit to it. Once you set the tone of a development it is hard to change it. And the wrong public perception can lead to costly losses in sales.

## Working with a Team

Working with a team of real estate professionals is an excellent way to develop your own sales projections. Real estate brokers will often work with developers in the creation of sales projections. In most cases, the brokers don't charge for their services. They do the work in hope of getting the listings on property in the development. Real estate appraisers can also provide deep insights into probable sales. Unlike brokers, most appraisers will expect to be paid for their services when they are rendered. Even at high hourly rates, the information derived from appraisers might be one of the best bargains you will find in the development business.

Some developers are members of a multiple listing service (MLS). Real estate brokerages nearly always subscribe to multiple listing services. If you are not able to access information from a multiple listing service on your own, you can gain access to it through a real estate broker who is a member of the system. The information available through an MLS is very valuable when developing sales projections. Details offered from an MLS vary, but most of the systems provide all data needed to predict comparable sales prices.

You could develop your own team of sales professionals to work with while creating sales projections. For example, you might hire an appraiser, work with several brokers, and track the results of an MLS. While doing all of this, you might also talk to local builders to get their input on potential sales. If you choose to hire a consulting firm to produce sale projections, you can factor in their findings with those of the rest of your team. In the end, you should have the makings for a pretty significant projection.

## Land Only

If you are developing land only, you may be able to get by with a lot less research than a developer who is also a builder. However, don't assume automatically that just because you will not be building houses that you don't have to know about housing prices. The value of building lots is often based on the value of completed housing packages. In my area, builders and banks usually consider the value of land to be about 20 percent of a total housing package. In other words, a complete house on a building lot might sell for $200,000. If this were the case, the value of the land might well be estimated at $40,000. There are certainly times when land is worth more or less than the rule-of-thumb 20 percent.

How will you establish the sales value of your land? The safest route is to have a complete appraisal done. This is an expensive way to go, but it is one that you can count on beyond any other type of sales projection. The appraisal method is so simple and involves so little time or effort that it seems like more developers would use it. But the cost can be prohibitive. If the appraiser used for the job is on the approved lists of local lenders, you can rest comfortably knowing that you are playing with real numbers. Any other approach leaves more room for error.

The next best method of putting a price on your property is, in my opinion, the comparable sale method. This is where having access to an MLS is invaluable. By looking at closed sales in the MLS you can see what people have really been paying for land like yours. The comparables, or *comps* as brokers call them, should be near your land and the sales should be less than 6 months old. If you find three developments in an area near where your lots will be and the lots in those developments are selling for prices between $32,000 and $35,000, a price of $40,000 could be a stretch for your project. If you expect to get much more, you are going to have to make it enticing for buyers. But convincing buyers to pay the price may not be enough. If the land is being financed, the appraised value will be what counts when it comes to loan approval. Even if buyers are willing to pay $40,000 for lots, their lenders might loan against the lots as if they are worth only $35,000, or less.

Before you gamble on the hope of getting more money for your development by adding new twists to your development, make sure that the improvements will pay for themselves. You can do this only by working with an appraiser. It's good business to expect a return on your investment. The return doesn't have to be in the form of cash. For example, an improvement that makes a development sell faster, but for no more money, can be justified. However, not all improvements are worth their expense. Investing money and getting back less than what you put in is an excellent way to go out of business in a hurry. Assuming that you want to stick around as a successful developer, you have to make investments that pay for themselves.

## Land and Improvements

If you are developing to sell land and improvements, you have more work to do. Not only will you have to peg a price for the land, you will have to pin down a value for the improvements. In the case of houses, this shouldn't be difficult. But, if you are developing something that is a bit rare, the prospect of picking the right prices can be dismal. Let's say, for example, that you are building a development of duplexes in a section of town where there are no duplexes. Your idea might be terrific and sales may be brisk, but how will you nail down a price? Since there are no other duplexes in the area, you will have no comparable sales data to pull from. It can be tough to pick a price and predict sales in such a case.

Will buyers flock to your duplex development? How can you know? Demographic studies and local research are about all that you can go on in this type of situation. Most of your projections will be difficult to prove. When you get into a deal that is unique enough to be without historical data on comparable sales, you are flying solo. Without closed sales to compare your development to, it is nearly impossible to make a comfortable projection on price and sales.

Should you avoid developments that can't be supported by comparable sales? If you are a conservative person who doesn't like to gamble, you should. However, if you are looking for the next major trend or a windfall of money, going where no one has gone before might be the only way to realize your goals. It is risky. You don't know what to expect. Sometimes you just have to go with your gut feelings and hope for the best. The biggest money is often made from the most dangerous deals. But, a deal doesn't have to be dangerous to be profitable. Savvy developers learn to predict the future in order to make their fortunes.

## Beware of Hype

Beware of the hype that some real estate professionals will heap upon you. In addition to being a builder and developer, I'm also a designated real estate broker and own a brokerage. I can tell you that some listing agents will push the envelope considerably to secure a listing. Personally, I don't approve of too much hype, but I see it happen from both sides of the table. In the real estate industry the hype is often identified as "puffing." There can be a thin line between puffing and misrepresentation.

If you are working on a major development, there can be a lot of money to be made by the listing broker. Plenty of brokers will want your business. Most of them will be honest with you, but you might run into a few who will embellish the reality of your situation, and this is putting it nicely. It's common for brokers who are trying to secure listings to offer every type of promise imaginable to a seller.

Be careful if you go to brokers for help in creating sales projections. Some brokers want high sales prices for two main reasons. The first reason is that the commission earned from a sale is higher when the sales price is higher. As for the second reason, sellers are more likely to list their properties with brokerages who suggest the highest market value. None of this means anything if you don't get sales. Listing agents get a brownie point with their sales manager and a brokerage loses money advertising overpriced property, but you—the seller—will not see sales in quantity or quality.

Real estate brokers can be very helpful in projecting sales prices and sales activity. But check over their data to make sure that the numbers that you are working with are reasonable. Don't get caught up in the hype of talk that is not substantiated with facts. Base your sales projections on proved facts.

Anyway you cut it, sales projections are little more than guesstimates. Some are better than others, but none of them are a sure bet. The accuracy of even the most formal, best-researched projections is unknown. Until you are knee-deep in the development process, you will not know how accurate your projections are. A sudden shift in interest rates can kill your projections. Other elements, such as tax-law changes, the closing of military bases, and other outside forces can ruin the best plans for a development. The best insurance is to get in and out fast, before there are significant changes in the market. Make the best projections that you can and then run with the wind to make your deal happen while the conditions are right.

# Financing

M ost developers will tell you that financing is the most important part of any deal. It easily can be. Getting even a small development deal off the ground without financial backing is difficult. There are very few people who can pay cash as they go for their development expenses. Most people have to finance their deals, and even developers who could come up with the cash often prefer to use financing. Let's face it, most of us don't pay cash for cars and we use plastic to buy a bunch of stuff that we don't really need. Financing is a part of American culture. But, for developers, it can be the pivot point between success and failure.

It is common for developers to create entire project plans before seeking financing. To get approval for a development loan, a lot of paperwork has to be done. However, you can make some preliminary inquiries before making a formal loan application. And you should consider all potential sources of financing before you cast your net for borrowed dollars. Commercial banks are the most common source of development money, but they are far from the only source. You might find money with a credit union, a private investor, a mortgage broker, a mortgage banker, or even the seller of the land that you are looking to buy. There is also the possibility of using limited partners to generate cash. And builders may participate with you, as might material suppliers. There is potential for a lot of creative deal making when it comes to land development.

Where do you plan to look for your development money? Most inexperienced developers go to their regular bank as a starting point. This is not a bad move, but don't take rejection from your bank as a death blow. Many lenders simply don't like to loan money for land deals, which are generally considered a major risk. You may have to talk to dozens of loan officers to find a few who are willing to gamble on development projects. The time you spend in prospecting lenders is well spent. If you are like most developers, there isn't going to be much activity to brag about until you have a willing lender.

If you are new to the land developing business, your search for money and favorable loan terms is likely to be more arduous than it would be for a developer who has a successful track record. Lenders are usually nervous about development deals regardless of who is doing them, and if you are trying to do one without any past performance to judge, you are going to have a tougher time getting financing. But, a good deal is a good deal, and lenders who know the land business can recognize a good deal when they see one. So, with or without a successful history, you can get the money you want if your deal is good enough.

Putting together a winning proposal for prospective lenders can take weeks. Don't think that you can walk into the office of a loan officer and chat for a while and leave with a loan commitment. You need a written proposal for how you are going to make your development grow and prosper. If the proposal is solid, you have a good chance of gaining loan approval.

Many developers are intimidated by lenders. You shouldn't be. Lenders make their money by lending money to others. You are a lender's customer. The lender is not doing you a favor by loaning you the money you want. In reality, the lender is hoping to turn a profit by getting you to borrow money. This whole concept is difficult for some developers to adjust to. So many borrowers feel that their banks are doing them a favor. The truth is, you are entering into a business deal with your lender. You hope to make money on the development and the lender hopes to make money on the loan. It should be a reciprocal relationship. Don't bow and scrape. Stand tall and pitch your development as a prize catch. Think of yourself as interviewing the lender, rather than being interviewed by the lender.

It's difficult for many people to face lenders on equal ground. Most borrowers go into a bank as if they were begging for something. Don't do this. Cast a positive, authoritative view of yourself. Would you feel intimidated talking to subcontractors who are going to haul dirt for you? I doubt it. Think of your lender as just another subcontractor. Yes, you need the money, but you have many lenders to choose from. You are not dependent on a single source of money. Remember this. A positive attitude can take you a long way in the banking world.

## Commercial Banks

Commercial banks are the most common source of financing for land development. Are they the best source? They can be and often are. But keep in mind that banks are not the only source of funds for developing projects. Commercial banks lend money for a variety of reasons. Most of them will at least consider land loans and development projects. To get a project approved by a loan committee you may have to offer substantial paperwork. Much of what a bank wants to see is reports from your experts.

Loan officers probably won't have much interest in your specific visual plans. They won't care if a house has a roof pitch of 8/12 or 10/12. Most of what the lender will be interested in is the financial solutions. You will need solid sales projections, a sales plan, and reports on what the value of your development will be. Banks do care that developers know their business. You will have to impress the bank of your ability to complete a project successfully. Long story short, you have to give your loan officer detailed reports and proposals that will support the likelihood of your success with a particular project (Fig. 21.1). Anything less than a convincing proposal is likely to be shot down by the loan committee. Bottom line: You have to sell your development to your lender before you can sell it to buying customers.

Conventional lenders generally like a lot of documentation. For some reason, the quantity of paper seems to make a loan request feel safer for most bankers. Give them what they want—that's what I always say. To get a loan from a commercial lender you have to know what the lender is looking for. This is easy enough to figure out. Make an appointment to meet with the loan officer. When you meet with your banker, ask plenty of questions. Find out what the lender is interested in and then go back to your office and create it.

---

Form RD 1922-15
(Rev. 6-97)

## ADMINISTRATIVE APPRAISAL REVIEW
## FOR SINGLE FAMILY HOUSING

| 1. Rural Development Office | 2. Appraiser Name |
|---|---|
| 3. Borrower/Former Borrower/Applicant | 4. Date of Appraisal |
| 5. Property Address | 6. Borrower Case Number |

The purpose of this review is for loan underwriting, processing a conditional commitment for a dwelling to be built, rehabilitated, or developed as a manufactured home package, issuance of a conditional commitment for a Guaranteed Rural Housing loan, and/or loan servicing purposes. The reasons for disagreement by the reviewer to any of the following statements are to be documented and attached herewith.

1. Uniform Residential Appraisal Report for the subject property is attached. The report correctly identifies the property and has been completed, signed, and dated by the appraiser.

2. The mathematical calculations and adjustments are correct, or errors, if any, have been noted and determined to have no significant impact on the final market value conclusion of the appraisal.

3. In preparing this report, the appraiser has used three comparable properties sold within the past twelve months from the date of the report. The comparable properties appear to be similar to the subject and are from the same or like market. The market value appears to be reasonable.

4. The appraiser has used both the comparable sales and the cost approach in preparing the appraisal report as prescribed in RD Instruction 1922-C or the Direct Single Family Housing Handbooks, as appropriate.

5. For Guaranteed Rural Housing only, the land value (does, does not) exceed 30% of the value of the total package. (circle one)

6. The appraisal is acceptable for the intended purpose and I recommend: (check one)

_____ Authorization of payment to contract appraiser.

_____ Acceptance of appraisal for Guaranteed Rural Housing Loan.

_____ Issuance of a Conditional Commitment under 7 CFR 3550.70.

_____ Other: (explain) _____

| SIGNATURE OF REVIEWER | TITLE | DATE OF REVIEW |
|---|---|---|

RD 1922-15 (Rev. 6-97)

**FIGURE 21.1**

---

Appraisal review form.

Talking to lenders is the best way to find out what they want to see in order to approve your loan. I could give you samples of loan applications and loan packages, but they might mean very little to you. It is a much surer bet to ask your particular lenders what they want from you. They will typically want a lot, but it should all be material that you are having prepared for your purposes anyway.

There are certain basics that nearly every lender will want. It's common for a developer to provide copies of tax returns for the last 2 years. A profit-and-loss statement on your business will probably be required. A financial statement of your personal worth will most likely be required. Unless you are a heavy hitter with strong corporate assets, expect to put your personal assets on the line. Very few lenders will accept a loan document signed by you as a corporate officer with no personal liability.

When applying for a development loan you will normally have to provide full details on the development. This will generally include a site plan, a master plan, detail plans, sale projections, a sales procedure, and so forth. Basically, you have to lay it all out for the banker. It helps to have reams of documentation when meeting for a loan application. Before you invest the time and money required to create such a package you should ask prospective lenders what they want to see. Their requirements will probably be similar, but not identical. It's best to customize each loan package according to the requirements of individual lenders.

## Mortgage Brokers

Mortgage brokers are to money what real estate brokers are to property. A mortgage broker is a person who puts you, a person in search of financing, in touch with a lender. The broker charges someone a fee for services rendered. The fee is usually in the form of points on the loan, but it can be structured in various ways. Good mortgage brokers have long lists of lenders for various types of projects. When a borrower comes to a broker, the broker reviews the loan request and then circulates it among perspective lenders. The result can be quick financing. But, it can also be a waste of time. Not all mortgage brokers are well connected, and some of their financial sources may not be typical lenders. You have to be careful when dealing with a broker, but you should not rule out this line of financing.

Money borrowed through a mortgage broker may cost you more than if you borrowed the money directly from a bank. Before you agree to work with a broker, request a written disclosure of all terms and conditions for your dealings with the broker. Assuming that the broker is on the up and up, it doesn't hurt to explore this option.

If your development plan carries a risk factor that is higher than normal, a mortgage broker may be your best bet for financing. Many private investors work with brokers to lend money at interest rates somewhat above going bank rates. It might sting a bit to pay more for the money that you borrow, but if it is the only way that you can get funding, the increased cost may be justified. The key in working with brokers is to know, beyond any doubt, exactly what you are agreeing to before you agree to it. You would be wise to have your attorney inspect all paperwork before you sign any of it.

## Mortgage Bankers

Don't confuse mortgage brokers with mortgage bankers. Most mortgage bankers will have little interest in development loans. They can be an excellent source of financing for people buying homes in your development, but you will probably not find many mortgage bankers who are interested in working with raw land. There are, as usual, exceptions to the rule. A quick phone call will tell you if the mortgage bankers in your area are interested in speculative loans.

## Private Investors

Private investors are a common source of money for developers. If you are working on a deal that will be difficult to obtain conventional financing for, private investors could be your ticket to success. Working with private investors may be more risky than dealing with banks. You can avoid many problems by having your attorney review all documents before you sign them. It is common for private investors to charge higher interest rates than banks. So long as you are willing to accept the rate of interest and the terms, there is nothing wrong with private deals. But some investors set very tight criteria that can hurt you if anything goes wrong during the term of your loan.

When you agree to terms for financing, you may not be thinking of potential problems. This could be a financially fatal mistake. Unfortunately, there are people doing business who are concerned only about their personal gains. Let me give you an example of how you might suffer from entering into a deal that has tight criteria and little room for error.

Assume that you have gone to a private investor and obtained financing for land acquisition and improvements. The deal that you enter into seems innocent enough when you sign it. You are happy to get the money that you want so badly. In your excitement, you have failed to read all of the fine print. As your project begins, you get involved in doing your job and don't think much about the financing terms. Your private lender provides money regularly, in keeping with the terms of your agreement. Everything is going along fine. After several months of activity, your project is starting to take shape. You have done all of the hard work. Now it is a matter of putting the subcontractors on autopilot. What you don't know is that your world is about to explode.

You've been so busy taking care of business that you have been a bit remiss in keeping your files cleaned up. Paperwork has been piling up. You've been meaning to hire an assistant to help you stay on top of everything, but you just haven't had the time. As it stands, you missed two payments on your development loan. It's not that you couldn't have paid it, you just failed to stay on top of the administrative duties in your office. All of your time has been spent on the job site. Well, there is one piece of paper that you paid attention to. It is the certified mail that notified you of your loan default.

You figure that the default was no big deal. You'll pay the payments and pay the late charges and everything would be fine. If you were dealing with a commercial bank, your assessment of what would happen probably would be correct. But this is not the case, since you are dealing with a private investor. When you send a check for the two payments and the late fees you think all is well. But your payments are returned to you and papers are delivered that announce that your property is in foreclosure. Whoa! Could this really happen? It could. Loan terms with private investors can be almost anything that all parties to the agreement agree to.

I knew a real estate developer who was honest, but very hard to take. He would build shell cabins on land and then owner-finance the deals to people. In many cases, the buyers would improve the properties. For example, they would have wells drilled and septic systems installed. If the buyers missed two payments, the developer would foreclose on the property. This gave him a financial victory every time. Not only did he keep the down payment given to him by the buyers and the monthly payments that they made, he also got to keep the improvements made on the property. If someone had paid $7000 for a well and septic system out of their own money, the developer reaped the reward when he foreclosed on the loan for the property. It was an honest deal, but it was held to the letter of the law, and many people suffered from short bouts with hard times.

The story I just told you is true. Though it dealt with real estate packages, similar situations could arise with raw land that you are developing. Think about it. If you do all the work and get a development rolling and then lose it to foreclosure, the investor who loaned you the money profits greatly. It stinks, it's scary, but it could happen. Be very careful with any documents that you sign.

## Builders and Contractors

Builders might be willing to work with you to get a new development up and running. They may lend you money or do work on speculation. If you are interested in bringing in partners, builders are good sources to consider. Having you in the deal as the developer and builders on board for construction makes a nice package. Other contractors are also possible partners who may help to either finance your deal or to defer payment for their services until you start making sales. If you can get a site contractor to do the work either on spec or at a net-cost basis until sales come in, it can be a big financial help. It's customary to pay contractors who work this way more for the work that they do. You are increasing your expenses, but you are deferring the time when the payment has to be made. Think of the increased cost as interest on a loan.

Some contractors are happy to buy into a development deal. They sometimes do it with cash and at other times with their services. Structuring deals with builders and contractors is a creative way to get a project going that would otherwise be stalled. As with all deals, get your agreements in writing and have your attorney approve everything before you offer it or sign it.

## Partnerships

Partnerships are another way to raise money for a new deal. I've used partners before, but all of my experiences with partnerships have ended with regrets. Personally, I would not enter into another partnership arrangement, but that's just my personal view. Using partners to launch a development can be a wise business move. Your partners might include your parents, your friends, business associates, people involved in the development process, general investors, or even your bank. Yes, some banks do take a role in development deals from time to time.

If you go into business with partners, you will have to decide on what type of partnership to set up. You could go with a general partnership or a limited partnership. Most investors will prefer a limited partnership, since it limits their liability. Talk to your attorney to see how you should structure your partnerships if you decide to create them.

## Creative Terms

Creative terms can be set up for most development loans. Loans that are sold on the secondary mortgage market, like most loans for houses, must adhere to strict rules and regulations. However, loans that are not sold can be written to any variety of terms and conditions. Basically, whatever you and your lender agree to will work. This pertains to banks, as well as private sources of financing.

When you finance a development there can be a lot of money at stake. How you structure the disbursement and repayment plans can have a lot to do with your success as a developer. Many first-time developers fail to think much about the terms of their loans. They are so consumed with the stress of getting a loan that they overlook key issues that will affect their projects. The way in which you negotiate the terms of your financing is crucial.

The schedule for disbursements is one of the first major considerations. You know the lump sum of your loan, but how will the money be parceled out to you? Will the lender advance you all of the money you need to acquire the land? Will you have to put a substantial amount of the land purchase up with money out of your own pocket. A down payment of 30 percent is not unusual with land deals, but some lenders will advance the full amount of the land cost to get the ball rolling. This is certainly one of the first questions that you should be concerned about.

Once you have the land, how will the lender decide when to advance more money to you? Will the lender pay bills for you when work is done and invoices are submitted, or will you have to pay the bills and then request a draw against your loan? This is important, because if you have to pay for expenses out of your own money and then get reimbursed by your lender you could need a lot of cash. Many lenders will pay invoices once work is done and inspected by a representative of the lender.

Your loan request should detail all elements of your project and the cost of all of the major portions of work to be done. Will the lender pay in accordance with your costs, or will your bank draws be based on a percentage of completion? Find out how and when you will have access to the money that you will need. Don't wait until you are under way to find out that you don't have enough reserve capital to float the project between disbursements from your lender.

Once you know the schedule for getting borrowed money, you need to know what your requirements for repaying the loan will be. Are you going to be paying interest only, with the total loan amount coming due upon completion? Will the lender allow interest to accrue with no payments being made for some period of time? How long will the lender allow your loan to remain active after the completion of your project? Some lenders will let a loan run for a long time as long as payments are made, but others want to be paid off, in full, shortly after the completion of a project. If you will be dealing with a different lender for long-term financing, how will that affect your short-term financing?

In the case of developing a residential subdivision you might be able to tie the repayment plan to the sale of lots. For example, you might make a deal where a percentage of each lot sale is applied to the loan amount until the loan is paid off. This type of deal is sweet when you can get it. What are the terms and conditions dealing with late payments or missed payments? How long after missing a payment will you have to correct the deficiency before foreclosure proceedings begin?

What type of insurance policies will you be required to maintain to satisfy the lender? Don't forget this question, because insurance can be expensive. Some developers fail to allow for the cost of insurance premiums when they do their cost projections. You should insure your project to protect yourself, but your lender may require a more extensive policy than what you would be satisfied with.

Don't feel as though you have no say in how the terms of your financing will be structured. Some lenders may be very firm in their loan guidelines, but you should be able to negotiate some elements of your deal. It's well worth your time to think carefully about the type of terms and conditions that will work best for you. Some developers would rather pay higher loan expenses in exchange for less money out of pocket. Developers who have plenty of cash will prefer to get lower loan rates by putting more cash into a deal. Each developer has individual needs and desires. Establish what you want and then attempt to set up a loan that meets your approval.

# Zoning

Zoning has much to do with what developers are allowed to create. The laws, rules, and regulations for zoning can vary greatly. These variations can run from town to town and city to city. You can't go on a state-by-state formula when it comes to zoning laws. Every organized community is likely to have its own zoning regulations. And zoning laws can be changed fairly quickly, so don't rely on old zoning decisions. Every piece of land can fall under different zoning ordinances.

Zoning regulations can be very complicated. Even experienced real estate attorneys can have trouble interpreting the laws. Trying to make sense, on your own, of all the zoning issues that you will deal with as a developer would be crazy. You will need a good lawyer to work with you when it comes to cutting through all of the red tape associated with zoning. However, there is a lot about zoning that you can understand and work with. These issues are what we will cover here. But remember this: Consult your attorney for clear interpretations of zoning before you make a buying decision on a parcel of land.

## Zoning Maps

Zoning maps are good starting points for checking the zoning of land. One purpose of zoning is to prevent conflicts in land use. It is the zoning laws that balance a community in what is believed to be the best means possible. Zoning maps are drawn to show specific zoning regions. For example, you might see that one part of town is zoned for retail use while another section is zoned for industrial use and another section is zoned for residential use. It is common for zoning maps to be altered periodically. Requests for zoning changes are sometimes approved. When they are, some reference to the changes must be recorded. Eventually, the zoning maps reflect the changes.

If you are researching a particular piece of land, you can look on a zoning map and see what the existing zoning is. When the established zoning is compatible with the type of project that you want to develop, you have it made. It is a simple matter to move forward when you don't need a zoning change to do it. If, however, you find that the land that you want to purchase is not zoned for a use that will allow your type of development, you have some possible trouble to consider.

If a change in zoning will be required for a project, you could be looking at many months of legal maneuvering and a lot of out-of-pocket cash expenses. Your choices are to pass on the property and look for another parcel that will be zoned for your needs, or to file for a change in zoning. Some types of zoning changes can be reasonably simple to obtain, but others are very difficult. It is certainly easier and less expensive to develop a piece of land that is already zoned for the proposed use.

I have had my share of dealings with zoning officials and zoning boards of appeals. The experiences have not been fun. Fortunately, I can't remember a time when I did not prevail. But, this is not to say that winning was easy or that it came without a fight. Some of my zoning battles have been very expensive. They have also been quite time-consuming. If a project doesn't have enough potential, fighting the system isn't worthwhile. Before you engage in a major zoning battle, make sure that the time and money that you will invest in it will be rewarded in the end.

Zoning boards usually have a lot of latitude in how they handle their zoning regulations. A landowner might obtain a variance with relative ease. When a variance is approved, it is usually in the form of a minor variation from existing zoning requirements. As an example, a variance might be issued for a garage to be built 2 feet closer to a property sideline than present zoning requirements allow for. It would be common in such a case for a developer to be required to talk with neighbors who might be affected by the variance and to gain permission from the neighbors, before the variance is issued.

Zoning maps show you what existing conditions are. The maps do not indicate that the land use might not be changed. In some cases, the zoning maps might tip you off to great opportunities. Finding land where zoning has been changed for a higher and better use can result in much higher profits for a developer. If you can buy land that the owner believes is zoned as residential use only and then use it for commercial purposes, the value of the land should soar. This is not all that uncommon.

Many residential areas slowly change over to other types of land use. This usually happens as an area grows. Car dealers, fast-food restaurants, hardware stores, and all sorts of other nonresidential uses move into an area. As this happens, the houses are sometimes converted to new uses or they may be removed to allow a higher use of the land. People who live in the houses sometimes sell their property for huge profits. But some sellers are not aware of how much more their homes have become worth as the zoning laws and land use have changed. Astute developers scour zoning changes in search of rare opportunities. Zoning maps may not show the changes soon enough. Dig deeply when you are researching permitted land use. Your research can keep you out of trouble and may make you much more wealthy.

## Cumulative Zoning

Cumulative zoning is a type of zoning that often allows for changes in zoning regulations. Developers tend to like this type of zoning, since it can allow a great deal of freedom. Communities, however, sometimes suffer from cumulative zoning. The purpose of zoning is to manage land use and to maintain certain separations. Some strange things can occur with cumulative zoning. For example, you might find housing developments mixed in with commercial projects.

The value of land is often in direct relation to the zoning laws. Obviously, a piece of land that can have a shopping mall built on it should be worth more money than the same piece of land if it is limited to single-family housing. Striving for the highest and best use is a good goal, but it is one that some communities cannot afford to enforce. The result is often a mixed-use community, which allows different types of land use in the same area.

Why would a community vote for mixed use? Deriving tax dollars from landowners might be one reason. In some areas, strict zoning keeps residential areas so far from places of employment that traffic becomes a problem. If people have to move into fringe areas and commute to work, the traffic flow can be more than the roads in a community can handle. There can be any number of reasons for cumulative zoning.

## Floating Zones

Floating zones are usually districts that are not mapped for specific zoning uses. Communities may use floating zones to give themselves flexibility in applying their zoning regulations. Since floating zones are often unmapped, they can be difficult to pin down during preliminary research. A floating zone may be used as a means to move into transitional zoning. And planned unit developments often come into floating zones.

## Transitional Zoning

What is transitional zoning? It is a type of zoning that starts with one region of land use and gradually changes the land use as distance increases. This type of zoning usually works well. It can facilitate a number of land uses without hurting the look of a city. For example, the most strict end of the zoning might contain heavy commercial properties. As a development sprawls out, the zoning could go to light commercial, then to office space, and eventually to residential use. You might even find regulations that require office space to be developed to appear as residential architecture.

There is a town in Maine where low-impact features are required of many types of business property. For example, a major fast-food chain is housed in what could appear to be a large farmhouse. Many of the restaurants and businesses are required to be housed in buildings that are compatible with the residential area. This can make it confusing for people who are looking for the business image that they have come to be so familiar with, but it does enhance the quaint appearance of the town.

# Planned Unit Developments

Planned unit developments (PUDs) are quite common. This type of development may house everything from single-family homes to commercial retail stores. It is common for a PUD to be a stand-alone community. The community may include all forms of service businesses, medical facilities of some sort, and a variety of housing types. Because of the mixed use in a PUD, careful planning is needed on the developer's part.

Floating zones are common areas for PUDs. Many communities encourage the development of PUDs. But, there is no guarantee of having a project approved, and this is a risk. The money spent designing a PUD for application approval can run into thousands of dollars. This is money that will be wasted if the project is not approved. Gaining approval for a PUD can mean major profits for developers, but the venture capital invested to get the approval can prove to be a substantial risk.

When a PUD is designed, it can contain many types of buildings and land uses. Most commercial uses are required to be neighborhood-serving establishments. Generally, PUDs are required to provide open space, recreational facilities, and other amenities. It is common for some provision to be made for local fire prevention and protection. Schools may also be a part of a PUD. The expense of developing a PUD runs high. But a PUD that is well planned should sell well. Few first-time developers start with PUDs.

When a PUD is designed, sections of the land are set aside for different types of land uses. These sections are identified on a site plan. For example, one section may be given a rating of R-1, which could mean low-density use. A section with a rating of R-20 could be set aside for ultrahigh density, and there could be other ratings between the two extremes.

# Cluster Housing

Cluster housing is popular in large urban areas. The general concept behind cluster zoning is a compromise of smaller house lots and larger open areas to balance the mix. Some communities approve cluster developments in an attempt to preserve land around historic sites or even valuable farmland. Developers who can gain cluster approval can turn a small parcel of land into a valuable housing project. There usually is not as much flexibility with cluster zoning as there is with planned unit developments.

Zoning density is usually maintained in a cluster development. However, the lot size and setback requirements are often forgiven. There is not as much freedom with a cluster development as you might think. Even though you can reduce lot size, you may not be able to increase the number of housing units. Remember, the goal of clusters is to give more open space per dwelling unit. Many developers think of clusters as a way of squeezing a lot of housing into a small space. This is sometimes possible, but don't expect it to be the rule. Rather, it is the exception in terms of density.

## Exclusionary Zoning

Exclusionary zoning is intended to prohibit specific types of development. This type of zoning is used to keep a certain type of development out of a region where general zoning would allow the use. Take for example a region where buildings for clubs are allowed. There might be exclusionary zoning to prevent the creation of a gun club that includes a shooting range. The noise from the firing range might be the reason for excluding the land use. Noise, odor, and pollution are common reasons why exclusionary zoning is used.

Gun clubs might not be the only target of exclusionary zoning. This type of zoning can limit any type of land use, at least in theory. For example, the zoning might exclude the construction of apartments or mobile homes. Minimum house sizes might be required. This is not uncommon for a developer to find in covenants and restrictions, but it is odd to have a zoning regulation of this type. In fact, exclusionary zoning often comes under fire as being a form of discrimination.

## Inclusionary Zoning

Inclusionary zoning is designed to promote the development of both low- and moderate-income housing. To do this, communities offer more flexibility in their zoning regulations. For example, a developer may be allowed to increase the density of a development in exchange for controlled-price dwellings. This can sound good on paper, but it may not work so well in reality. Not all land parcels can be maximized with the type of housing that you may want. For example, you may have to include town house designs to achieve the higher density.

## Other Types of Zoning

There are other types of zoning. In fact, you may run into any number of zoning situations as you move from one jurisdiction to another. Zoning laws are similar to building and plumbing codes. They are usually offered in a generic form that is adopted and adapted by local governing bodies. The adaptation can be extreme. You and your attorney will have to read all of the fine print to stay out of trouble. Don't make any assumptions. Zoning is a major part of the development process, and it is a topic that you will have to become acquainted with.

# Closing Your Land Deal

Closing your land deal can be simple and require little of your time. Or, it can be a challenge to your patience unlike any other. In theory, getting from an accepted purchase agreement to ownership should be a routine matter that merely takes time. Most closings take between 30 to 60 days. Once you have a fully executed contract to buy land, your dealings with that part of the job should be in the hands of others and off of your plate, but don't count on it. It is not uncommon for major problems to arise somewhere along the way during the closing process.

Given normal conditions, your attorney and other professionals will be running the show to get your purchase settled. There can be a great number of people involved in the overall process. Some of the players may include your lawyer, the seller's lawyer, real estate brokers, surveyors, title companies, insurance companies, property inspectors, appraisers, and the list goes on. Developers hope to be hammering out details for development while papers are being shuffled for closing. There are many deals that do close smoothly, but there are some that don't.

By the time you reach a point of being ready to close a deal you may have invested a substantial amount of money on a deal that you don't yet own the land for. Engineering reports, soil tests, and similar work done to give you the green light to buy a property are all paid for out of your pocket. If the sale doesn't close, you are out the money. You won't be able to have the seller reimburse you, and few experts are going to return their fees if you can't close your deal. It's possible to lose thousands of dollars before you ever own a piece of land.

How can you protect yourself during closing procedures? Having a good lawyer is a start, but even that doesn't guarantee success. There is so much that can go wrong that you can't protect yourself from everything. Much of what might happen is hidden until the closing process begins. You can, however, do some work ahead of time to limit your risks.

If you are not an expert at dealing with real estate you will be limited as to what you can do personally. But you can still maintain an active role and keep your closing on track. I'm fortunate to be a designated real estate broker with many years of experience. I know the ropes, so to speak, so I can do a lot of my own work. You may not have this advantage, but you can still do more than most developers do to ensure a timely closing.

## The Closing Process

The closing process begins once a buyer and seller agree to a transaction. There are usually many contingencies that must be removed from a contract for purchase. Time is needed to clear the contingencies. One of the early steps in the closing process, for most buyers, is the application for financing. If you have your loan package prepared, this step only takes an hour or so. Once a relationship is established with a lender, the rest of the closing process moves into gear.

Lenders will want current appraisals on the property being bought. The appraisal process for a home might take less than a day, but the same process for a development project could take several days, or more. It is during this process that information is collected to place a value on the existing property and the property as it will be after proposed development plans take place.

Someone, usually a lawyer or a representative from a title company, has to perform a title search (Figs. 23.1 and 23.2). This aspect of the closing process can go quickly, but delays may occur with some

Form RD 1927-10
(Rev. 7-98)

UNITED STATES DEPARTMENT OF AGRICULTURE
RURAL DEVELOPMENT
FARM SERVICE AGENCY

FORM APPROVED
OMB NO. 0575-0147

**FINAL TITLE OPINION**

| LOAN APPLICANT | ADDRESS OR PROPERTY COVERED BY THIS OPINION | |
| --- | --- | --- |
| APPLICANT FOR TITLE EXAMINATION | COUNTY | STATE |

I.  I have examined title to the property described in the security instrument described in paragraph II. B. below. My examination covered the period from the time of termination of title search covered by my Preliminary Title Opinion on Form RD 1927-9; or the time of recordation of the initial loan security instrument if this opinion covers land already owned by the loan applicant in a

subsequent loan case, to _____, _____, at _____ a.m. (including the time of filing the current security
instrument).                *(Date)*                               p.m.

II.  Based on said title examination, my preliminary title examination if any, and any additional information concerning the title which has come to my attention, it is my opionion that:

A.  Good and marketable title, in accordance with title examination standards prevailing in the area, to said property (real estate and

any water rights offered as security) is now vested in _____

_____

as_____.
             *(Joint tenants, tenants by the entirety, etc.)*

B.  The United States of America holds a valid _____   _____lien on said property as required by Rural
                                          *(Priority)*      *(Mortgage, etc.)*

Development or the Farm Service Agency, or their successor (Agency), which lien was filed for record on _____,
                                                                                      *(Date)*

_____, at _____ a.m.  and is recorded in _____.
                        p.m.                        *(Book, page, and office)*

C.  Said property and lien are subject only to encumbrances, reservations, exceptions, and defects which were approved by written administrative waivers of the Agency attached hereto or to my Preliminary Title Opinion.

III.  If a water right is involved and is not covered by the current security instrument, it is subject only to the encumbrances, reservations, exceptions, and defects set forth in said administrative waivers and was made available as security in the following manner (Water stock would normally be reissued in the names of said land owners and the United States of America and delivered to the Agency Official at the time of loan closing):

**FIGURE 23.1**

**Final title opinion form.**

properties. A typical title search involves tracking all activity with the title to the land over the past several decades. The search could go back to ownership for the last 40 years, or more.

Current surveys are often a requirement of the closing process. Depending on circumstances, the field work for a survey may take a

IV. The term "encumbrances, reservations, exceptions, and defects" means all matters which would prevent the United States from obtaining the required lien on the property identified in paragraph I, including but not limited to (a) mortgages, deeds of trust, and vendors', mechanics', materialmen's, and all other liens, including any provisions thereof for future advances which could take priority over the said lien to the United States, (b) Federal, State, and local taxes, including county, school, improvement, water, drainage, sewer, inheritance, personal property, and income, (c) State and Federal bankruptcy, insolvency, receivership, and probate proceedings, (d) judgments and pending suits, in State and Federal courts, (e) recorded covenants; conditions; restrictions; reservations; liens; encumbrances; easements; rights-of-way; leases; mineral, oil, gas, and geothermal rights (regardless of the right of surface entry); timber rights; water rights; pending court proceedings and other matters of record which affect the title of the property or the ability of the buyer or seller to convey or accept title.

V. This opinion is issued expressly for the benefit of the above-named applicant for title examination and the United States of America acting through the United States Department of Agriculture Agency which provided the assistance, and I assume liability to each hereunder.

_____
*(Date)*

_____
*(Attorney's signature)*

Attachments

_____
*(Address, include ZIP Code)*

**FIGURE 14.1**

RD 1927-10, Page 2 of 2

**Final title opinion form. (*Continued*)**

few hours or several days. The time and expense is related to how difficult it is to pin down property boundaries. Some properties have iron stakes and benchmarks that are easy to locate. Other properties may be much more difficult to survey, such as a property cut from a larger parcel or one that has not been surveyed in recent years.

Employment verifications are a part of the closing process, and they are handled by the lender. Many developers are self-employed.

USDA
Form RD 400-4
(Rev. 3-97)

**ASSURANCE AGREEMENT**
(Under Title VI, Civil Rights Act of 1964)

FORM APPROVED
OMB No. 0575-0018

The_____

*(name of recipient)*

_____

*(address)*

("Recipient" herein) hereby assures the U. S. Department of Agriculture that Recipient is in compliance with and will continue to comply with Title VI of the Civil Rights Act of 1964 (42 USC 2000d et. seq.), 7 CFR Part 15, and Rural Housing Service, Rural Business-Cooperative Service, Rural Utilities Service, or the Farm Service Agency, (hereafter known as the " Agency") regulations promulgated thereunder, 7 C.F.R. §1901.202. In accordance with that Act and the regulations referred to above, Recipient agrees that in connection with any program or activity for which Recipient receives Federal financial assistance (as such term is defined in 7 C.F.R. §14.2) no person in the United States shall, on the ground of race, color, or national origin, be excluded from participation in, be denied the benefits of, or be otherwise subjected to discrimination.

1. Recipient agrees that any transfer of any aided facility, other than personal property, by sale, lease or other conveyance of contract, shall be, and shall be made expressly, subject to the obligations of this agreement and transferee's assumption thereof.

2. Recipient shall:

   (a)   Keep such records and submit to the Government such timely, complete, and accurate information as the Government may determine to be necessary to ascertain our/my compliance with this agreement and the regulations.

   (b)   Permit access by authorized employees of the Agency or the U.S. Department of Agriculture during normal business hours to such books, records, accounts and other sources of information and its facilities as may be pertinent to ascertaining such compliance.

   (c)   Make available to users, participants, beneficiaries and other interested persons such information regarding the provisions of this agreement and the regulations, and in such manner as the Agency or the U.S. Department of Agriculture finds necessary to inform such persons of the protection assured them against discrimination.

3. The obligations of this agreement shall continue:

   (a)   As to any real property, including any structure, acquired or improved with the aid of the Federal financial assistance, so long as such real property is used for the purpose for which the Federal financial assistance is made or for another purpose which affords similar services or benefits, or for as long as the Recipient retains ownership or possession of the property, whichever is longer.

   (b)   As to any personal property acquired or improved with the aid of the Federal financial assistance, so long as Recipient retains ownership or possession of the property.

   (c)   As to any other aided facility or activity, until the last advance of funds under the loan or grant has been made.

4. Upon any breach or violation this agreement the Government may, at its option:

   (a)   Terminate or refuse to render or continue financial assistance for the aid of the property, facility, project, service or activity.

   (b)   Enforce this agreement by suit for specific performance or by any other available remedy under the laws of the United States or the State in which the breach or violation occurs.

Rights and remedies provided for under this agreement shall be cumulative.

In witness whereof,_____ on this

*(name of recipient)*

date has caused this agreement to be executed by its duly authorized officers and its seal affixed hereto, or, if a natural person, has hereunto executed this agreement.

_____
Recipient

(SEAL)      _____
Date

Attest:_____      _____
Title                                  Title

*According to the Paperwork Reduction Act of 1995, no persons are required to respond to a collection of information unless it displays a valid OMB control number. The valid OMB control number for this information collection is 0570-0018. The time required to complete this information is estimated to average 15 minutes per response, including the time for reviewing instructions, searching existing data sources, gathering and maintaining the data needed, and completing and reviewing the collection of information.*

**FIGURE 23.2**

**Assurance agreement form.**

For most, this means providing tax returns for at least the last 2 years. The verification process includes checking bank accounts, income, credit history, debt service, and other factors that may be deemed important to a repayment plan.

In simple form, closings are not complicated or difficult. There can, however, be much more to the closing process than what we have discussed. For example, you may have to apply for and receive permits for development before you can close your loan. It could be necessary for you to provide detailed documentation on development costs before closing, and this might mean having many written quotes from contractors. You probably won't conduct your own title search or perform your own appraisal, but there is work for you to do.

## The Appraisal Process

The appraisal process starts early during closing procedures and is very important. If the land that you are trying to finance doesn't appraise well, you will not be able to borrow as much money against it. You can't do your own appraisal, but you can work with the appraiser. All good real estate brokers know the value of working with appraisers. If you want to make sure that you get a high appraisal, you may have to do some research for your appraiser. The appraiser might be appointed by the lender or may be someone whom you have hired that the lender will accept. You can have an impact on the appraised value of your property. Let me show you what you can do.

Appraisers look for all sorts of information when putting a price on a piece of land. Much of their research is done by computer and with multiple listing service (MLS) books. If you have any access to information that may not be in a current MLS you should make it available to your appraiser. For example, if you know of a private sale that closed within the last 6 months that would be comparable to the property that you are having appraised, the information could be very valuable to you.

Many developers, such as myself, do a lot of preliminary research on a parcel of land before ever offering a contract to purchase it. The results of the research done can be very helpful to an appraiser. There is a lot of latitude in a appraiser's decision of comparable properties to be used for valuation purposes. Depending upon the current market conditions, an appraiser may have 10 to 12 potential comparable properties to choose from for appraisal purposes. The appraiser may use only three pieces of property as comparables. The three chosen can have much to do with the value placed on your land.

Appraisers should look for comparable properties that are the best match with your land. But many appraisers are short on time and pressured by their employers. This can lead to grabbing the first few comparables that are "close enough" for setting a value on your land. You don't want this to happen. It is in your best interest to have the absolute best comps used for setting a price.

When your deal is assigned an appraiser, find out who the appraiser is and how to make contact. Call the appraiser and share any information that you have regarding comparable properties that you would like used. You can even enclose data on the comps with your loan application. I've done this many times and the comps have often been used. If you provide the comps, you make life easier for the appraiser. You also get a good shot at getting your comps on the appraisal report.

Getting to know the appraisers in your area is time well spent. Putting together your own comparables is the most productive way to control your own destiny. In many ways, the appraisal process may be the most critical part of a closing. If your land doesn't come in with a value high enough, you will either have to walk away from it or put a larger portion of money on the table as a down payment.

## The Title Search

The title search of a property is often done by a developer's attorney. Sometimes the search is done by a title company or someone else. Searching a title is not particularly difficult, but it is a critical part of long-term success. I often do my own title searches before making an offer to buy land. Then I have my attorney do a title search before closing on a property. While I know how to do a search, it suits my style to have the backup of an attorney. And most lenders want a title search to be done by someone in the legal profession.

What do title searches turn up? In most cases, they are just part of the closing process and don't prove to be monumental. But there are times when a title search kills a deal. This is why I like to search a title before I spend much in preliminary investments prior to a purchase. Title searches are intended to find anything that might cloud a title. A clouded title is one where there are problems, or potential problems, that might make the transfer of a title difficult. Some title defects can be insured to make a property fairly safe to buy, but other problems are almost insurmountable.

The types of problems found during a title search can be numerous. For example, there may be unpaid taxes and a tax lien. This type of problem can usually be solved quickly with cash, but you wouldn't want to take ownership of a property and then discover the need for more money to pay off back taxes. More serious problems could include ownership disputes or a specter of an illegal subdivision. I've run into problems with alleged illegal subdivision and beaten them, but it is not the best foot forward in a new deal.

A title search might reveal various types of liens on a property. Normally, the liens have to be paid before a clean transfer can be made. A property that is up for sale due to a divorce could be a candidate for lien problems. Liens can be placed on property that is not the centerpiece of a legal problem. For example, if a person was in deep debt, a creditor might be awarded a judgment through the courts. In some cases, any real property owned by the debtor might have a lien placed on it for security. It's important to know of any liens that may exist prior to buying a parcel of land.

Title searches don't usually require a lot of time to complete. The work can often be done in a matter of hours, rather than days. It is wise to do a search before putting much money into preliminary expenses. But it is also a good idea to do a new title search right before closing. A lien can be filed in a day, so a search done a week before may not be good enough. Make sure that you have the most recent title search possible before closing on a property.

## Surveys

Surveys are almost always a part of the closing process. It's possible that a seller will have a current survey available that will relieve the need for a survey during the closing process. If this the case, it's fine. However, if there is not a recent survey available, you should insist on one. Land is often what it seems to be, but sometimes it is not. You can't depend on boundary markers provided by sellers. Many owners lose some of their memory over where exact boundaries are. Unless you are able to find verifiable survey markers, you should question the boundaries of a property.

During the closing process, a survey can turn up undesirable information. If a section of land is not as it has been reported to be, a closing might be stopped. I remember a closing once where a buyer believed that the land being purchased included a nice, paved parking lot. I was working with the buyer as his real estate broker. The selling broker had advertised the property with a drawing that included the entire parking area. It was not until a site survey was done that we discovered most of the paved parking area was on town property. It seems that a previous owner had paved municipal property at some point with no complaints. The present owner had assumed, for years, that the parking lot was part of the property. It was not.

The problem with the parking lot was not known to us until we were all gathered around the closing table. I was reviewing the closing documents when I noticed the discrepancy. Once I saw it, I immediately told my customer of the problem. We went into the hallway to discuss it. The deal was good enough to take as it was, so the buyer went forward with the closing. In this case, the mix-up with the survey was unfortunate, but not a deal-stopper. It could have been.

## Income Verifications

Income verifications are another part of the closing process. There shouldn't be any surprises in this procedure. As long as you report your income as it really is, there shouldn't be any problem. However, you may have to provide more verification than what you are expecting to, and this might be a problem. If you are self-employed, you can expect to provide a minimum of the last 2 years' tax returns. Generally, a lender will average the earnings of the two tax returns to arrive at your income. You may, however, have to provide more detailed information. If you do have to, and if you don't have it readily available, you could lose time. If your purchase contract has a "time is of the essence" clause in it, you could lose your closing by not having your documentation handy. When you make loan application, make sure of exactly what will be required of you and comply as quickly as possible.

## Credit Reports

Credit reports are a part of the closing process. Typically, a lender will pull a credit report on you before sending a loan to the closing process. But things can change between the time that you start a closing and finish it. Just as you will want a "fresh" title search, a lender is likely to want a fresh credit report before closing. If anything happens during the closing process to taint your credit rating, you could lose your deal.

Credit problems can come from a variety of reasons. Usually, these are associated with situations that people who suffer from them are aware of. But this is not always the case. There are times when dark spots can appear on your credit report without you suspecting it. Sometimes reporting agencies make mistakes. This happened to me once, and it was very weird.

I was living in Virginia and doing my work as a builder and developer. When I applied for a construction loan, I was turned down. The lender was one with whom I'd worked with in the past, and he was confused by the credit report. When the lender called, he told me what he was seeing on my credit report. It showed me having terrible credit. I knew that there was a mistake, but I didn't know what it was. With some research, I found a surprising situation.

As it turned out, there was another man with the same first and last name as mine living on the same road that I lived on. My credit was golden, and his was not so good. The problem was that the credit-reporting agency thought that I was responsible for the problems that actually belonged to the other individual. The tipoff came when it showed that my neighbor had three children. I didn't have any children at the time. Our middle names were different and so were the names of our wives. It was not a huge problem to straighten out the mess, but it did take time, and it was very confusing at first.

The point to my story is that you can be hit with bad credit that is not supposed to be your problem. If you are, it can put the skids on your closing in a hurry. The odds of getting saddled with someone else's credit problems are probably pretty low, but it can happen. It's also possible for a divorced spouse to mess up your credit. However your credit gets compromised, you have to be able to right the wrong quickly.

## Tracking

A typical real estate closing involves a lot of people. It would seem logical to assume that these professionals will do their jobs independently. Don't count on it. It's almost scary how unorganized some closing procedures are. Having been in the real estate business for decades, I've dealt with too many closings to count. The number of times that one hand doesn't know what the other one is doing is simply incredible at times. The level of poor communication between players in the closing process can be extremely frustrating. This is where a broker's intervention or a developer's supervision can make the difference between a timely closing and a busted deal.

The closing process is not usually overseen by a single supervisor. All of the people involved in the process are working independently. Lenders are the closest thing to an overall supervisor, but they don't always keep as tight a rope on the closing process as some developers would like. If you have a good broker representing you, the broker will take care of your closing for you. Developers who are not working with brokers, or who don't have enough confidence in the brokers with whom they are working, should track their own closing process. Failure to track a closing can result in a blown deal and lost money (Fig. 23.3).

Keeping tabs on your closing is not a major task. It will, however, require you to make some phone calls to make sure that everyone is on schedule. Assuming that you will be doing your own supervision, you will need the names and phone numbers, maybe the e-mail addresses, of all the players on your team. Your goal will be to track all elements of your closing. This will basically be a weekly task that could last for up to 8 weeks, and maybe more.

Essentially, you will check in with everyone involved in your closing. If a survey is supposed to be delivered by a certain date, you will call on the following day to make sure it arrived. If it did not, you will call the survey firm to establish the status of the survey. This process will apply to appraisers, attorneys, lenders, inspectors, and so forth. You should have a complete list of everyone working on your closing. The list should be set into a schedule, so that you can know if the closing is on time. You can lay out your table of players and tasks on a computer or on a sheet of ruled paper. The important thing is to have every category, every player, and every date in place.

Once you have your schedule, post it in a place where you will see it regularly. It's easy to become distracted by the many hats you wear as a developer. Putting your schedule in plain view can be quite helpful. Record anticipated dates. Insert space to note when tasks are completed. If there is a problem, and there will probably be some, make more notes of what you need to do to solve them. Stay on top of your list. Work it daily if need be.

**C. Note:** This form is furnished to give you a statement of actual settlement costs. Amounts paid to and by the settlement agent are shown, items marked (p.o.c.) were paid outside the closing; they are shwon here for infromational purposes and are not included in the totals.

| D. Name & Address of Borrower: | E. Name & Address of Seller: | F. Name & Address of Lender: |
|---|---|---|

| G. Property Location: | H. Settlement Agent: | |
|---|---|---|
| | Place of Settlement: | I. Settlement Date: |

| J. Summary of Borrower's Transaction | | K. Summary of Seller's Transaction | |
|---|---|---|---|
| **100. Gross Amount Due From Borrower** | | **400. Gross Amount Due To Seller** | |
| 101. Contract sales price | | 401. Contract sales price | |
| 102. Personal property | | 402. Personal property | |
| 103. Settlement charges to borrower (line 1400) | | 403. | |
| 104. | | 404. | |
| 105. | | 405. | |
| **Adjustments for items paid by seller in advance** | | **Adjustments for items paid by seller in advance** | |
| 106. City/town taxes    to | | 406. City/town taxes    to | |
| 107. County taxes    to | | 407. County taxes    to | |
| 108. Assessments    to | | 408. Assessments    to | |
| 109. | | 409. | |
| 110. | | 410. | |
| 111. | | 411. | |
| 112. | | 412. | |
| **120. Gross Amount Due From Borrower** | | **420. Gross Amount Due To Seller** | |
| **200. Amounts Paid By Or In Behalf Of Borrower** | | **500. Reductions In Amount Due To Seller** | |
| 201. Deposit or earnest money | | 501. Excess deposit (see instructions) | |
| 202. Principal amount of new loan(s) | | 502. Settlement charges to seller (line 1400) | |
| 203. Existing loan(s) taken subject to | | 503. Existing loan(s) taken subject to | |
| 204. | | 504. Payoff of first mortgage loan | |
| 205. | | 505. Payoff of second mortgage loan | |
| 206. | | 506. | |
| 207. | | 507. | |
| 208. | | 508. | |
| 209. | | 509. | |
| **Adjustments for items unpaid by seller** | | **Adjustments for items unpaid by seller** | |
| 210. City/town taxes    to | | 510. City/town taxes    to | |
| 211. County taxes    to | | 511. County taxes    to | |
| 212. Assessments    to | | 512. Assessments    to | |
| 213. | | 513. | |
| 214. | | 514. | |
| 215. | | 515. | |
| 216. | | 516. | |
| 217. | | 517. | |
| 218. | | 518. | |
| 219. | | 519. | |
| **220. Total Paid By/For Borrower** | | **520. Total Reduction Amount Due Seller** | |
| **300. Cash At Settlement From/To Borrower** | | **600. Cash At Settlement To/From Seller** | |
| 301. Gross Amount due from borrower (line 120) | | 601. Gross amount due to seller (line 420) | |
| 302. Less amounts paid by/for borrower (line 220) | ( ) | 602. Less reductions in amt. due seller (line 520) | ( ) |
| **303. Cash** ☐ From  ☐ To Borrower | | **603. Cash** ☐ To  ☐ From Seller | |

Section 5 of the Real Estate Settlement Procedures Act (RESPA) requires the following: • HUD must develop a Special Information Booklet to help persons borrowing money to finance the purchase of residential real estate to better understand the nature and costs of real estate settlement services; • Each lender must provide the booklet to all applicants from whom it receives or for whom it prepares a written application to borrow money to finance the

Section 4(a) of RESPA mandates that HUD develop and prescribe this standard form to be used at the time of loan settlement to provide full disclosure of all charges imposed upon the borrower and seller. These are third party disclosures that are designed to provide the borrower with pertinent information during the settlement process in order to be a better shopper.

## FIGURE 23.3

Settlement cost form

| | | | |
|---|---|---|---|
| **800. Items Payable In Connection With Loan** | | | |
| 801. Loan Origination Fee | % | | |
| 802. Loan Discount | % | | |
| 803. Appraisal Fee | to | | |
| 804. Credit Report | to | | |
| 805. Lender's Inspection Fee | | | |
| 806. Mortgage Insurance Application Fee to | | | |
| 807. Assumption Fee | | | |
| 808. | | | |
| 809. | | | |
| 810. | | | |
| 811. | | | |
| **900. Items Required By Lender To Be Paid In Advance** | | | |
| 901. Interest from to | @$ | /day | |
| 902. Mortgage Insurance Premium for | | months to | |
| 903. Hazard Insurance Premium for | | years to | |
| 904. | | years to | |
| 905. | | | |
| **1000. Reserves Deposited With Lender** | | | |
| 1001. Hazard insurance | months @ $ | per month | |
| 1002. Mortgage insurance | months @ $ | per month | |
| 1003. City property taxes | months @ $ | per month | |
| 1004. County property taxes | months @ $ | per month | |
| 1005. Annual assessments | months @ $ | per month | |
| 1006. | months @ $ | per month | |
| 1007. | months @ $ | per month | |
| 1008. | months @ $ | per month | |
| **1100. Title Charges** | | | |
| 1101. Settlement or closing fee | to | | |
| 1102. Abstract or title search | to | | |
| 1103. Title examination | to | | |
| 1104. Title insurance binder | to | | |
| 1105. Document preparation | to | | |
| 1106. Notary fees | to | | |
| 1107. Attorney's fees | to | | |
| (includes above items numbers: | | ) | |
| 1108. Title insurance | to | | |
| (includes above items numbers: | | ) | |
| 1109. Lender's coverage | $ | | |
| 1110. Owner's coverage | $ | | |
| 1111. | | | |
| 1112. | | | |
| 1113. | | | |
| **1200. Government Recording and Transfer Charges** | | | |
| 1201. Recording fees: Deed $ ; Mortgage $ ; Releases $ | | | |
| 1202. City/county tax/stamps: Deed $ ; Mortgage $ | | | |
| 1203. State tax/stamps: Deed $ ; Mortgage $ | | | |
| 1204. | | | |
| 1205. | | | |
| **1300. Additional Settlement Charges** | | | |
| 1301. Survey to | | | |
| 1302. Pest inspection to | | | |
| 1303. | | | |
| 1304. | | | |
| 1305. | | | |
| **1400. Total Settlement Charges (enter on lines 103, Section J and 502, Section K)** | | | |

**FIGURE 23.3**

**Settlement cost form.** (*Continued*)

Your active participation in the closing process can make the difference between a successful closing and a lost opportunity. Developers who rely too heavily on others are often disappointed in their success ratios. You can swing the odds in your favor by keeping an active hand in the closing process. Remember, without a successful closing, you can't do much development work. One key to the success of developers is building each block of the development step by step, and the closing process is one of those building blocks.

# Insurance and Subcontractor Needs

What are your insurance and subcontractor needs as a developer? This is a big question that can have many answers. A lot of people don't think much about insurance when they own only raw land. While it is not practical to insure raw land for a replacement value, you should still have insurance on the property. Normally, it's not feasible to get insurance to cover the loss of trees or ground cover. Insurance policies that protect homes and buildings don't usually extend to the land. So, if you can't get replacement coverage for the attributes of a piece of land, why do you need insurance at all? You need insurance to protect you from liability claims that might be filed against you as a result of your land ownership. For example, if a tree that grows on your land falls on someone else's property, you could be facing a lawsuit. Having someone on your land could put you at risk. If a person is injured on your property, you may be a target for a liability lawsuit.

The needs for and pertaining to subcontractors is a much broader issue. Most developers rely on subcontractors for most of the work done during a development project. There are many factors that developers must face when working with subcontractors. There is the obvious need for finding good subcontractors. Insurance is also a factor in dealing with subcontractors. In the case of subcontractors, there can be many aspects of insurance to consider, such as liability insurance and workers' compensation insurance. Then there are the contractual arrangements that must be evaluated.

It's easy to get caught up in the excitement of a development and let some things slip through the cracks. But you simply can't afford to do this. It is imperative that you pay attention to details. Staying focused and organized is critical for success as a developer. Most developers and contractors despise paperwork. Yet it is often paperwork that makes the difference between success and failure. If it is your goal to prosper as a developer, you must be willing to deal with the details.

## Insurance for Your Land

Buying insurance for your land can be expensive, but you would be foolish to do business without any insurance. Liability insurance coverage is one of the first types of insurance to buy. As soon as you become responsible for a piece of land, and this can happen during the period that a parcel is under contract, but not yet closed on, you should place liability coverage on the real estate. The liability laws (Fig. 24.1) in different states vary. Some states provide a certain amount of protection for landowners. But other states have tough laws that don't favor landowners when anyone is injured on the landowner's property. Regardless of individual laws, every developer should acquire insurance to reduce financial risks.

Title insurance is another type of coverage that you should invest in. This type of insurance is not too expensive, and it can save you from numerous problems. Basically, title insurance protects you in the event that the title to your land is defective. Even when title searches are done well, things can be missed. It's possible to close on a piece of land and later discover that your ownership is in question.

Title insurance cannot guarantee that you will be able to keep your land if there is a title defect. However, the title insurance does guarantee that you will not lose the money that you spent on land. In other words, you may have to give up the land, but your financial investment of the purchase price will be returned to you from the insurance policy. Don't expect to be reimbursed for your other expenses. Each policy can differ, so read yours carefully. Normally, the exposure for the insurance policy is limited to the purchase price of a property.

Once you begin to make improvements on your land, you need to arrange for insurance coverage to protect them. This type of coverage will normally be required by the lender who is financing the improvements. It is common for lenders to require minimum insurance requirements. Even so, you may want to purchase more than minimal

---

Your Company Name
Your Company Address
Your Company Phone and Fax Numbers

### LIABILITY WAIVER FORM

Customer: _____

Customer address: _____

Job name: _____

Job address: _____

I, _____, (Customer) hereby acknowledge and accept the

following: _____

_____

_____

_____

_____

_____

_____

_____

_____

_____

_____

_____     _____
Customer                       Contractor

_____     _____
Date                           Date

**FIGURE 24.1**

Sample liability waiver form

insurance. It doesn't make sense to overinsure a property, but you should be certain that your coverage is adequate to relieve you of pressure if a loss occurs.

The value of your property will escalate as improvements are made. Your insurance coverage should increase as the value of your property and improvements climbs. There is also the issue of insurance coverage on equipment and materials that is left on a job site. Most developers insist that their subcontractors assume responsibility for their own materials and equipment. This is, in my opinion, the best solution to the situation. However, if you will have any liability for either equipment or materials, you need to protect your exposure to a lawsuit. Don't skimp on insurance. You hope that you will never need it, and maybe you never will. But, if you ever do, it's very comforting to have the proper coverage in place.

## Insurance for Subcontractors

Insurance for subcontractors is an important issue for developers. Since subcontractors are independent contractors, they should carry their own insurance coverage, but not all contractors do. If you have contractors working for you who are not properly insured, you might be held responsible for their problems. The types of problems could range from basic liability issues to workers' compensation premiums. If your contractors are not abiding by the local laws pertaining to worker's compensation, you may have to pay the premiums that the subcontractors should have been paying. This is a fact that some general contractors and developers are not aware of.

If you are in business for yourself and have employees, you are probably aware of the overhead expenses related to employees. We are not talking only about hourly pay rates. No, it's the other overhead that may become important to you. If you don't establish a clear, defined, independent contractor agreement with your workers, you may be held responsible for employee-related expenses (Figs. 24.2 and 24.3). This can become extremely expensive.

When you decide to use subcontractors, you owe it to yourself to make sure that all of your dealings are recorded in writing. The contracts between you and your subcontractors should detail all aspects of insurance coverage, among other items. A good starting point is liability insurance. All subcontractors should have proof of liability insurance available. You need to request proof of this insurance and keep the certificate of proof on file. It will need to be updated annually.

I've had many subcontractors show me photocopies of their liability certificates. Don't accept this type of proof. A photocopy proves only that the subcontractor had insurance at the time that the copy was made. It does not guarantee that the coverage is still in full force and in effect. The proper way to verify current insurance status is to receive a certificate directly from the insurance agency holding the policy. All insurance companies that provide contractors with liability insurance will provide proof of insurance on request of the policyholder. Simply require your contractors to contact their insurers so that the insurers can mail or fax you a copy of the insurance certificate.

When you get a certificate of insurance, check the dates carefully. Observe the limits and types of coverage. If you don't understand the document, have your attorney review it. Keep the certificate on file. If you are audited by your insurance company, the certificates that you are holding on your subcontractors can keep you out of trouble with your own insurance company.

Workers' compensation insurance is a major expense for employers. It's bad enough paying the premiums when you are supposed to; it's worse when you have to pay them for subcontractors who should be paying the expense themselves. The contract between you and your subcontractors should state clearly who will be responsible for the cost of workers' compensation insurance. Make sure that you bear no responsibility for anyone who is not your employee.

While on the subject of employees, another issue to keep in mind is payroll taxes. This is not an insurance issue, but it can run hand in hand with the workers' comp issue. When there are employees on a payroll, the employer has to make tax deposits in proportion to the wages of the employees. You could get nailed on this one, too, if you are not careful.

Just as you will define responsibility for workers' comp premiums, you should make the same type of definition for payroll taxes. If you have a subcontractor working for you without a clear independent contractor, you might find yourself being told that your contractor was really an employee. If this happens, you could be lined up to pay payroll taxes on the contractor. Don't let this happen. Make it very clear, and very legal, that your subcontractors are independent contractors who are responsible for their own business expenses.

Your Company Name
Your Company Address
Your Company Phone and Fax Numbers

### INDEPENDENT CONTRACTOR AGREEMENT

I understand that as an Independent Contractor I am solely responsible for my health, actions, taxes, insurance, transportation, and any other responsibilities that may be involved with the work I will be doing as an Independent Contractor.

I will not hold anyone else responsible for any claims or liabilities that may arise from this work or from any cause related to this work. I waive any rights I have or may have to hold anyone liable for any reason as a result of this work.

_____
Independent Contractor                               Date

_____
Witness                                              Date

**FIGURE 24.2**

Independent contractor agreement.

Your Company Name
Your Company Address
Your Company Phone and Fax Numbers

## INDEPENDENT CONTRACTOR ACKNOWLEDGMENT

Undersigned hereby enters into a certain arrangement or affiliation with Your Company Name, as of this date. The Undersigned confirms:

1. Undersigned is an independent contractor and is not an employee, agent, partner or joint venturer of or with the Company.

2. Undersigned shall not be entitled to participate in any vacation, medical or other fringe benefit or retirement program of the Company and shall not make claim of entitlement to any such employee program or benefit.

3. Undersigned shall be solely responsible for the payment of withholding taxes, FICA and other such tax deductions on any earnings or payments made, and the Company shall withhold no such payroll tax deductions from any payments due. The Undersigned agrees to indemnify and reimburse the Company from any claim or assessment by any taxing authority arising from this paragraph.

4. Undersigned and Company acknowledge that the Undersigned shall not be subject to the provisions of any personnel policy or rules and regulations applicable to employees, as the Undersigned shall fulfill his/her responsibility independent of and without supervisory control by the Company.

Signed under seal this _____ day of _____, 19 ___.


_____          _____
Independent Contractor                  Company Representative

                                        _____
                                        Title

**FIGURE 24.3**

Independent contractor acknowledgment.

You may have other insurance needs. For example, you may have a need to be bonded. There are many types of bonds that are used in development and construction. For example, you might require performance bonds from your subcontractors. Talk to your attorney for advice on the type of protection that you should put in place. The main thing is to avoid leaving yourself exposed. It only takes one lawsuit to sink a business.

## Subcontractor Needs

Subcontractor needs vary from trade to trade. The requirements for an earthmoving contractor can be different from those pertaining to a framing crew. Once you begin negotiating with and working with subcontractors, you could have your hands full. Poor communication with your subcontractors can result in serious problems. Since you are the boss, the responsibility is yours. The best way that I know of to reduce problems is to keep all dealings in writing.

As a developer, you have to know enough about each type of subcontractor used on your project to predict their needs. This isn't always easy. The only real way to avoid having some personal knowledge of your needs and those of your subcontractors is to hire a project manager who has the knowledge.

I've used a lot of project superintendents, but I like to be my own project manager. You may not share my feeling for remaining in control. It may be in your best interest to hire someone to tend to your project for you. If you elect to hire a project manager, that's fine. Your time requirements will be less if you have a project manager. Yet, you will still have to know something about the needs of your subcontractors.

The best way that I've found to know the needs of subcontractors is to ask them directly what they need. Why guess when you can simply ask? For example, is your site contractor going to need to leave heavy equipment on your site? Well, unless it's a very small job, the answer to this question will always be yes. But, will that contractor need space to put a site trailer on the land for supervision? Not all site contractors do this, but many do. If site trailers are required, you will have to be prepared to make some arrangements for the trailers. You need to know this in advance. If a theft occurs on your site, document it (Fig. 24.4).

Are your contractors expecting you to provide a fenced enclosure for the storage of equipment and materials? Do you have any plans for offering private security patrols on your site during development? Had you even considered the possibility of providing security? Depending on your level of development, you may have many types of subcontractors working on your site. If you do, you may have to make special provisions for them.

Are you going to have temporary electrical power installed at various points on the job site? Will it be your responsibility to have temporary water outlets installed at points on the site? Who is going to take care of dust control? When big trucks are rolling, a lot of dust can get in the air. Neighbors won't like the dust. Are you going to take responsibility for the dust? What about cleaning up mud that gets on public roadways; who is going to clean that up? As you can see, there can be a lot of questions that you might not think of when first starting a development project. You need to pin down as much as you can with your contractors before going into a contract with them (Fig. 24.5).

## Your Needs

Just as subcontractors have needs, so do developers. You must make your needs known early in a relationship with subcontractors. And your needs should be detailed in your written contracts with the subcontractors. The needs of developers are as individual as the developers. For example, you might be developing land that is near a medical facility. Maybe the patients in the facility require a specific amount of sleep. This might influence you to have your contractors begin work later in the day than what they might normally be used to. If this is the case, you must stipulate in your contracts what the allowable work hours are.

Who is going to supply and install erosion barriers for your project? Are you expecting your site contractor to do the erosion control? If you are, the terms of your understanding should be recorded in your written agreements. Most work-related tasks should be covered in the quotes that you receive. Then the terms of the quotes should be included in your contracts. When this is the case, you are off to a good start.

Your Company Name
Your Company Address
Your Company Phone and Fax Numbers

### LOST/STOLEN EQUIPMENT REPORT

Date of report: _____

Date of loss: _____

Time of loss (when was item last seen): _____

Location of loss: _____

Type of item lost/stolen (include serial number): _____

_____

Item was  lost/stolen (circle appropriate word)

Name of person in charge of equipment at time of loss: _____

Was notification given to the police?: _____

Additional comments: _____

_____

_____

_____

_____

_____

_____

_____

_____

**FIGURE 24.4**

Lost/stolen equipment report.

Your Company Name
Your Company Address
Your Company Phone and Fax Numbers

## SUBCONTRACTOR AGREEMENT

This agreement, made this _____ day of _____, 19__, shall set forth the whole agreement, in its entirety, between Contractor and Subcontractor.

Contractor: _____, referred to herein as Contractor.

Job location: _____

Subcontractor: _____, referred to herein as Subcontractor.

The Contractor and Subcontractor agree to the following.

### SCOPE OF WORK

Subcontractor shall perform all work as described below and provide all material to complete the work described below.

Subcontractor shall supply all labor and material to complete the work according to the attached plans and specifications. These attached plans and specifications have been initialed and signed by all parties. The work shall include, but is not limited to, the following: _____

_____
_____
_____
_____
_____
_____
_____
_____
_____
_____
_____

### COMMENCEMENT AND COMPLETION SCHEDULE

The work described above shall be started within _____ (____) days of verbal notice from Contractor; the projected start date is _____. The Subcontractor shall complete the above work in a professional and expedient manner by no later than _____ (____) days from the start date. Time is of the essence in this contract. No extension of time will be valid without the Contractor's written consent. If Subcontractor does not complete the work in the time allowed, and if the lack of completion is not caused by the Contractor, the Subcontractor will be charged _____ ($_____) dollars per day, for every day work extends beyond the completion date. This charge will be deducted from any payments due to the Subcontractor for work performed.

(Page 1 of 3. Please initial _____.)

**FIGURE 24.5**

Subcontractor agreement.

## CONTRACT SUM

The Contractor shall pay the Subcontractor for the performance of completed work subject to additions and deductions as authorized by this agreement or attached addendum. The contract sum is _____($_____).

## PROGRESS PAYMENTS

The Contractor shall pay the Subcontractor installments as detailed below, once an acceptable insurance certificate has been filed by the Subcontractor with the Contractor. Contractor shall pay the Subcontractor as described: _____

_____

_____

_____

All payments are subject to a site inspection and approval of work by the Contractor. Before final payment, the Subcontractor shall submit satisfactory evidence to the Contractor that no lien risk exists on the subject property.

## WORKING CONDITIONS

Working hours will be _____ a.m. through _____ p.m., Monday through Friday. Subcontractor is required to clean work debris from the job site on a daily basis and leave the site in a clean and neat condition. Subcontractor shall be responsible for removal and disposal of all debris related to the job description.

## CONTRACT ASSIGNMENT

Subcontractor shall not assign this contract or further subcontract the whole of this subcontract, without the written consent of the Contractor.

## LAWS, PERMITS, FEES, AND NOTICES

Subcontractor shall be responsible for all required laws, permits, fees, or notices, required to perform the work stated herein.

## WORK OF OTHERS

Subcontractor shall be responsible for any damage caused to existing conditions or other contractors' work. This damage will be repaired, and the Subcontractor charged for the expense and supervision of this work. The Subcontractor shall have the opportunity to quote a price for said repairs, but the Contractor is under no obligation to engage the Subcontractor to make said repairs. If a different subcontractor repairs the damage, the Subcontractor may be backcharged for the cost of the repairs. Any repair costs will be deducted from any payments due to the Subcontractor. If no payments are due the Subcontractor, the Subcontractor shall pay the invoiced amount within _____ (_____) days.

## WARRANTY

Subcontractor warrants to the Contractor, all work and materials for _____ from the final day of work performed.

(Page 2 of 3. Please initial _____.)

**FIGURE 24.5**

Subcontractor agreement. (*Continued*)

### INDEMNIFICATION

To the fullest extent allowed by law, the Subcontractor shall indemnify and hold harmless the Owner, the Contractor, and all of their agents and employees from and against all claims, damages, losses, and expenses.

This agreement, entered into on _____, 19____, shall constitute the whole agreement between Contractor and Subcontractor.

_____          _____
Contractor                        Date          Subcontractor                  Date

(Page 3 of 3)

**FIGURE 24.5**

**Subcontractor agreement.** (*Continued*)

Contracts are an integral part of working with subcontractors. I suggest that you don't use generic forms as contracts. Many states require specific language in contracts to make the contracts enforceable. A contract can be legal without being enforceable, and this is a significant factor to consider.

I sometimes testify as an expert witness. In doing this, I have seen where the language in a contract can make a huge difference in the outcome of a court case. Presently, I live in Maine. Verbal contracts are legal in Maine, but they are not enforceable. This seems stupid, but it's true. How can a contract be legal and not be enforceable? Well, it's just a fact of life in Maine. Many verbal agreements are not enforceable, which is why written contracts are so important.

One case where I was an expert witness involved a lawsuit that was ultimately lost because of a lack of appropriate language in the contract between the plaintiff and the defendant. Maine law requires specific language in some types of contracts. In the case that I testified in, the defendant had used a generic form to draft a contract on. In doing so, the contractor thought that he was covered. The contract was signed by all parties and seemed perfectly legal. Well, it was legal, but it was not enforceable. Since the stock form did not contain the specific language required in the state of Maine to make the contract enforceable, the judge ruled for the plaintiff.

The case was one in which the defendant was being denied final payment for work completed. All indications pointed to the fact that the defendant would have prevailed and got his money, if his contract had been enforceable. But the end result was a financial loss due to a generic contract form. Don't allow this to happen to you. Have your attorney create legal forms for you that you can fill in the blanks on for individual jobs. The legal expenses are a one-time cost that is well worth the investment.

## The Paperwork

The paperwork that you use with your subcontractors may be extensive. There will be contracts, but there will probably be much more paperwork. For example, when you pay subcontractors you should have them sign lien waivers (Fig. 24.6). The waivers protect your property from liens that may be placed for alleged nonpayment for services

Your Company Name

Your Company Address

Your Company Phone and Fax Numbers

## SHORT-FORM LIEN WAIVER

Customer name: _____

Customer address: _____

Customer city/state/zip: _____

Customer phone number: _____

Job location: _____

Date: _____

Type of work: _____

Contractor: _____

Contractor address: _____

Subcontractor: _____

Subcontractor address: _____

Description of work completed to date: _____

_____

_____

_____

_____

Payments received to date: _____

Payment received on this date: _____

Total amount paid, including this payment: _____

The contractor/subcontractor signing below acknowledges receipt of all payments stated above. These payments are in compliance with the written contract between the parties above. The contractor/subcontractor signing below hereby states payment for all work done to this date has been paid in full.

The contractor/subcontractor signing below releases and relinquishes any and all rights available to place a mechanic or materialman lien against the subject property for the above described work. All parties agree that all work performed to date has been paid for in full and in compliance with their written contract.

The undersigned contractor/subcontractor releases the general contractor/customer from any liability for nonpayment of material or services extended through this date. The undersigned contractor/subcontractor has read this entire agreement and understands the agreement.

_____

Contractor/Subcontractor                    Date

**FIGURE 24.6**

Short-form lien waiver

or materials. Most lenders require contractors and material suppliers to sign lien waivers when they are paid. If your lender doesn't require this, and I've known some who don't, you should require the signatures.

How many times do needs change once a job is in progress? A multitude of changes can be needed before a project is completed. When a change is required, you should have your subcontractor sign a change order that specifies all details of the change. The change order should describe the actual work and materials being changed, as well as payment adjustments and terms.

Over the years, I have developed a list of close to 100 forms that I use with subcontractors. Some of them are not used often, but I have them when they are needed. Having been through many projects and a good number of battles, I have learned the value of written records (Figs. 24.7 and 24.8). I strongly suggest that you have your attorney provide you with forms for every type of situation that you anticipate. It may seem like a waste of time, but sometimes a single sheet of paper can mean the difference between success and failure.

## Payment Schedules

Payment schedules are always a matter of discussion with subcontractors. Some subcontractors want substantial deposits when a contract is signed. I suggest that you refuse to pay large deposits. It's reasonable to pay some form of a deposit with a contract, but I rarely do this. Even though some contractors say that they will not enter into an agreement without a third of the contract amount as a deposit, they often will if it's a matter of winning a bid or losing it.

Giving subcontractors money before services have been rendered is very risky. It's possible that the contractors will disappear with the cash. Established developers have more clout when it comes to refusing to put up deposits. But even rookies have the power to control subcontractors. You may run into contractors who attempt to make you feel guilty about not paying large deposits. Don't buy into it. There are contractors who simply will not work without a sizable deposit, but there should be many others available to take their place. You have to do what you are comfortable with and feel justified in doing. Remember, however, that handing out money for work that hasn't been done

Your Company Name
Your Company Address
Your Company Phone and Fax Numbers

## CERTIFICATE OF SUBCONTRACTOR
## COMPLETION AND ACCEPTANCE

Contractor: _____

Subcontractor: _____

Job Name: _____

Job Location: _____

Job Description: _____

_____

_____

_____

Date of completion: _____

Date of final inspection by contractor: _____

Date of code compliance inspection and approval: _____

Defects found in material or workmanship: _____

_____

_____

_____

### ACKNOWLEDGMENT

Contractor acknowledges the completion of all contracted work and accepts all workmanship and materials as being satisfactory. Upon signing this certificate, the contractor releases the subcontractor from any responsibility for additional work, except warranty work. Warranty work will be performed for a period of _____ from the date of completion. Warranty work will include the repair of any material or workmanship defects occurring between now and the end of the warranty period. All existing workmanship and materials are acceptable to the contractor and payment will be made, in full, according to the payment schedule in the contract, between the two parties.

_____     _____
Contractor              Date          Subcontractor           Date

**FIGURE 24.7**

Certificate of completion.

Your Company Name
Your Company Address
Your Company Phone and Fax Numbers

**NOTICE OF BREACH OF CONTRACT**

Date: _____

To: _____        From: _____

_____        _____

_____        _____

TAKE NOTICE that under Contract made _____, 19 _____, as evidenced by the following documents: _____, we are hereby holding you IN BREACH for the following reasons: _____

_____

_____

If your Breach is not cured within _____ days (i.e., cure must be completed by _____, 19 _____), we will take all further actions necessary to mitigate our damages and protect our rights, which may include, but are not necessarily limited to, the right to "Cover" by obtaining substitute performance and chargeback to you of all additional costs and damages incurred.

This Notice is made under the Uniform Commercial Code (if applicable) and all other applicable laws. All rights are hereby reserved, none of which are waived. Any forbearance or temporary waiver from enforcement shall not constitute permanent waiver or waiver of any other right.

You are urged to cure your Breach forthwith.

_____
Contractor

By: _____

Authorized Signatory

**FIGURE 24.8**

Notice of breach of contract.

could result in having to pay more than once for the work to get it done.

I generally don't offer any type of deposit to my subcontractors. My payment schedules are based on percentages of the contract amount and they are paid only after work is completed, inspected, and approved by me. This is the safest way I know of to protect your own interest. I do, however, usually pay within 7 days of receiving an invoice, and this is much better for the subcontractors than the standard 30-day payment schedule.

Learning to deal with subcontractors may take some time. You will probably get burned a few times along the way. This is a cost of doing business that most developers and general contractors face. Working closely with your attorney to create solid contracts that leave no room for confusion is the best protection that I know of. Different regions have different trends. You must match your business procedures to the conditions that exist in your region. Ideally, never sign a contract provided by a subcontractor. Insist on using only your own contracts, and make sure that your lawyer has created the best legal documents available for you. If you feel the need, have a different attorney review the drafts prepared by your primary attorney. Keep in mind that if you wind up in a lawsuit, your legal documents will be of the utmost importance.

# Rolling Out the Big Rigs

When site contractors begin rolling out the big rigs, developers have to be ready. It's exciting to see heavy equipment being stocked on a job. But once work begins, there can be a number of problems to deal with. Up until the time that earth is disturbed a project is done mostly on paper. It's much easier to make matters work on a computer or piece of paper than it is on a development site. Some of the best plans will prove to be unsuitable. Developers and their experts must be prepared for potential problems.

Seemingly simple tasks can turn to trouble. This is true on projects of all sizes. While it is generally the responsibility of various contractors to take care of their own jobs, developers are often pulled into the loop. Not all developers are as active as they should be in monitoring job progress. It is not mandatory for a developer to be on a site every day, but projects are more likely to run smoothly when developers are around.

Much of the early work done on a project is difficult to undo if a mistake is made. A carpenter who bends a nail while driving it can remove the nail and start over without much fuss. If an equipment operator scars a tree by hitting it with heavy equipment, the scar is visible for a long time to come. Worse yet, the contractor who fells a tree that was meant to be preserved can do almost nothing to overcome the mistake. Stripping dirt from the wrong area will result in a situation that is difficult to repair. There is much that can go wrong during the early stages on site development.

Confusion is often the primary cause of problems on job sites. Negligence is sometimes a problem. Then there are the accidents that occur from time to time. The odds of getting through a development without problems are very low. Smart developers prepare as best they can and they stay as active as possible to prevent problems and mistakes. The developers who sit in their offices and don't make personal appearances on sites are much more likely to face struggles with problems.

Preparing a site for work to begin is not a small job. A great deal of thought has to go into the various elements of developing land. We've touched on some of the preliminary work in previous chapters. In some cases, equipment is needed on a site in order to make preparations. Getting your site ready for the big equipment to work effectively is a pivotal point in your success.

All development sites require some amount of preparation work. Even a single house lot needs a certain amount of work before you open the site to your contractors. There is always something to do before you can do what you want to do. Developers like to see heavy equipment and crews working busily. But jumping the gun and starting a project too soon can set you back considerably in both time and money. To better explain the type of prep work that you may become involved in, let's review an example of preparing a small residential development for site work.

## A Simple Residential Development

Let's assume that you are doing a simple residential development. The land has substantial road frontage and is wide, but not deep. You have decided to create the house lots by just dividing the land from front to rear. This type of development is about as simple as it gets. You have your surveyors establish one front line, one back line, and then the various side lines. Since every lot will have frontage on a public road, you don't have to build any roads, just driveways. Each building lot will have its own private well and septic system. The land has already been tested by a soils engineer and the septic sites have been clearly marked. You are working with a builder who will build the houses in your development. All of the preliminary testing has been done and permits for development have been issued. It appears that you are ready to put equipment on the site to start clearing for construction. But are you?

## Underground Utilities

Underground utilities are sometimes damaged during land development. Some serious injuries can occur if underground utilities are disturbed. All sites should be checked for the existence of unseen obstacles and utilities. Most areas have a phone number listed in the local phone directory that contractors can call to arrange a site assessment. It is common for small flags to be used to mark the paths of utilities. The marking is usually accurate, but there are times when mistakes are made. Even when all utilities are marked, contractors should exercise care in digging.

Many regions have laws that require contractors to call about underground utilities before any digging is done. Site contractors normally take responsibility for having site markings done for utilities. However, I have found that it is important for developers to stay right on top of this part of the preparation work. Over the years, I've had some contractors who were negligent in calling for site assessments. By having my follow-up procedures, I caught the problems and solved them before they became serious.

Don't assume that working in rural locations will keep you from dealing with underground utilities. I've done a lot of work in country locations, and there can be underground pipes and wires where you would least expect them. Don't make any assumptions on this issue. Make sure that you, or someone, has done all the homework needed to make digging safe and legal.

## Permits

Most jurisdictions require that permits be posted in plain view of the road. There are different ways to do the postings. Some contractors simply wrap the permits in plastic and staple them to trees. This method works, but the permits don't always hold up well in weather. Other contractors build small boxes that have a hinged, plexiglass front. Permits are placed in the box and are visible through the plexiglass. Small locks are sometimes used to keep people from opening the box cover. The boxes are often mounted on a 4x4 inch post that is used over and over, from site to site. The post is simply set in a posthole and backfilled with dirt. The permit box protects the permits nicely and gives a much more professional appearance to a job than permits stapled to trees would.

## Culverts

Culverts are usually required where driveways intersect with roads. The size and location of the culvert pipe is normally established before a permit is authorized for the installation of the culvert. Many contractors have their surveyors stake the location for all culverts, and this is a good idea. Before you put equipment on a site to install a driveway culvert, you must have the location established, the permit posted, and the installation instructions clearly stated. It's normally possible to get equipment on a site before a culvert is installed, but culverts are often one of the first orders of business when the development process begins on a site.

## Driveway

A driveway installation may have to wait until land is cleared. Lots that don't have many trees can have a driveway installed before the clearing process. It is common for driveway locations to be shown on a site plan. If you are working to tight tolerances and must keep the driveway in the location that is shown on the plan, you should have your surveyors stake the edges of the proposed driveway location. Don't make the mistake of having the stakes installed on the actual edges of the driveway. If you do, your contractor's equipment will be hitting the stakes and will make verifying the driveway location difficult. Have the stakes installed a certain distance from the driveway edges. For example, have the stakes set 10 feet from the edges. Then you can measure from the stakes to the edges even after the driveway is done to confirm placement.

## Clearing

Clearing wooded land can be a big job. This phase of work can prove to be dangerous. Any time there are mature trees being cut down or knocked over there is an element of risk. It's common for electrical and telephone wires to run along the edges of roads. Having a tree fall into the wires can be serious. Experienced contractors don't usually have problems with trees falling in the wrong direction. However, there is always some element of risk.

When clearing begins, it can take many forms. Some developers have trees pushed over and then cut up. Other developers have the trees cut and then have excavators remove the stumps. Either way, there are stumps to get rid of. Brush has to be dealt with, and something has to be done with the wood from the trees. Large parcels of wooded land are sometimes offered to logging companies to clear. Small developments don't offer enough timber to make the work worthwhile for a logging company. In these situations, the wood is sometimes sold as firewood. Brush is often run through a chipper and is sometimes used for landscaping. There are times when stumps are ground up, but they are usually hauled off to special landfills.

Your site contractor will be responsible for most of the aspects of clearing a parcel of land, but you have to decide what to do with the debris of clearing. This is a decision that should be made before quotes are taken. Ideally, you should have all aspects of what you want done detailed in your contract. If you have forgotten something, think of it before you have trees coming down and equipment and workers standing idle while you try to figure out what to do with wood or stumps.

It's rare to strip a project of all its trees. Most builders and developers keep as many trees as they reasonably can. In doing this, someone has to mark the trees. Depending on the amount of trees, some contractors mark the trees to be removed. Other developers mark the trees to be saved. When doing a single house lot, I usually run flagging tape around sections of the lot where clearing will be done. For example, I might circle a large section of trees where a house will be situated. If there are certain trees within the cut zone that I want to keep, I mark them individually. If I used yellow flagging tape to establish the cut zone, I would use red flagging tape to mark the trees to be saved.

Equipment operators sometimes hit valuable trees by accident. Even dedicated operators sometimes make mistakes. After learning this the hard way on more than one occasion, I created a way to reduce the losses. To prevent scarring, I marked small trees that were between the major cut area and the preservation area. By doing this, it keeps equipment away from the best trees. Once the major clearing is done, the smaller trees can be cut and removed by hand.

Taking such extra effort to keep trees from being damaged may seem strange to some people. But, if you have ever had to be yelled at by lot buyers who discovered that their favorite trees were hit by back-hoes and front-end loaders, you would understand. People can be very upset when their trees are marred.

When you are working directly with a builder, as in our example, you might leave tree selection to the builder. In this type of a situation, you may have the builder mark trees for you. If the decision is yours, you or your employees should mark the trees. Don't leave the decision up to your site contractor. Trees are too hard to replace to leave their removal to chance. The selection of trees should be made either by the developer or the lot buyer.

### Erosion Barriers

Erosion barriers are required on some sites. The barriers should be in place before land is disturbed. One of your contractors should be taking care of this for you. But you should do a site check to make sure that the barriers are installed when they are supposed to be. Failing to get the barriers in place on time could result in some stiff fines. If you don't want to face financial expenses beyond your budget, make sure that all environmental precautions are in place before you begin site work.

### Rough Grading

Rough grading is done once a lot is cleared. Moving dirt seems simple enough, but don't let your guard down. Your site workers may be doing their job by tight elevation specifications. If they are, your protection will come in the form of inspections. Many small projects don't require strict elevation plans. Many jobs are done on an eyeball basis. By this, I mean that the rough grading is done so that it suits the eye of the site contractor. Most of these types of jobs turn out all right. However, you should have some written requirements for how a site will be graded out. Once the rough grading is done on a small project, you can generally turn the lot over to a builder or begin construction yourself.

# Larger Projects

Larger projects are more complicated to develop. In some ways, however, larger projects are easier to work with than small ones. The extensive planning that goes into a large development removes a considerable amount of responsibilities from developers. While you might have to make decisions on your own with a small project, the decisions will often be made for you on larger projects. Builders run into this all the time. When builders are working with large commercial jobs, they have blueprints that guide them along every step of the construction. This is not often the case with builders who build single homes. The blueprints for an individual home rarely have anywhere near the details that commercial blueprints have. Development plans are similar to blueprints. When you are doing a large development, most details will be specified on the plans.

Even when the actual development details are covered clearly, there is still prep work that needs to be done before equipment begins to roll. You may have to decide how to handle traffic concerns as trucks are entering and exiting your site. Will you have to hire a company to provide traffic control? Is this an issue that you are expecting your site contractor to take care of? What provisions will be made for keeping the big rigs on your site? How will the equipment be protected from vandalism and theft?

While small projects may require your personal presence to mark trees or driveway locations, larger jobs may put different responsibilities on you. A land planner will probably take care of most of the site planning details for you on a large project. One of your experts will have all the major issues covered. However, you still should not authorize work to begin until you do your own checking to see that everything up to the site work has been done properly. This may mean making a lot of phone calls. You might find it worthwhile to visit your site to see that all permits are posted and that environmental controls are in place. More of your work will be in the form of checking on the actions of others when you are dealing with a big job.

If you are using a project manager or site supervisors, you should communicate daily. Staying on top of your project can be time-consuming, but it is the best way to ensure success. Resist any urges to jump ahead with work before your site is ready for it. Once work begins, maintain regular supervision of the project. Some developers feel pressured by their jobs and grow to feel that their projects are running them. You should be running your project, not letting it run you.

# Site Supervision

Once your project is seeing site activity, you need to make arrangements for regular supervision. Most developments benefit from daily supervision. However, not all developments require such active supervision. You should pattern your supervision to your individual property. There is no reason to drive out to a site daily if there is nothing happening there. On the other hand, you may find that it is in the best interest of your project to have a site trailer that you can work out of. How much attention will your project need? The answer is not as simple as a single sentence. You have to weigh the needs of your project and then adapt to them.

How much time will you have to devote to your project? Not all developers earn their livings as developers. It's not uncommon for developers to have full-time jobs outside of their development ventures. When this is the case, it can make supervision a bit tricky. But there are still ways to maintain decent supervision. You don't have to spend every waking hour babysitting your project if you set the production schedule up properly.

Do you have to hire a project manager to keep an eye on your development? Maybe, but you might not. Hiring a project manager can be a substantial mistake. Good managers don't work for peanuts. If you hire an experienced manager, you can expect to pay a substantial fee for the services rendered. There are certainly times when the overhead of a manager is warranted, but you must think carefully before committing to the expense.

Not only do project managers add to a developer's overhead, they remove much of the developer's responsibilities. This is good in one sense, and not so good in another. Being relieved of supervision duties will free you up to perform other tasks. This may be the most cost-effective way for you to run your project. But when you engage a site manager you lose some control over your project. Basically, you are trusting the manager to see that your best interest is protected. The right managers can do this well, probably better than many developers could do it for themselves. However, hiring a bad manager can cripple your project. This is the main concern when thinking of putting your project into the hands of someone else.

If you are a part-time developer, you may have to make special arrangements for the supervision of your project. There are many ways to go about this. One way is to juggle your day job and your development by putting in a lot of hours. This is the normal way of going about the task. But there may be ways to get some help. And there is always the problem of meeting with contractors during normal working hours. A lot of these meetings can be avoided, but some of them must be kept. How will you get time off to make the meetings? It's possible that you won't have to. Well, let's look at supervision needs and how you might meet them best.

## Types of Supervision

What types of supervision will be needed for your project? To answer this question, you must know what type of project you are developing and what your production schedule is. The amount of supervision required can be kept to a minimum with proper site preparation. However, if you are a person who likes to stay busy for hours, you can make plenty of busy work for yourself. Some aspects of site supervision can be dealt with in many ways. Some ways are more cost-effective than others.

Some developers thrive on meeting with people and staying busy. Land developing is a good business for these people. You could spend hours of your time driving out to your project and meeting with people. The meetings could be justified as work, so you would feel as if you were doing your job. However, avoiding the time lost in meeting this way could mean a lot more money in your pocket. Time management is essential in nearly all businesses, and it certainly counts in land developing.

People will need to be able to locate your site easily. At times, this might require you to meet at known locations to escort people to your site. A more effective means would be to put good signs on your property to make it visible. Take a ride from your site to known locations and record the mileage. Being able to offer people precise directions takes a lot less time than driving all over town to meet them. Using established landmarks, good directions, and eye-catching signs is one of the first steps in site supervision.

Good preparation will help you avoid lost time. There will, however, be some meetings that must be kept. There are many times when you can simply send people to your site if what they need to see is clearly marked. But there comes a time when face-to-face meetings on the site are required. Who's going to make these meetings? If you are a full-time developer, you can do it. If you have a regular job that allows you freedom in your schedule, you can probably make the meetings. But, if you are tied to a desk for 8 hours a day, you will have to meet after hours. When this is the case, make sure that you are working with contractors who will be willing to meet you during times that you have available.

## Production Supervision

Production supervision can require that you, or your manager, be on the site most of each day. This could be the case with a large project, especially if you are doing building construction as a part of your development. In other cases, you might go by your site each day after your crews leave to see what was done during the day. Many developers attend their sites during the early morning hours to confirm that workers show up and get started without problems. This is good procedure, but you don't have to hold the hands of good contractors.

Unless you are involved in a major development, checking your site daily at any time during the day should suffice. You will know enough about what is happening to stay in control. However, don't think that you can cruise by your job site every weekend and maintain good supervision. You have to be willing and able to commit time to supervision if you expect to be successful.

## Code Compliance

Maintaining code compliance is mostly a job for your subcontractors. Permits are usually issued to the contractors performing the work that is controlled by code requirements. Unless you are your own contractor, your supervision of codes for the subcontractors will be minimum. This doesn't mean that it should be nonexistent. At the least, you should require proof of approved code inspections before paying subcontractors for their work. This type of supervision doesn't require a lot of time, and the compliance checks can be done when you have the time.

## Phone Calls

You might not think of phone calls as supervision, but they are a strong form of supervision. Many forms of supervision can be conducted with the use of telephone conversations. Phone calls do save a lot of travel time, but they can also eat into a large part of your business day. Contractors and developers are often swamped by phone calls. Returning calls and making calls can take several hours each day. Are you prepared for this? How will you handle the likelihood of countless phone calls each week?

Answering services can cover most of your bases when you are not available to take calls, but returning the calls that accumulate can take a lot of time. Some of the calls will be able to be returned only during business hours. This can be a problem for developers who hold down full-time jobs while doing land developing. Pagers are excellent for developers who want to be readily available when they are away from their offices. Cell phones are about the best option, but using cell phones extensively becomes quite expensive. It's common for developers to utilize answering services, pagers, and cell phones to maintain active communication.

Your availability for quick communication may well be one of your most important forms of supervision. If you have contractors who run into problems and who cannot reach you quickly, your job could be shut down until you are back in touch. Having crews sitting idle on a job site is expensive in many ways, so you need to avoid it whenever possible. Being accessible by telephone is one of the best ways to reduce downtime on a job.

## Security

Security can be a major issue with some projects. Many projects get by without special security provisions. But others are often patrolled by private security agencies. A lot of developers don't feel right if they don't shut their projects down for the night. Are you going to check padlocks and gates every night? Will you call or visit your site to be sure that your security force is in place? Most small and medium projects don't call for much security. Locked impounds for materials and vehicles are often assumed to be enough. Once you determine what type of security your project will have, you can better judge your needs for supervision in that area.

## Administrative Supervision

Administrative supervision is often one of the most overlooked aspects of land developing. It's easy for developers with limited staff to struggle with administrative duties. Developers who don't maintain administrative assistants often become so involved in the field work that they neglect the piles of paper building up in their offices. In some ways, this lack of supervision is just as serious as not keeping an eye on your bulldozers.

The good thing about administrative supervision is that it can generally be done at most any hour of the day or night. If you feel like staying up into the middle of the night to catch up on paperwork, you can. The work is very important, but it's the type of supervision that you can handle even if you are holding down a full-time job.

## Building Supervision

If you are a builder or if you are working with builders, you will have building supervision to consider. This type of supervision requires extensive time. Whether you are building houses or hospitals, the day-to-day supervision required for the construction can be extremely demanding. It is possible to do a housing development with part-time supervision, but it can be grueling. If your plans call for overseeing construction, you had better give some serious thought as to your skills and available time.

Watching construction go up is fun for most developers. Not only is the construction a signal of income being generated, it is satisfying to see a development coming together. As much fun as construction can be, it can also be a major drain on your supervision time. Running construction on a large site is basically a full-time job. If you have extremely good subcontractors, you might get by with supervision at the end of each day. Otherwise, you may be needed several times during the course of a day. Don't commit yourself to a building project unless you have excellent subcontractors, the skills and time to perform supervision yourself, or a competent project manager.

## Get Organized

Before you can hope to supervise a project properly, you must get organized. This is easy for some people and very difficult for others. Being organized is crucial to efficiency. A good filing system is only part of what is needed. You have to have everything organized. This means phone messages, production schedules, contracts, accounts payable, and much, much more. Fortunately, getting organized is not all that difficult. Staying organized, however, can be more stressful.

Your organizational process should begin as soon as you start any aspect of a project. By the time you get started on site work, you should have your system set up. If you design the system properly, it will almost run itself. The use of computers today is at an all-time high. Computers are wonderful tools and they can streamline the needs of more conventional organizational methods. However, many old-school developers, myself included, still rely on boxes and file cabinets full of paper records to keep our projects on target. Don't get me wrong, I use computers as an enhancement and can't imagine how I used to do what I did without them.

Everyone organizes work a little differently. I like working with lists and bulletins boards that hold time-sensitive duties. Some people prefer dry-erase boards and still others are firmly committed to doing everything via computer. Your means of organization are not nearly as important as your ability to be organized. If you need to produce evidence of a driveway permit, you should be able to put your hands on it quickly. When you are looking at how your next week will shape up, you should have a clear picture of all the chores that will be addressed throughout the week.

Letting administrative work pile up on you can be very bad for business. The development business is one that generates a lot of paperwork. You have to maintain an effective way to deal with the workload in the time that you have available. If you are running a large project, you may have a full-time person doing nothing but document work. There was a time when I had one person who worked full time doing photocopying, filing, and correspondence. My in-office administrative staff has included as many as six people at a time. When you consider that my development work has been on a small to medium scale, this is a lot of people and a lot of overhead, but the people were needed and proved to be cost-effective.

If you are going to hire an administrative person to help you with supervision, you must be aware of your responsibilities as an employer. We won't go into all of the requirements of having employees on your payroll, but they add up. The same could be true if you hired a field supervisor. However, you might be able to hire a project manager on an independent contractor basis to avoid the snags associated with employees.

An entire book could be filled with organizational tips. This book is about land developing, so it doesn't tell you, step-by-step, how to get organized. Yet, organization is so very important that you must take it seriously. Your supervisory duties will prove more effective if you have yourself and your business well organized.

## Site Visits

The number of site visits required for your project will depend on many factors. You may want to go to your project at least once a day. Many new developers spend as much time as they can on their development sites. Their presence may not be needed, but being on the site helps to convince the new developers that their dreams are coming true. I like to either visit or have my sites visited daily. This may be excessive for some types of projects, but I find it works well. When a site is active with workers, I often make several trips a day to the site. A personal presence on the job is usually good motivation that keeps workers working a little harder.

If you have a site that has inactive days, you can avoid making visits on those days. As to how often you need to be on site, it depends on your project and your contractors. Most of my contractors have proved themselves. Frankly, I could probably sit in my office and wait for certificates of completion to roll in without many drawbacks. If you have exceptional contractors, you can cut back on your personal inspections. However, if you are working with new talent, being on the site is the best way to assess that the job is getting done.

If you are juggling your development with a full-time job, you might make site visits early in the morning, on your way to work. Perhaps you could stop by the site on your way back from your job each day as you are returning home. Many developers who are just starting out have to juggle their time. I remember running a building business, a plumbing business, and a real estate business while keeping tabs on my early development projects. There were a lot of balls in the air, but I had flexibility in my time. This made it possible to keep my supervision up to snuff. If you want to be a developer badly enough, you will find a way to meet the time demands. Part of your supervisory requirements is to keep your project on time and on budget. This is a different type of supervision, but nonetheless important. So, let's turn to the next chapter and see how you can control your schedule and budget.

# Keeping Your Project on Time and on Budget

**K**eeping your project on time and on budget is instrumental to your success. There are so many elements of land development that are critical to success that it's hard to pinpoint one that is the most important. Surely, your production schedule and budget rank high on the list of key factors in making a project successful. How will you keep your project on track? Most developers do it with personal attention to their projects.

When we talk about personal attention, it doesn't always mean that you will take a regular role in day-to-day activities for tracking your budget and production schedule. Maybe you will have a project manager who will track jobs for you. An accountant might supervise your financial issues as your project develops. Field superintendents might bring you weekly reports to keep you up to speed on the production schedule. Your role might be reviewing reports, rather than taking a more hands-on position. Reducing your work by having others tend to daily matters will not reduce your responsibility.

Assuming that you did your advance work properly, staying on budget should be fairly simple. If you have firm contracts that lock in all prices, you shouldn't encounter too many surprises. But there are almost always some surprises to deal with. Maintaining a production schedule depends on so many factors, some of which you just can't control, that it can be difficult to bring a project in on time. Since budgets and schedules are two different aspects of the development business, let's bring them down and take them one at a time.

# Tracking Your Budget

Tracking your budget isn't difficult. Staying within the budget can be troublesome, but it should not be hard to tell where you are from one week to the next. Developers create budgets before they begin site work. The budgets are often on file with the lenders who finance developments. Anyone with experience as a developer expects the budget to come out differently from projections. Occasionally, a job comes in under budget. No one gets upset about a job that costs less than expected. But when a job is over budget, there can be a number of problems to deal with. Not only will a developer realize less profit, the developer may run into trouble with lenders and contractors.

Following the expenditures on a development can be pretty simple. Computer programs can provide you with a ledger on a daily basis that will show all of the expenses to date. Even simple records maintained on ruled paper can keep you up to date on your spending. If you are running a large project, you might want to retain a financial wizard to count your pennies for you. Overall, though, tracking the money being paid is a simple task.

It's not hard to count the money that you've spent, but making sure that you don't spend more money than you have to is somewhat more complicated. Keeping your purse strings tight is wise. If you have cost overruns on something, you need to be concerned. Some overruns are to be expected, but you need to identify why you had to spend more money and evaluate if the added expense could have been avoided. The lessons learned won't help you on the present project, but they will benefit you on future projects.

Your predevelopment work should include extensive budget forecasting. If you do enough of it and do it right, you should have minimal trouble once field work begins. But don't think for a moment that you will not run into unexpected expenses. You should have entered into your project with some expectation of budget overruns. Most developers factor in some figure to anticipate the unexpected costs.

You hope not to need the extra room in the budget, but you hope even more not to exceed it.

Once you are fully engaged in a project, you are pretty much committed, even when prices are higher than what you had planned for. This can feel like a helpless situation. If you are way off, it may be extremely serious. But, in most cases, cost overruns only amount to making less money. If they are so substantial that they reach beyond your profit margin and into your actual expense account, then you have real trouble.

Huge problems are more often than not the result of poor planning. This is why it is so important to pay full attention to all possible expenses during your planning stage. Once your crews are rolling, you are locked into your role and your budget. The best you can do is to limit your losses as best you can, and there may be times when there is little that you can do about your losses. Your best defense is a well-planned offense.

## Routine Reports

Routine reports are a good way to keep an eye on your expenses. The reports will tell you where you stand at any given time. However, you should not get too caught up in reports and projections. I knew a developer several years ago who had an entire wall in his office plastered with reports. He would stand there and stare at them for hours. He lost so much time studying his reports that he could probably have gotten another development well under way with the lost time. Use the reports as tools, but remember that you have many duties, so don't become consumed by the paperwork.

## Invoices

When invoices come in, you should check them carefully before paying them. It is quite common for invoices for materials to be more than what you bargained for. Developers who are in a hurry often overlook a few hundred dollars here and there. In the scheme of land developing, $200 is not a lot of money. But, if you overpay bills routinely, the amounts add up to a considerable sum.

Invoices for materials that are higher than what you were quoted should be questioned. Hopefully, you have rock-solid quotes on file to prevent you from having to pay more than you expected to. Sometimes material suppliers simply make mistakes when computing invoices. You have to look for the mistakes. This can be time-consuming, tedious work, but it is very important if you want to stay on budget. Over the years, I have caught countless mistakes that would have cost me considerable money. Take the time to review all invoices before paying them.

Invoices submitted by subcontractors should be fast and easy to confirm. Compare the invoices to the contracts and see if the numbers match. Assuming that they do, you are all set. When there is a discrepancy, you should call your contractor to find out why. Don't just pay the bill. Investigate all charges and question any that are not in line with your established contracts.

If you have contractors who will be charging more for additional services, the added costs should be referenced in change orders. You should limit your exposure to surprise bills. Don't let contractors get away with tacking on extra costs if you have not agreed to them beforehand. Your contracts should have language in them that relieves you of any responsibility for cost overruns that are not first negotiated and agreed to in writing.

## Price Increases

Price increases sometimes put developers in bad situations. The cost of stone, for example, might go up without notice. You can lock in prices for some period of time, but you may not be able to keep them locked in throughout the full term of a large project. Big projects can take years to complete. When this is the case, the best that you can do is predict price increases as accurately as you can. There will be risk, but there is no other reasonable way to do it.

Contractors should honor their contract prices for the term of a project. They may lose money if they have to offer pay increases to their workers, but the cost should not be passed on to you. Your biggest risk with price increases comes from the suppliers of materials. If your development can move quickly, you should be able to get prices locked in. Your subcontractors will often be responsible for supplying their own materials. When they are, you should have some type of arrangement in your contracts with them to deal with the risk of material prices escalating.

# Staying on Schedule

Staying on schedule is a good way to avoid cost overruns. Projects that run late in their completion schedule normally go over budget. The delay can cost a developer money in various ways. Most projects are financed. Developers budget for a certain amount of finance expense, which is usually called *carry cost*. When a project runs beyond its intended schedule, the carry costs go up. They can go up quickly and in large amounts. A month or two of additional carry cost on a large project could be quite substantial.

Other reasons that delays cost money can be increases in prices once the locked-in time goes past. If your lock-in periods expire before your project is complete, you are susceptible to what could be major price increases. Projects that come in late can lose their presale buyers. Having buyers lined up for a project is good, but the buyers may be counting on delivery by a certain date. If the date comes and goes without you being able to deliver, the buyers may lose their financing or face higher financing rates. There are plenty of ways for delays to turn into lost money.

Keeping your project on a tight schedule can prove more difficult than you might think. There will be some circumstances that you simply cannot control, such as the weather. A late spring or an early winter could really put you behind. Unusually large amounts of rain could shut you down for weeks. Since you can't control the weather, the best that you can do is plan your job on the basis of past weather records. Once you get into the working stage of site development, you simply have to live with the weather.

Losing 3 days of production because of rain may not sound like a lot of downtime. But, the 3 days that you lose can throw off work schedules for different contractors. For example, if your clearing crew is set back by 3 days, it will hold up your excavation crew. If the excavation crew is very busy, your job might get bumped back if it is not ready when it is supposed to be. Your excavation contractor might have to tend to other jobs on their committed start dates. All of a sudden, you could be looking at several more days of downtime.

Every time one element of a job is delayed it can impact other areas. You may have to scurry around letting contractors know that their anticipated start dates have to be moved to later dates. The amount of time spent on rearranging the schedules can take away from your other duties. A ripple effect often occurs when some part of a job is compromised. It is your job to keep your project running as smoothly as possible and to correct problems when they occur.

We talked in the last chapter about supervision. The supervision is a cornerstone to your production control. If you have your supervision set up properly, it will protect you from a number of setbacks that would be likely with lack of supervision. However, your best field supervision is not going to stop the ground from becoming muddy after hard rains. You can think of your production control as a part of your supervisory duties, but don't assume that good supervision will automatically result in a timely completion.

Organization is another fact that we talked about previously. Just as supervision is a factor in bringing in a development on time, so is organization. Communication with your subcontractors and vendors is another part of the puzzle. Legwork can speed up a project. By legwork, I'm referring to the act of taking an active role in delivering documents and such. The amount of control that you have over your workers can be a factor in getting a job done on time. Money is almost always a motivator, and it can help to bring projects in ahead of schedule. Backup plans can help you to overcome problems that are slowing your project down. The lure of another project can be enough to keep your contractors grinding out extra hours to complete a present project. Provisions to charge a daily cash penalty to any contractor who is slowing down your project might make a difference. To expand on these issues, let's look at them individually.

## Supervision

We've talked enough about supervision to avoid a lengthy section here. When you need to get a project done on time, having someone with authority on your job site is a good way to meet your goal. The person might well be you, your project manager, or your site superintendent. As long as the person has the teeth to back up the barks of command, your project may move along faster. However, if the person is a jerk, you may have any number of problems with your subcontractors and suffer more setbacks than you would have without the supervisor. It takes talent to run a development properly. You have to be strong, firm, and willing to back up your threats. Yet, you should strive to gain the respect of your workers, so that threats are not needed. Putting the wrong person in a position of power can be a major mistake. And, remember this, *you* may be the wrong person. If you are not good when it comes to managing crews, hire someone who is.

The constant presence of an authority figure on a job site can greatly reduce the goofing off that goes on at some projects. However, the patrolling authority may make workers nervous and slow them down or bring about mistakes that might not have happened without the supervision. There can be a thin line between too little and too much supervision. Once you, or your supervisor, perfect the skills for handling crews in various situations, the hourly presence should make a difference. Even if you are sitting in a climate-controlled site trailer and looking out the door periodically, the knowledge that a boss is on the job should keep things moving along a little better.

## Organization

Good organization can help nearly every job come to a close quicker. You don't need a massive office and several assistants to maintain good organization. If you are into computers, a good notebook computer may be your primary means of organization. You can take it with you when you visit a site, you can hook it up to your cell phone to check your e-mail, and you can make notes as needed. A computer can even beep and remind you of your next appointment. For those who are not so much into the computer age, a spiral notebook can be pretty efficient.

If you have to travel from your office to your site, you may need some travel files. Developers who put site trailers on their projects can keep files in them. However, if you do most of your work out of your truck, you should have copies of files with you. No, you won't need a full filing cabinet in the back of your vehicle. An expandable file folder or a cardboard file box will do nicely. The key is to have copies of active files with you in the event that a question or conflict comes up. For example, if your clearing crew is working your site, have a file with all the documentation for the clearing crew in it. Make sure you have another set of files in your office. Field files sometimes get lost.

Pulling onto a job site and being faced with questions that you cannot answer is bad. It makes you look unprofessional, and it can slow down your job. If there is an assistant in your office that you can call, that's helpful. But, it is better to have active files with you so that you can solve situations on the spot.

Over the years, I have found that expandable file folders work very nicely when it comes to holding truck files. The folders tuck away behind the seat of a pickup truck with no problem. Cardboard boxes are okay in vehicles like my jeep, where they can be kept dry and in the back storage area. If your job is small, you may be able to simply put files in your briefcase before leaving your office. Each developer and each project has different needs. The bottom line is to have the information with you when you need it to keep your project from slowing down or shutting down.

## Communication

Communication is probably one of the largest factors in successful business operations. Developing land is no exception to the rule. You need to be able to reach your subcontractors quickly and easily. They should be able to contact you in the same manner. Cell phones have made communication a lot easier for people who are on the road a lot and out of their offices. When I contract a subcontractor, I make sure of what means of communication are available. You should too. If you are dealing with subcontractors where all you get is an answering machine when you call, you should probably be looking for different subcontractors. Answering machines have their place, but you need contractors who you can reach quickly when the need arises.

There is much more to communication than being able to contact someone. Once you've made contact, you need a viable means of communicating your needs and feelings. This type of communication is easier with some contractors than it is with others. It's common to have minor personality glitches with some people. While some of your contractors may not be the type of people that you would like to invite over for a party, you have to set aside personal differences if you are going to do business together.

Before I contract with a subcontractor, I conduct a few interview meetings. These meetings are designed to let us get to know each other. One meeting is not always enough. You and your subcontractors have to decide if you can work together well. Sometimes one of you will feel that the other one is not compatible for a working relationship. If this is going to happen, find it out early to avoid production problems. One of the last things that you need are subcontractors who don't want to work for you. The meetings take some of your time, but it is far better to spend the time before work begins on a project than it is to scramble to find a replacement subcontractor when your project is in full production.

## Legwork

We live in a time when e-mail makes almost instantaneous delivery of documents possible. Fax machines are vital to many businesses. Private delivery services can work wonders in getting packages from one place to another in record time. Even with all of this, there are times when you simply can't beat old-fashioned legwork. Sooner or later, you will run into a situation where a soil sample has to be delivered by a certain time or a lien waiver has to get to a lender in a hurry. If you are available to make deliveries personally, you can save the day. I can't count the number of times that I've acted as a courier for time-sensitive deliveries. Missing a deadline on some deliveries can set a project back by days. This, of course, is not acceptable.

Many cities have courier services, but developers who work out of the city lights can't count on such services. You might be in a position where you will need to meet an engineer on your site and then drive the engineer's findings to some place 50 miles away. Getting the same-day turnaround could make a real difference in your production schedule. It's desirable to avoid legwork whenever you can, but don't be lazy and allow it to cost you valuable production time.

## Control

Control is an issue that some people don't like to talk about. The crowd who wears rose-colored glasses like to believe that everyone will do the job in the right manner, without the need for controlling supervisors. I've been in the trenches long enough to know that this simply isn't true. A lot can be accomplished with a smile and respect, but there are certainly times when good old control is the only way to win. Most of your control as a developer will come from your contractual agreements.

Subcontractors are entitled to run their own shows, so long as they meet your needs, as per your contract. It wouldn't be right for you to insist on having all red dump trucks on your job site, but you should have the right to demand a certain amount of production. If a subcontractor wants to take 2 hours off for lunch, you may not be able to do anything but fume about it. But, if the subcontractor's action puts your job behind schedule and is not allowable by your contract, then you have some power to speak up firmly.

Control is a tool. It is one you hope will not be needed but will be thankful for when it is. Make sure that your contracts give you plenty of authority. The authority can come in many forms. For instance, you should have a clause in your contract that allows you to replace a subcontractor who is not fulfilling the terms of a contract. Having a clause that allows you to deduct money from a contract amount to cover the losses caused by the contractor is a good idea. Talk with your lawyer and come up with contract elements that will protect you in as many circumstances as you can envision.

## Money

Money is almost always a good motivator. With the right bonus structure, you might have some of the happiest subcontractors around and some of the fastest projects in town. I often use bonus programs to stimulate production. It's common for me to take quotes from contractors and add a percentage to them for the payment of possible bonuses. This gives me an existing budget to use and my contractors love to finish early and receive bonuses.

You can use bonus money to get a sluggish project moving even if you don't have a bonus budget. It will be painful to give up your profits, but it will work out to be better than having a late project. In fact, if you consider all of the money lost from carry costs and other elements of the probable delay, the payment of bonuses might be saving you money compared to what you stand to lose.

## Backup Plans

Backup, or contingency, plans should be in place to protect your project from slowdowns. For example, you should have a depth of contractors to call on if something happens to your first choice. I usually maintain a roster of at least three contractors for each phase of work to be done. If my primary contractor fails to perform, I have two other candidates in position for replacement. This type of advance planning can make a huge difference in keeping a project on time.

It's impossible to plan a contingency for every event that might slow a project down. But the more plans you have, the better off you will be. For example, if you have trouble getting a delivery of sewer pipe, what else can you have your backhoe or excavator work on? Think about this type of situation in advance and have an answer ready when you need it.

## Another Project

If you have another project coming up as you are nearing completion of an existing project, you might see faster work from your contractors. One reason for this is that they will want to please you, so that you will use them on the next project. Another reason is that they will not be worried about what they will be doing when they finish your existing project. This may seem silly, since they are independent contractors being paid by the job, not by the hour. Believe it or not, I have had subcontractors admit to me that they were working slowly because they didn't have another job to go to. Their slow pace didn't earn them any additional money, but it did cost me some in delay factors. Why someone being paid by the job, rather than by the hour would work slowly is beyond me. If I didn't have another job to go to, I'd finish up as soon as I could and start prospecting for more work. If you will have another project waiting, it could be worth your while to let your contractors know about it.

## Penalty Payments

Penalty payments take on different looks in different states. Contract law varies from state to state. I have used one form or another of penalty contracts for years. Basically, my contracts allow me to deduct a dollar amount from a contractor's earnings for each day that work is not completed beyond the completion date. If a contractor is going to lose $100 a day for being late, you might see faster work.

Some contractors balk at signing my contracts because of the penalty fees. This is an immediate red flag to me. I don't mind giving contractors adequate time. In fact, I usually ask how long a job will take to complete and then tack some time onto it as insurance for the contractor. But, when I have a contractor who is unwilling to make a commitment to a completion date where a penalty clause is present, I won't use the contractor. Check with your attorney to see what your rights are and how your contracts will have to be worded to take advantage of penalties for contractors who are late. Personally, I have found the clause to be a good motivator, and I've rarely used the leverage.

As your development takes shape, you should be seeking advance sales. If you planned your project right, you have a basic marketing plan in place. However, things may have changed a bit. Don't wait until your development is ready to sell to start marketing it. Get customers interested early. To discuss this more fully, let's move to the next chapter.

# A Marketing Plan and Sales Team

Creating a marketing plan is a big part of land developing. You may find it beneficial to create your own sales team, or you may choose to list your property with a real estate brokerage. In one way or another, you will need a plan for making sales. After all, what is a good development worth if you can't sell it? Seriously, having a strong marketing plan and sales force is most likely what will make your deal profitable. There are many sayings in the business, and some of them ring true. It's common to be told that good marketing can sell a bad development, but that bad marketing can't sell a good development. This is one of the true statements. Sales are sales, and sales are what make the developing process profitable.

Every developer needs a solid sales plan. The type of plan can vary considerably from project to project. For example, selling building lots will require different talent than selling spec houses. Leasing professional space in a new development requires another type of talent. You have to look at your project and form your sales approach accordingly.

Some developers concentrate heavily on sales, but a lot of developers are so consumed in their development work that they don't spend a lot of time on sales. Some developers make their own sales, but most developers rely on others to close deals. The two ways that they normally work involve either a professional brokerage or an in-house sales force. Both methods can be effective.

As a builder and developer, I have used real estate professionals and my own staff to make sales. Most of my success has come from an in-house sales team. However, I have had brokerages who served me well. There are pros and cons to both approaches. When I became a developer, I knew little about sales, but I took the time to learn the ropes, and it paid off. You may not be making your own sales, but it doesn't hurt to know the business.

If you are doing a small development, listing your property with a brokerage is probably your best bet, if you don't feel that you can sell it yourself. Larger projects can easily justify an in-house sales staff. The commission rates for sales can vary greatly, but they are usually pretty close to each other. There is no rule that sets a commission rate. In fact, it is illegal to fix commission rates. Being your own salesperson is the least expensive route, but the other options may be better for you. Let's spend a little time considering how you might make the most money from your development.

## Independent Sales

Independent sales are good in that you don't have to maintain an overhead expense for employees. While this is good on one hand, it can be bad on the other. Choosing between an employee-based sales force and a commission-based sales team can be tough. Simple math will tell you what each type of sales attack will cost. Is it better for you to pay only for what is sold? Could you make more money by having an in-house sales team? Part of your decision will probably be based on the value of what you have to sell. It is a large responsibility to take on in-house sales. If you, or someone who is working for you, is not skilled in sales, an in-house team will probably result in failure. Listing your property with a professional brokerage doesn't cost you a cent until you get a closed sale. This means that you don't have to pay for advertising or employees. But, when a sale is made, you have to cough up a lot of cash for a commission. So, which way is going to be right for your development?

Many developers who have medium-to-large projects maintain an in-house sales staff. More often than not, however, developers list their properties with outside agencies. Both ways can prove profitable, but one should be better than the other, depending on your personal circumstances. Volume is a definite consideration. How much are you going to have to sell? What number of sales will it take to sell most of your development? Can you afford the overhead expense of advertising and salaries until sales close? There can be a multitude of questions to ask yourself prior to making a firm decision. There is no cookie-cutter answer. Each developer and each project has specific needs. With this in mind, let's look at the option of using an independent brokerage to sell your development.

## Commission Rate

What is the commission rate that you will be charged? Independent brokerages usually charge for their services by having their clients pay a percentage of the price paid by a buyer at a closing. The percentage of the price is called a *sales commission*, and the precise percentage can vary considerably. Commission rates are not fixed, and it is illegal to fix them. However, they do tend to be very similar from one brokerage to another. Commission rates are negotiable. It is illegal to fix the rate, so it is always negotiable. A brokerage that paid an 8 percent commission on one deal might sell a different deal for a 6 percent commission. Some sales agents try to convince sellers that commission rates have to be a certain amount. This is not true. A brokerage may decide that a minimum rate is required to make the sales effort worthwhile, but you can always ask for a lower rate.

There is a downside to cutting a brokerage's commission rate. If you don't make it attractive for a brokerage to sell a property, you may not see a lot of sales activity. When a brokerage has a large commission at stake, it can be a great motivator for making a sale. Having been on all sides of this table, as a builder, a developer, and a brokerage owner, I've seen the angles from all perspectives. I believe in keeping the reward for a brokerage high enough to stimulate fast sales.

When you first look at the amount of a commission, it can seem very high. Assume that you are selling a new house for $200,000 and paying a 7 percent commission. The amount that you would pay in commission would be $14,000. This is a lot of money. But what will the brokerage have to do to earn it? There will be advertising, and that can be costly. Usually, there is a lot of wasted time working with people who don't buy. Time, effort, and expense have to come out of the commission. It's still a lot of money to pay for one sale. How much would it cost you to sell the house yourself? If you have the ability, you might save several thousands of dollars selling your own properties. I did plenty of this in my early years.

If you are your own salesperson, you can sell for a lower price and still net the same amount of profit. Or you can sell for the market rate and pocket more profit. You clearly have more options and more control. However, you do have the expense of advertising and the burden of showing the property. You have to decide what your skills are and what you are willing to do to limit the cost of commissions.

Paying large commissions can be difficult to swallow. But having independent, commissioned sales people moving your property can be a good way to go. If you are not sales-oriented, don't have your own sales team, and simply are not interested in being active in your sales, an independent brokerage should look pretty good. The good thing about commissions is that you don't pay them until you have sales. Brokerages take all the risks up front and get paid only if they sell your property.

What's the bottom line? Commissioned sales are not bad. If you don't want to risk your money on advertising, commissioned brokerages are a good idea. Negotiate for a fair commission rate, but don't make the figure so low that your brokerage will put your property on a back burner. If you have a large project, consider building an in-house sales team. Selling a spot lot or a spec house here or there should be done either by yourself or by a commissioned brokerage. Small deals don't warrant salaried sales staff.

## Listing Agreements

There are many types of listing agreements that may be used when you engage an independent brokerage. The most common type of listing agreement is an exclusive listing agreement. There are, however, many other types of listing agreements. Exclusive agency agreements can offer advantages to you that don't exist with exclusive listing agreements. If you enter into an exclusive listing, often called an *exclusive right-to-sell agreement*, you will have to pay a commission to the listing brokerage even if you sell the property yourself. This is not the case with an exclusive agency agreement. When you have an exclusive agency agreement, you can sell your property yourself and pay no commission. This is the type of listing that I would want to use as a developer. Brokerages don't like having anything less than an exclusive right-to-sell listing, but they will usually accept an exclusive agency listing.

When you enter into a listing agreement, you must set a term for the listing. It's common for a brokerage to want your property listed for a minimum of 6 months. This may be too long, but it does take time to generate sales, so it is really a matter of the market conditions. A 90-day listing is short and some brokerages will not accept such a short listing. I recommend a 6-month listing, but one that can be terminated if the brokerage is not performing. As a developer and builder, I can't recall signing many standard listing forms. I generally require special language. For example, I want to see a marketing plan from the brokerage and I want the plan included in the listing agreement. If the brokerage doesn't deliver the advertising promised, I can cancel the listing.

Brokerages don't like to give much control to their clients. However, they usually will give in to firm clients who are willing to list their properties elsewhere. Strong business owners know that they must work hard to drive solid deals, and this applies to working with brokerages. Listing agreements are not that different from subcontractor agreements. The listing agreements are legal contracts, and like other contracts, they are negotiable. Treat listing agreements just as you would a subcontractor agreement. In other words, make sure that the contracts favor you.

It is your right, and in fact, your duty, to ensure that the listing agreements that you enter into will prove beneficial to you. Signing an exclusive listing with an agency is a major commitment. There have been times in my career when a brokerage took a listing and did very little. Your hands can be tied in this situation. You need some control over your listing agreement. If you don't have a right to terminate a listing agreement, you could be left hanging in the wind for months. Don't allow yourself to be put into this type of position. Have clauses in your agreements that allow you to cancel the agreement if the listing brokerage is not living up to the agreement between the two of you. I suggest that you consult your attorney to arrive at the proper wording to insert into listing agreements.

## Requirements

There are many requirements that you might wish to put on your listing brokerage. I'm not qualified to offer you legal advice. But I can give you a few tips to run past your attorney. Don't consider these suggestions as complete and comprehensive. Take them for what they are worth. Every deal has individual needs. Anyway, here are some topics that you may do well to address in your listing agreements.

**Term:**  The term of the listing should be established and tied to performance requirements. It is reasonable to expect a term of 6 months for a simple house sale. In the case of a large development, the term might be much longer. The term of the agreement is not nearly as important as your rights to terminate the agreement. It's fine to sign a long listing as long as you can terminate it if necessary.

**Advertising:**  You should detail a complete schedule of advertising for your project. The advertising plan should indicate where and when your project will be advertised. A good plan will detail such items as the size of the advertisements, how they will be placed, if they will be in color, and in what media they will be placed. If you are expecting radio or television advertising, you should have a projected schedule on it. In simple terms, spell out all aspects of what you expect your brokerage to do when it comes to advertising and make the plan a part of the listing agreement.

**Open House Events:**  Open house events can sell property on the spot. If you want your brokerage to hold open house events, put it in your listing agreement. Specify when the events will be staged, how long they will last, and what type of demographics will be kept on visitors. The demographics can tell you a lot about how the marketing plan is working. If you are pulling in the wrong types of people, you can make adjustments.

**Signs:**  What types of signs will be used to promote your property? Where will they be placed? Determine how signs will be used to make sales and then carve the plan into stone. Put the requirements in writing in your listing agreements. If local laws allow the use of lead-in signs, you should require them in your listing agreements. Lead-in signs are usually made of cardboard and are generally posted on stakes or trees. The signs have the name of a development and directional arrows to lead prospective buyers to the site.

**Telemarketing:** Do you expect your brokerage to use telemarketing? If you want telemarketing on a large scale, you should include your desire in your listing agreement. Very few brokerages do a lot of tele-marketing for buyers. It's common for telemarketing to be used in search of listings, but it is not normally used for making sales. Tele-marketing can be effective, but few companies enjoy using it.

**Trailers:** Will your brokerage provide on-site sales trailers? Having a sales trailer on site when you are in the early stages of development can increase sales. It doesn't cost a brokerage a lot of money to put a sales trailer on a site. Yet, many brokerages either don't think about putting a trailer on a site or they are too cheap to place a trailer and staff it. If you have a substantial project, getting a sales trailer on the site is well worth requesting.

**Other Stuff:** There is plenty of other stuff that you might want to set up as special provisions in your listing agreements. Talk with your lawyer to get the legal language right. Think about your personal needs to give you ideas for what to put into the listings. When you combine your desires with the legal clauses, you have effective listing agreements.

## Being Your Own Salesperson

Being your own salesperson can take a lot of your time. The expenses of advertising will come out of your pocket if you sell your own prop-erties. I am not aware of any state that requires a developer to be a licensed real estate professional to sell property owned personally. This means that you should be allowed to sell property that you own without any special license. It does not mean, however, that you can sell spec houses for builders who bought lots from you. If you are going to sell property that is owned by someone else, you are most likely going to need a real estate license.

Selling your own property can save you a lot of money. Commission rates add up. If you are good at sales, you might find that you can enhance your profit potential substantially by selling your own projects. Remember, though, the sales game takes time. If you are able to make sales, the money saved can relate to payment for your time. Deciding to be your own sales force is a big commitment.

Not all developers are good at sales. I never thought that I would be good at sales when I started selling my own properties. After some trial-and-error experience and a lot of reading, I got pretty good at sales. Most people can learn to sell. If you are interested in taking care of sales, you should be able to learn the ropes, but it will take some time. The time needed to refine the skills could be detrimental to your project. You may find that it makes more sense to hire sales professionals or to list your property with a brokerage than to sell it yourself. Sales is a specialized field of endeavor. You might be better off to concentrate on developing and leaving sales to others.

## Your Sales Team

Having your own sales team makes a lot of sense if you have enough to sell. Run the numbers and look at them for yourself. Assume that you have a 12-house development. By most standards, this is a small development, but it can be large enough to justify your own sales team. Assume that the sales commission on each house will be $10,000. With 12 houses, this works out to $120,000 in sales money. You will need a chunk of it for advertising. If you hire an in-house sales person, you will have to pay a salary. Once you have an employee, there are other expenses that get tacked onto the basic salary. Let's say that your sales pro is going to cost you $50,000 a year when all costs are factored in. This leaves you $70,000 to use on advertising, and that's a lot of money for a small development. If you can get by with $15,000 in ads, you pocket $55,000 that would have gone to a brokerage. You could even give your sales pro a bonus and still keep a handsome sum for having done your deals in house.

If the numbers work on a small development, you can imagine how well they might work on a larger project. Say you had 24 houses to sell. Just do the math. You might be putting an extra $100,000 in your bank account by having your own sales pro. I used to sell over 60 houses a year with a sales staff of only two people and myself. It was common for me to sell about 30 of the homes and the other sales people sold the rest. I had other duties and was not selling full time. It's easy to see how much money can be saved by having an in-house sales staff, but there are downsides to the deal.

If you are thinking of hiring an in-house sales staff you should check local laws and regulations to see if the employees will need any special type of licensing. In many cases, the employees of a company can sell real estate owned by the company without any special licensing needs. Assuming this is the case, you will only have to deal with typical employee overhead and responsibilities. However, you should see to it that your sales team is trained to avoid legal confrontations.

The sale of real estate can result in lawsuits. Having inexperienced people who are not familiar with real estate law can be very risky. If you are not up to speed on real estate law yourself, require your sales team to attend training classes on the subject of real estate principles and practices. Invest in some errors-and-omissions insurance to protect you and your company if the sales team makes a mistake. The insurance is added overhead, but it is an expense that you should not attempt to operate without. One lawsuit could wipe out your entire company, and the insurance could protect you from such a disaster.

Deciding to create your own sales team opens a can of worms that you must be willing to deal with. You don't get to keep all the commission money for nothing. In other words, there is added responsibility required if you want to keep the cost of sales in your bank account. It is desirable to hire people with a background in real estate sales and to make sure that they are kept current in their knowledge of real estate law.

# A Marketing Plan

Once you know who will be selling your development, you need a marketing plan. We touched on this in talking about listing agreements. You, or your sales experts, have to come up with a plan for selling your lots, space, or buildings. Some developments require only simple plans, but other developments can be worth investing heavy money in for a marketing plan. You have to weigh your personal situation. Obviously, you would not pay a marketing consultant $25,000 to tell you how to sell one or two houses. But, if you were developing a complex of 300 houses, paying a consultant might make a lot of sense.

When you begin to think of marketing plans, you could be considering a number of possibilities. To say that you will spend $5000 or $50,000 on advertising is not enough. You have to pinpoint how you will advertise. Are you going to rent space on billboards? Will direct mail be a part of your marketing plan? What success would you expect from television commercials? Would radio spots work for you? How much are you willing to spend on signs and where will they be placed? How soon will you start your marketing campaign? These are just some of the questions that you should be asking yourself.

Your marketing plan will depend a lot on who your buyers will be. For instance, if you are planning to sell blocks of lots to builders, a direct-mail campaign should work nicely. It wouldn't be feasible to use direct mail to general consumers, but if your target market is small and identifiable, such as it would be with home builders, direct mail could produce great results. Running radio spots should work for home buyers, but they wouldn't be worthwhile if you are after builders. You have to match your marketing to your audience.

Let's assume that your primary market is composed of home builders. You might want to tell the builders that you will be running ongoing ads for the development to make home buyers want to live in it. This could influence builders to buy from you. When this is the case, you should have a defined advertising schedule to show the builders. The schedule should be in writing and it should be firm. For example, you might promise the builders that you will run 3 radio spots a day for the first 120 days after the development is ready to be bought into. This type of promotion can be expensive and you might want to avoid it. But if it helps you sell out to builders quickly, the added expense will be well worthwhile.

An entire book could be written on marketing and advertising. In fact, many have. You should read some of them to get a feel for what might work with your development. There is not enough room here to teach you how to build a formidable marketing plan. It is, however, crucial that you be aware of the need for such a plan. You have to establish an advertising budget and a viable means for making people aware of your project. Getting quick sales at good prices is the key to winning in the developing game.

You should turn your attention to a marketing plan early in your development. It is advisable to have your plan completed before you even begin construction. Don't wait until you have something to sell to figure out how to sell it. Concentrate on getting sales before you have a finished product. Presales are always welcome. Go get them as soon as you can. Once you have your sales rolling, you can begin to think about new deals. With this in mind, let's move to the next chapter and see how you might move on smoothly to new projects.

# New Projects

Once developers are well into a project, they often start thinking about new projects. This is okay, but you should stay focused on the project in progress. Yet, you should plan in advance for new projects. When is the right time for a new project? Some developers juggle multiple projects all at one time. Experienced developers who have enough cash and credit can run more than one project at a time. Depending on the size of the projects, it's possible to run many jobs simultaneously.

When I started out as a developer, I kept my work simple by doing one project at a time. As I gained experience and money, I branched out. There have been many times when I've had several projects going at once. It has not been uncommon for me to have a basic land development deal going while working on a shopping center project and doing three or four housing projects. This, of course, is a lot to bite off, and it can choke you if you are not careful.

Should you tackle multiple projects? Only you can answer this question. The odds are that you should start small and work your way up. However, some people simply don't have the patience to climb a ladder one rung at a time. If you are willing to move slowly, you will still have some overlap between existing projects and future projects.

Waiting for one project to come to full completion to begin a new project is a mistake. There is too much downtime if you are not in the process of getting your next project rolling while you are wrapping up an existing project.

Your first decision has to be whether you want to get into another project. Some developers find that the business is not all that they thought it was before they got involved with it. If this is the case with you, there is no reason to give new projects any thought. But most developers do want to move onto new projects. Even if you were not happy with the results of your first deal, you will probably want a chance to do better on a next deal. So, let's look at the various ways that you can step up to your next project.

## Timing

The timing for a new project is a sensitive issue. If you wait too late, you will be without work or income for some time. Starting too early can complicate your life and conflict with your existing project. Another problem with starting too soon is that your financial resources may be tied up in your existing project. You will have to decide what timing will work for you, but I can give you some suggestions to consider.

Let's say that you are involved in a basic land deal, one where you are cutting a parcel into lots and selling them without building on them. This is normally a low-impact type of project. You have decided you want to do another project similar to the one you are doing. In this case, it would be reasonable to start your preliminary work for the new project any time after the existing project is approved and surveyed. Before you put much money into a new project, you might want to wait until some of your lots are sold. You might even set a timetable that has you buying into the new project when one-half of your existing project is sold out. You will control the timing according to your comfort level and your financial ability.

In this example, once you have your lots cut up and on the market, you can devote a lot of time to a new project. Even if you are doing your own sales, you can still have plenty of time to think about your new project. The type of project that you are developing has a lot to do with the timing that you select for new projects.

For our second example, assume that you are doing a residential housing development that contains 20 building lots. You are cutting up the land and acting as the general contractor for the construction of the homes. This type of project requires considerably more effort than a simple land deal. When can you break away from this type of project to start another one? You should probably wait until several of the homes have been built and sold.

When you are involved in construction, the problems can amount to a lot more demands on your time than when you stick with basic land developing. Even after buildings or houses are complete, there can be warranty work that eats into your time. This can go on for a year or so. If you are going to be involved in the building process, you have a lot more profit potential, but you also have much more responsibility.

Getting the timing right can be difficult. As a rule-of-thumb, you should start planning your new project long before your existing one closes out, but you should make sure that the work on the new project doesn't hamper the work on the present project. Some developers allocate a certain segment of their day to concentrate on new projects. I often do this. It's common for me to do what I call my productive work for several hours and then to hide out for an hour or two to plan future projects. Then, I go back to the production work to wrap up the day. If you have enough self-discipline to limit your planning of new projects to set times that don't interfere with your present project, you can start planning at almost anytime.

## Using Your Past Projects as Stepping Stones

Using your past projects as stepping stones can make getting into new projects easier. Lenders are much more willing to loan money to developers who have proved their abilities. With each project you complete successfully, you become a better risk for lenders. Every time you post a winner on the board, you become a more viable developer. This is often why developers start small and work their way up.

If you work through some small jobs you can reach goals quickly. Going to a lender for a large development before you have a track record can prove frustrating, to say the least. But if you take on small projects and complete them successfully and quickly, each project gives you experience and a track record. As you begin to stack up the small projects, they give you the ability to reach out for larger projects. Not only will lenders be more likely to support your interest in larger projects, you will be better prepared to take the projects on.

## Routines

Some developers get into routines. There are times when routines are good, but there can also be problems associated with routines. As a developer, you will find that there is a good deal of repetition from one job to the next. However, you should not assume that each job will be a carbon copy of the previous job. You have to take on each project as an individual deal. Much of what you do for one project will be about the same as what you will do for future projects, but this is not always the case. If you change stride in the types of developments that you are doing, the playing field can change considerably. For example, there is a big difference between developing houses on spot lots and developing dozens of houses in a subdivision. You have to make adjustments, as needed, for each project that you undertake.

The types of routines that are likely to hold true from job to job include your supervision of the project. Status reports, charts, tables, files, and similar tracking methods can be used in almost all types of jobs. What you are tracking may be different, but the way in which you track it could be the same. This is where a routine is good.

Experienced developers create systems that they can work with to keep their jobs running smoothly. There can be more than one system in place. For example, you may have one system for straight land developing, another system for land developing that includes building construction, and a third system that is used for commercial projects. It certainly helps to have a defined, proven method for keeping your project profitable. While each job will be different, they should be similar enough to allow most of your preestablished system to work well.

## Changing Styles

Changing styles of developments is almost like starting from scratch. If your first project went only to the point of selling finished lots and your next project will include building houses, there is a lot of difference to be considered. Even so, your previous experience will help you up to the point of construction. Any experience that you have is an advantage.

Should you change styles, or should you stick with what you have learned? This is a tough question to answer. It's probably wise to stay within the same style for your first few projects. Get the feel for what you are doing and work the bugs out of your system. Once you perfect the style, consider moving into another style. You are likely to be more profitable by sticking with a single style, since it is what you have the most experience with. However, growth is usually desirable, and this means stepping out of your comfort level. Whenever you walk into the unknown, the risk factors increase. But sometimes moving up and moving on are the only way to increase your earnings for the time spent on a job.

## Just Land

Should you do just land, or should you become involved in the building process? There is potentially more money to be made if you get into building on the lots that you develop. Some people would say that there is less risk associated with land-only deals. To some extent, this is true. But, it can be much easier to sell an improved lot, one with a house on it, than it is to sell a bare building lot. Builders are a primary market for bare lots. Some consumers will buy bare lots and either build their own homes or hire builders for the construction. But if you are offering a total package, your pool of buyers is much larger. There is more risk, because of the increased investment of building a spec house, but there are also many more potential buyers to work with.

Many developers are quite happy with their earnings for basic land developing. People like me, who have a background in construction, tend to go for the larger view. There are pros and cons to both sides of the coin. Developers who limit themselves to land can get in and out of a project much quicker than developers who want to take part in the building process. While straight land developers may not turn over as much money, they can turn it over quicker and more often. Developers who are also builders get more mileage out of each development, but they are locked into the site for longer. If market conditions change quickly, the builder-developers are more likely to take financial hits than straight land developers would. Since the builder-developers have to stay in a project longer, they are more vulnerable to changing market conditions. This is clearly a factor worth considering. It can be much better to get in and out quickly as a straight land developer.

There is a lot to be said for sticking with straight land developing. Your job is easier when you are not involved in construction. Getting the return on your investment is faster when you are not building homes or commercial space. Fewer employees and subcontractors are needed when you are not building. Generally speaking, straight land developing is much less complicated than being a builder-developer. Does this mean that you should omit building from your plans? Not necessarily. Building can boost profits in a big way.

Finding prime parcels of land to develop can take a lot of time. There are only so many excellent pieces of land to work with. If you zip in, develop the land, sell the lots, and get out, you will be leaving a lot of potential money on the table. As difficult as finding good property can be, you may not want to cash out on just the building lots. There could be plenty of money waiting for you in the building process.

## Taking the Builder Angle

Taking the builder angle to developing can be very rewarding. It is, however, not a simple task. Building is a business that involves a lot of people. When a lot of people are involved in something, there are more chances for problems. Developers are sometimes general contractors. At other times, developers make deals with home builders to take care of construction, but for a lower price than they would normally charge. Some builders will lower their typical markup in return for a high volume of business.

It's not unusual for builders to have dozens of subcontractors and vendors. At one time, I had about 120 subcontractors and vendors, not counting my in-house crews and my administrative people. Land developing and building are two different businesses, but they both work together well. Either can be a full-time job. When you combine the two, you have the potential for a lot of work and responsibility.

Profit zones for builders vary, as you might imagine. Most builders I know figure a gross profit based on 20 percent of the appraised value of a home. The land developers I know try to double their money on the price of their lots. If you can cash in with both forms of profit potential, the result can be quite comforting.

Some builders will work for less when they have a guarantee of volume. I used to sell houses 10 at a time to partnerships. When I did this, I cut my profit margin in half. It went down to 10 percent, but the sales were solid, guaranteed, and often amounted to 30 houses at a time. If you want to branch out into building without becoming a builder, this might be a good way for you to do it. Consider offering a builder an exclusive on your lots in exchange for a piece of the building profit. For example, you might guarantee a builder contracts to build 12 houses in 6 months in exchange for a markup of only 10 percent. This opens the door for you to make 10 percent on the houses. Of course, the cost of the sale may have to come out of the markup. If this is the case, and you are paying a 5 percent commission, you are getting only 5 percent of the building deal. Still, 5 percent of 12 houses can add up nicely.

If you don't like the idea of dealing with builders and want to be your own builder, you will need a bevy of subcontractors and material suppliers. More important, you will need some expertise in the building trades. While you don't have to be competent to install roofing materials or plumbing, you need a general understanding of what will be required on a job.

Assuming that you are paying 5 percent in a sales commission, you should be looking at a gross profit of 15 percent for most types of homes. On a $200,000 home, 15 percent is $30,000. Depending on how many homes you are building, this type of money can add up very quickly, and it is money that you will miss out on if you don't take advantage of the building angle.

Deciding to get into the building side of developing is something that you should give a lot of thought to. It is a potentially lucrative business, but it is also a business that can be full of pitfalls. If you don't have experience in construction, find some seasoned people to work with. Don't venture out on your own as a builder if you don't know and understand the business. There is plenty of money to be made on straight land deals. You don't have to get into the building side of a project. But, if you have the right skills and personality, the building side of the business can be well worth your time.

## Building on Past Performances

Building on past performances is probably the best way for developers to grow safely. If you have done a small office building, you can probably do a larger office building with similar results. Building a subdivision of 8 houses after having completed one of 5 houses should be a snap. When you are ready for your next project, pick one where your experience and strengths can be used to improve your odds of success. A gradual climb is often the best means for reaching the most lofty goals. I wish you the best of luck as you grow as a developer.

# Resource Directory

## On-Line Real Estate Forums

www.creonline.com
**CREATIVE REAL ESTATE ONLINE**
   This site offers how-to articles, money-making ideas, a legal corner, a cash-flow forum, books, courses, a news group, a chat room, a players club, success stories, money sources, and classified ads. The site revolves around investing in real estate and creative financing.

www.timesunion.com
**REAL ESTATE PARLOR**
   This site has open forums for all sorts of real estate, business, and economy topics. This is a good site for networking with buyers and sellers.

## Information Sites

www.realtor.com
**REALTOR.COM**
   This is a huge site that is aimed at real estate professionals, but it also offers plenty for investors. You can find a home, find a neighbor-

hood, or find a real estate professional to work with. Public resources on the site include: real estate news, a resource center, a finance center, a place for commercial sources, and mortgage rates.

www.owners.com

## OWNERS.COM

This site offers homes for sale by their owners. You can search for a home, list a home for sale, visit the loan center, read reports, check out the resource guide, and so forth. This site is well worth a look.

www.credb.com

## COMMERCIAL REAL ESTATE ARENA

This site bills itself as the Internet's most powerful real estate database. Aimed mostly at investors who become members, this site does offer a public access area. The database contains information on properties that are for sale or lease. Presently, the site concentrates on northern California, but there are plans to expand the coverage.

www.webcom.com/~pcj/welcome.html

## PLANNING COMMISSIONER'S JOURNAL

Here is a fine site to visit for land planning. You will find articles and many links. Learn about access management, the transfer of development rights, and much more.

www.listnet.net/

## LISTNET

This site is basically an advertising site that offers a great deal of information on real estate listings ranging from rooms for rent to vacation properties. There are some good links here and information of all types for anyone interested in real estate.

www.zoning.net/

## ZONING

Do you need answers on zoning issues? Are you interested in knowing how zoning laws may affect your property. Well, visit this site for your zoning questions.

www.hud.gov/

## U.S. DEPARTMENT OF HOUSING AND URBAN DEVELOPMENT

Here is an official HUD site that is well worth some time examining.

www.usda.gov/

## U.S. DEPARTMENT OF AGRICULTURE

There is a wealth of information for developers at this site.

www.rliland.com/

**REALTORS LAND INSTITUTE**

This site is aimed at real estate professionals, but developers will find good information and links here, too.

# Mortgage Sites

www.mortgage101.com

**MORTGAGE 101**

This site provides a large resource of information when you are looking for a loan. There is information here about loan applications, appraisals, bankruptcy, credit ratings, FHA loans, VA loans, insurance, second mortgages, refinancing, interest rates, mortgage calculators, and much more. If you are in the market for a loan, this is a site you should visit.

www.mortgage-source.com

**THE MORTGAGE SOURCE ONLINE**

Here is a financial site that provides information on mortgages and mortgage rates. The site has an ability to help you find a lender online. There is a service that allows visitors to ask the mortgage experts questions.

www.blackburne.com

**1ST AAA COMMERCIAL MORTGAGE LENDER DATABANK**

This is a site that offers free information on lenders of all sorts. You can search a databank for commercial lenders, apply for a commercial mortgage online, compare interest rates, get business loans, home loans, or just enjoy the joke of the day. According to the site, an online commercial mortgage miniapplication can be filled out in less than 4 minutes.

www.capitalprofits.com/land_developers.htm

**GREAT NORTH AMERICAN CAPITAL**

This site is specialized for land developers. It offers sources of financing, a newsletter, links, and much more.

www.landfinance.net/

**LAND FINANCE COMPANY**

Here is another site that is aimed at filling the financing needs of land developers. This company will consider loans for everything from ranches to manufactured housing subdivisions.

# Foreclosures

www.bankhomes.net
**FORECLOSURES ON LINE**

Here is a site that gives you access 24 hours a day to a reported 20,000 listings of foreclosed property. The site boasts having 3000 lenders involved in all 50 states. This site offers a database, books, articles, news, resources, and a section about foreclosure talk, as well as a real estate library. There is a one-time cost of $195 and monthly dues of $19.95 if you want to take full advantage of this site.

www.foreclosuresusa.net
**FORECLOSURES USA**

This site lists bank and government foreclosures nationwide. The site explains a bit about foreclosures, speaks of homes selling for as low as $10,000, provides other real estate links, and offers debt management services.

# Magazines

*Affordable Housing Finance*—(415) 546-7255

This is a bimonthly magazine aimed at developers of affordable apartments.

*Business Facilities*—(908) 842-7433

This monthly magazine covers corporate expansion, economic development, and commercial and industrial real estate.

*Canadian Property Management*—(416) 588-6220

Published eight times a year, this magazine covers every type of real estate from residential properties to hospitals. The publication provides investors with industry news, case law reviews, technical updates, and more.

*Commercial Investment Real Estate Journal*—(312) 321-4460

This bimonthly magazine focuses on commercial real estate investment. It publishes pieces on trends and development ideas for commercial properties.

*Condo Management Magazine*—(508) 879-4744

This monthly magazine covers condo management in New England, Florida, and California. The pieces published range from roofing and painting to security and insurance.

*Financial Freedom Report Quarterly*—(801) 273-5301

This quarterly magazine is written for both professional and semi-pro investors. The magazine is packed with how-to articles and is well worth your time. I've written many articles for this one, and the content is always top drawer.

*Journal of Property Management*—(312) 329-6058

This bimonthly publication covers all aspects of real estate management. It is published by the Institute of Real Estate Management and can be counted on for timely and authoritative articles.

*Managers Report*—(407) 687-4700

This monthly magazine covers property management and condo issues. There are how-to articles, interviews, profiles, new product opinions, technical reports, and personal experiences to learn from. Many investors view this magazine as a problem-solver for technical trouble encountered with real estate.

## Online Bookstores to Check Out:

- Real Estate Bookstore—www.realestatebookstore.com
- Barnes and Noble—www.barnesandnoble.com
- Amazon—www.amazon.com
- Borders—www.borders.com
- Trendsetters—www.trendsetters.net
- BookBuyer's Outlet—www.bookbuyer.com

# INDEX